fun with the family
Oregon

Praise for the *Fun with the Family* series

"Enables parents to turn family travel into an exploration."
—Alexandra Kennedy, Editor, *Family Fun*

"Bound to lead you and your kids to fun-filled days, those times that help compose the memories of childhood."
—Dorothy Jordon, *Family Travel Times*

Help Us Keep This Guide Up to Date

We would love to hear from you concerning your experiences with this guide and how you feel it could be improved and kept up to date. Please send your comments and suggestions to:

editorial@GlobePequot.com

Thanks for your input, and happy travels!

fun with the family
Oregon

hundreds of ideas for day trips with the kids

Sixth Edition

Sarah Pagliasotti

travel

Guilford, Connecticut

All the information in this guidebook is subject to change. We recommend that you call ahead to obtain current information before traveling.

To buy books in quantity for corporate use or incentives, call **(800) 962-0973** or e-mail **premiums@GlobePequot.com.**

Editor: Amy Lyons
Project Editor: Heather Santiago
Layout: Joanna Beyer
Text Design: Nancy Freeborn and Linda R. Loiewski
Maps: Rusty Nelson © Morris Book Publishing, LLC
Spot photography throughout © Photodisc and © RubberBall Productions
Previous editions of this title were written by Cheryl R. McLean.

ISSN 1540-4366
ISBN 978-0-7627-5721-3

Printed in the United States of America
10 9 8 7 6 5 4 3 2

Contents

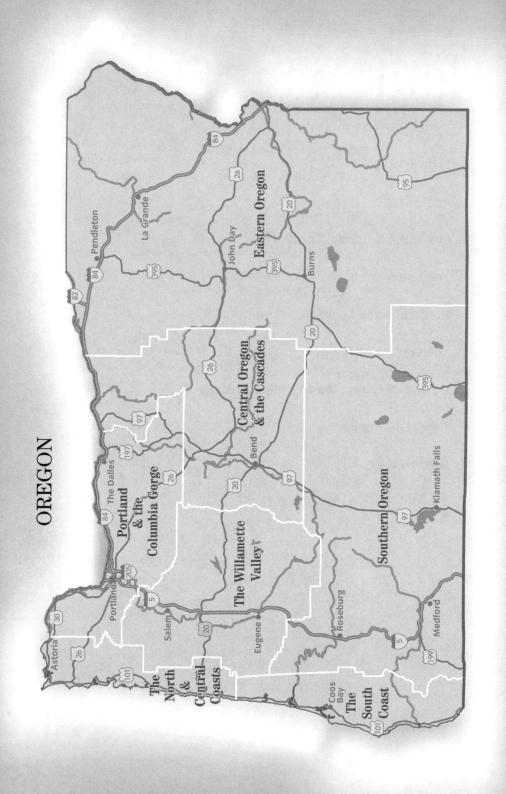

OREGON

Astoria
Pendleton
La Grande
The Dalles
Portland
& the
Columbia Gorge
Portland
Salem
Eugene
The
North
&
Central
Coasts
The Willamette
Valley
John Day
Eastern Oregon
Burns
Central Oregon
& the Cascades
Bend
Southern Oregon
Klamath Falls
Roseburg
Medford
The
South
Coast
Coos
Bay

84
26
95
20
395
20
82
84
395
26
20
97
197
26
20
97
395
97
5
30
26
205
5
20
101
199
5
101

To Josie, Julia and Mike, with whom life is a wondrous odyssey, and to my mom Judith, who finds adventure and beauty everywhere.

Acknowledgments

The author would like to thank some of the many colleagues, family and friends who helped make this book a success: Christina Katz for recommending me and for lots of guidance over the years. Amy Lyons for the opportunity and the professionalism. Sheila and Jack, for being my two amigos and partners in adventure. Susan for being a bright spot a good friend and a tireless cheerleader. Dad, for being my writing coach and Brookings expert. Mom, Tita, Kate, and the Newman clan for providing all manner of support and thoughtful insight.

Finally, thank you Mike. You made this possible by being SuperDad to the girls and a super partner while I renewed my vows with the laptop. I'm so glad we're in each others' corners. And thank you my sweet girls, Josie and Julia, for being great travel buddies and joyous, beautiful people.

About the Author

Sarah Pagliasotti is a freelance writer for parenting and travel publications, among others. She's a nearly native Oregonian who grew up splashing in the surf at Newport's Nye Beach, hiking the forests of the Cascade Mountains and waiting on a tow truck for the family VW bus on myriad roadsides throughout the state. With wanderlust in her DNA, she's now logging many miles with her own family exploring Oregon's bounty and searching out unique experiences for families. She lives in Portland with her husband and two curious daughters.

Preface

A sk any Oregonian why she loves the state and she'll likely mention the diversity of terrain: high deserts, beaches, mountains, rain forests, valleys, and rivers that offer a wealth of recreation. That variety makes Oregon a place to be enjoyed by people of all ages, interests, and abilities, but especially by families.

A wilderness ethos is still alive in every part of the state, from the ranchers of eastern Oregon to the crabbers of the Oregon coast; from the foresters of southern Oregon to the Native American tribes who still fish the rivers; and from the Lewis and Clark legacy of the Gorge and Astoria to the descendants of Oregon Territory homesteaders who keep its history alive.

At the same time, Oregon's cities and towns boast culture and urban interests beyond their size. In even some of the smallest towns, you'll find impressive arts performances, unique shopping, fascinating museums and history centers, and world-class restaurants.

In fact, there's so much to do that it can be overwhelming to know where to start, what to see, or how to spend a couple days or hours in any given locale. Though the Web is bursting with information, it's difficult to distinguish which experiences are worth a visit and how to prioritize if you don't have much time. Like having a friend in every corner of this state, this book offers insider advice to help you easily take advantage of the bounty that Oregon offers families.

This sixth edition is significantly updated with new listings for must-visit attractions and events, lodging, and restaurants. Though some of the key spots remain the same— places like Crater Lake and Cannon Beach, and events like the Pendleton Round-Up and the Oregon Country Fair— there are always interesting new finds popping up, and of course Oregon's incredibly active dining landscape is constantly evolving. On top of that, the fluctuating economy has created dramatic changes in some areas of the state in recent years, making older guidebooks less reliable. We've also added website addresses so you can find more information quickly, and reorganized some sections to make it easier to get the most out of the time you have in any one area.

Sources for Oregon **Information**

Travel Oregon: (800) 547-7842; www.traveloregon.com.
Welcome to Oregon website: www.el.com/to/oregon. This site also has city pages with links to various local attractions.
State Park Campsite Reservations and Information: (800) 452-5687 for reservations; (800) 551-6949 for general information; www.oregonstateparks.org.
Bureau of Land Management in Oregon: www.or.blm.gov/recreation.htm

Junior **Rangers**

The Oregon State Parks and Recreation Department likes to keep kids interested in nature, and its Junior Ranger program provides activities to help stimulate the imagination while teaching kids to protect and enjoy our natural resources. Children ages 6 to 12 can participate in programs offered at most campgrounds and selected day-use parks that have staff or hosts on hand. Find a complete list of sites and details about activities at www.oregonstate parks.org/juniorrangers.php, or call the general information line at (800) 551-6949.

Take advantage of visitor bureaus and chamber offices. The staff in these organizations are inevitably helpful and personable, and they are usually ready to provide suggestions on the best places to eat, stay overnight, or visit. And since Oregonians are notoriously friendly, you'll get lots of additional insider tips by striking up conversations with locals wherever you go.

I grew up road-tripping around this state, hiking its forests, driving its back roads, and playing in its icy ocean waters till my feet turned blue. Even so, I was amazed how many surprises awaited me as I researched this edition. There is no end to the family fun contained in this state. Oregon is a dynamic place, solidly steeped in a rich history but also constantly percolating with new opportunities for adventure.

—Sarah Pagliasotti

Introduction

I've lived in Oregon most of my life and have always marveled at the variety to be found in this state—ocean, mountains, gently rolling pastures, verdant valleys, giant old-growth forests, sagebrush deserts, mesas and canyon lands, and wide stretches of volcanic wasteland. The opportunities for family adventure are just as varied and vast as the landscapes.

Oregon has far more attractions, amusements, and family fun opportunities than can possibly be covered in a book this size, but in the following pages I've included those that have stood the test of time—or the test of my daughters.

In addition to the specific attractions listed in the book, here are some ideas for family fun in just about any town in Oregon:

- Head over to family swim time at the local pool.
- Visit the police department, fire station, and city or county government center or courthouse (call first to see if they'll give you a tour).
- Join family hour at the roller-skating rink.
- Grab a lane at the bowling alley (most now have inflatable gutter guards to help little ones play).
- Tour a recycling center, local industry, fast-food franchise restaurant, hospital, post office, or television or radio station (call in advance).
- Visit a U-pick farm and gather berries, beans, or whatever's in season.
- In winter grab your mittens and scarves, don your warmest coats, and head for the nearest snow hill with sleds, inner tubes, or just a cardboard box.
- In summer find a swimming hole at the nearest stream, river, or lake (there are plenty in just about every corner of Oregon).
- Find a wide open space (no overhead wires and few trees) where you can fly a kite on a windy day.

The following three price tables illustrate the price ranges that the dollar symbols represent. Rates for accommodations are for a one-night stay; rates for attractions are the price per person for adults and children; and rates for restaurants are the average cost of a single menu selection without beverages. Prices do not include tax or tip. All prices and hours of operation are subject to change, so be sure to call ahead before embarking on your adventure.

Rates for Accommodations

$	Less than $60
$$	$60 to $80
$$$	$80 to $100
$$$$	More than $100

Rates for Attractions

$	Less than $6
$$	$6 to $11
$$$	$11 to $20
$$$$	More than $20

Rates for Restaurants

$	Most selections less than $6
$$	$6 to $10
$$$	$11 to $20
$$$$	More than $20

Attractions Key

The following is a key to the icons found throughout the text.

SWIMMING		FOOD	
BOATING / BOAT TOUR		LODGING	
HISTORIC SITE		CAMPING	
HIKING / WALKING		MUSEUM	
FISHING		PERFORMING ARTS	
BIKING		SPORTS/ATHLETICS	
AMUSEMENT PARK		PICNICKING	
HORSEBACK RIDING		PLAYGROUND	
SKIING/WINTER SPORTS		SHOPPING	
PARK		PLANTS/GARDENS/NATURE TRAILS	
ANIMAL VIEWING		FARM	

The North & Central Coasts

Oregon's Pacific Coast National Scenic Byway (US 101) follows the entire 400-mile coastal edge. With few exceptions, it's hard to go even 10 miles without finding a scenic, historic, or just plain fascinating spot. It was along these shores that Captain James Cook landed in 1778 and discovered the bounty of animals that sparked the Northwest's fur trade. Less than three decades later, Lewis and Clark's Corps of Discovery set up Fort Clatsop as a base camp from which to explore the region for Thomas Jefferson. And in 1942 a Japanese submarine fired shells at Fort Stevens, making it the only spot on the continental United States to receive enemy fire since the War of 1812. So although you could drive the North and Central Coast's roughly 160 miles in a day, you wouldn't want to. To get a sense of the whole, plan at least four days to explore the many parks, waysides, lighthouses, and public beaches found along the stretch between Astoria and Yachats. Thanks to the foresight of the state legislature and the leadership of the late governor Tom McCall, who in 1967 enacted the Beach Bill, which made it so all of Oregon's beaches are open to the public.

In summer, traffic on US 101 sometimes seems to crawl in the early afternoon. Try leaving for your destination by 9 a.m. to avoid waiting in traffic or in lines at tourist attractions. During the fall and winter, the coastal highway is less congested, lines shrink in restaurants and on beaches, and life gets a little more laid-back. Take advantage of off-season rates to enjoy some of the more luxurious lodgings. Stroll through one of many amazing coastal bookshops to find a great read, then curl up in your room by the fire and enjoy the music of the waves while you relax. Winter is also the best time to view the gray whale migration and to visit the many historical museums that enrich Oregon's coastal communities.

This region provides the backdrop for all kinds of spontaneous family fun that doesn't require you to schlep any of the "stuff" that families usually seem to need. Most Oregon beaches have a built-in toybox in rocks, driftwood, and other natural tidbits. But a few helpful props can extend the fun: Frisbees, simple pails with shovels for building sand castles and digging clams, blankets for relaxing on the sand and towels for drying off, plus spare clothes to change into after a day spent tangoing with the waves.

THE NORTH & CENTRAL COASTS

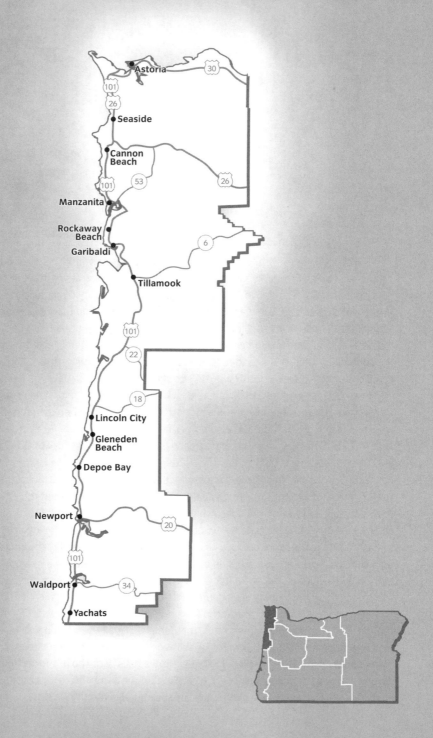

Astoria

30

101

26

Seaside

Cannon
Beach

53

26

Manzanita

101

Rockaway
Beach

Garibaldi

6

Tillamook

101

22

18

Lincoln City

Gleneden
Beach

Depoe Bay

Newport

20

101

Waldport

34

Yachats

In several places along the coast, the position of the tide will make a difference in both enjoyment and safety. Pick up a tide table when you get to the area and use it to plan your tide-pooling, beachcombing, and hiking to ensure the maximum fun for your family.

Safe Fun on the Beach

Keep in mind the following guidelines for beach safety and conservation. "Sneaker" or "rogue" waves are especially dangerous in areas such as jetties and rocky headlands where obstructions cause waves to crash with greater force. Riptides and undertows can pull children as well as adults underwater and out to sea.

Driftwood also can present dangers. If you see a log drifting in the surf, stay well away, and keep away from piles of logs on shore when waves are nearby. It's legal to build fires on the beach, but remember: Never build a fire in a large pile of driftwood or near grassy slopes that could keep burning after you leave. Before you go, douse the fire with water or wet sand. Don't bury hot coals, because someone walking along shortly after you've gone could be burned. More safety tips can be found online at www.visittheoregoncoast.com; click on "Beach Safety."

Preserving the Coast for Everyone

The Oregon coast is a popular destination for tourists because of its natural beauty and the many recreational opportunities to enjoy along its shores. Explain to your children the importance of leaving everything as they find it. As the saying goes, take nothing with you but memories; leave nothing but your footprints in the sand.

The North Coast
Astoria

Astoria was the first settlement west of the Rocky Mountains, famous for being the place where Lewis and Clark ended their 3,700-mile journey. It remains an important shipping port. Huge ships pass daily under the bridge that crosses the 4.1-mile-wide Columbia River to Washington. On the waterfront you'll find piers to walk on and shops to browse in. At **Smith Point** you can watch the shipping activity from a large viewing deck just west of

Take a **Stroll**

The Riverfront Walkway at the historic Astoria Waterfront features an ever-changing parade of sea lions, birds, freighters, tugboats, and fishing vessels. It's the perfect place for a predinner walk with your active toddlers and preschoolers.

Top Astoria **Events**

April
Astoria-Warrenton Crab & Seafood Festival. This celebration of the sea's bounty is held at Hammond Mooring Basin.

June
Scandinavian Midsummer Festival. This festival includes dances, food and craft booths, a beer garden, and performances by traditionally garbed singers and dancers. www.astoriascanfest.com.

June through July
Astoria Music Festival. This festival is held at the historic Liberty Theater in downtown Astoria and is sponsored by River Theater. (503) 325-7487.

August
Clatsop County Fair. The fair is located in the Astoria fairgrounds and features carnival rides, games, exhibitions, and a tempting array of foods. (503) 325-4600; http://clatsopfairgrounds.com.
Astoria Regatta. The century-old regatta is a week full of activities along the waterfront. Kids enjoy the demolition derby, Coast Guard drills, and boat races. www.astoriaregatta.org.

October
Fort Stevens War Reenactment. People in period costumes reenact battles and camp life at the Fort Stevens Historic Area. (503) 861-2000; www.nwcwc .org/fortstevens.html.
Great Columbia Crossing. Join the thousands who walk or run across the Columbia River over the 4.1-mile Astoria-Megler Bridge. Trek to the challenging midpoint at 205 feet above the ocean or catch a free pickup along the way. www.greatcolumbiacrossing.com.

November
St. Lucia Festival of Lights. The festival, held the day after Thanksgiving, celebrates the holiday season with an evening program honoring St. Lucia and featuring a dance. For information on Astoria events, call (800) 875-6807 or (503) 325-6311 or visit www .oldoregon.com.

Pier 1. Kids love watching the enormous cranes at work, lifting whole railroad cars onto ships that make everything else in the vicinity seem minuscule.

Astoria Column (ages 5 and up)

Reach Coxcomb Hill by driving south on Jerome Avenue and turning east onto 15th Avenue; then continue to the park entrance at Coxcomb; (503) 325-2963; www.astoriacolumn .org. Open daily dawn to dusk. $1 per car donation.

Built in 1926 for $32,550, this 125-foot landmark tower standing on Coxcomb Hill, 600 feet above the town, is a favorite with children. The mural painted on the monument's outside walls tells the history of the area as it spirals upward. To get a good view of the other community landmarks, climb the 164 winding steps.

Heritage Museum (ages 8 and up)

1618 Exchange St.; (503) 325-2203; www.cumtux.org. Open daily May through Sept 10 a.m. to 5 p.m.; Tues through Sat Oct through Apr 11 a.m. to 4 p.m. $ adults and children ages 6 to 17, under 6 free.

The museum, run by the Clatsop County Historical Society, is housed in the 1904 City Hall. The exhibits encompass all ingredients of the area's history—Native Americans, fur traders, pioneer settlers, geology and natural history, and timber and maritime industries, while the Emigrants' Gallery gives a feel for what it was like to start a new life here.

Flavel House (ages 8 and up)

Eighth and Duane Streets; (503) 325-2203; www.cumtux.org. Open daily May through Sept 10 a.m. to 5 p.m., Oct through Apr 11 a.m. to 4 p.m. $ adults and children ages 6 to 17; $$$ family (up to 3 adults and 4 children).

The Flavel House was built in 1885–87 by Captain George Flavel, the state's best-known Columbia River bar pilot. You'll start your tour in the rehabilitated Carriage House, which is now an interpretive center, and end in the regal home, one of the best-preserved examples of Queen Anne architecture in the Northwest.

Fun Fact

The Astoria Column is the only large piece of memorial architecture made of reinforced concrete. It was patterned after the famous Trajan's Column in Rome. The pictorial frieze illustrates the history of the Northwest Territory, from its discovery by Captain Gray to the arrival of the Great Northern Railroad.

Uppertown Fire Fighters Museum and Astoria Children's Museum (ages 5 and up)

30th Street and Marine Drive; (503) 325-2203; www.cumtux.org. Open Sun 1 to 4 p.m. or by appointment. **Free** (donations accepted).

There's lots of kid appeal here, including an extensive collection of old firefighting equipment and a horse-drawn fire wagon in use here in 1877.

Astoria Aquatic Center (all ages)

20th Street and Marine Drive; (503) 325-7027; www.astoriaparks.com. Open daily; call for swim times. $$ adults, $ children ages 2 to 17, $$$ family, under 2 **free.**

Opened in 1998, the Aquatic Center has 4 pools filled with nearly 200,000 gallons of water. Locker rooms are available for men and women, and parents with small children will appreciate the family changing rooms. The center also has a weight room, concession stand, waterslide, and "lazy river."

Columbia River Maritime Museum (ages 5 and up)

17th Street and Marine Drive; (503) 325-2323; www.crmm.org. Open daily 9:30 a.m. to 5 p.m. $$ adults, $ children ages 6 to 17, under 6 **free.**

Founded in 1962, the museum was recently renovated, adding interactive exhibits and oral histories that bring maritime history to life—including a new exhibit on the dangerous Columbia crossing and a map of the shipwrecks it has caused. The museum houses many miniature ships and several full-size vessels, including a WWII navy destroyer. Call for information on monthly children's programs.

Fort Clatsop National Memorial (all ages)

92343 Fort Clatsop Rd.; (503) 861-2471; www.nps.gov/lewi. Open daily 9 a.m. to 6 p.m. in summer and 9 a.m. to 5 p.m. in winter. Closed Dec 25. $.

Transport your kids back to the early 19th century with a visit to Fort Clatsop, which contains an exact replica of the stockade used by explorers Lewis and Clark when they led their Corps of Discovery into this area in 1805.

Fun Fact

The Columbia River bar is one of the most dangerous crossings in the world. When oceangoing vessels arrive at the river, they rely on the expert local river pilots to guide them across the bar.

An **Adventure** to Remember

Fort Clatsop National Memorial gives a lively lesson in 19th-century history and many rich details about the courageous Lewis and Clark expedition. From mid-June through Labor Day, buckskin-clad rangers demonstrate the art of candle making and canoe building and describe the trials of the 33-member party who camped here in the winter of 1805–06. A replica of the explorers' 50-foot-by-50-foot fort is the centerpiece of this 125-acre park. The rustic fort, a historic canoe landing, and a natural spring are surrounded by lush coastal forests and wetlands that merge with the Columbia River estuary. There is a visitor center with exhibits and audiovisual programs. Walking trails, which connect the visitor center, fort, and canoe landing, are about 1 mile in length and easy for preschoolers to navigate. For heartier legs, follow the path the Corps of Discovery made from the fort to the ocean. The 6½-mile Fort to Sea Trail starts at the visitor center, up a gentle hill where you can glimpse the ocean, then under Highway 101 and on to the shore. If you don't want to hike back, Warrenton's Old Gray Cab Company (503-861-1735) offers drop off and/ or pickup. Allow at least one to two hours to visit Fort Clatsop.

Fort Stevens State Park
and Fort Stevens Historic Area (all ages)

Located 10 miles west of Astoria off US 101 at 100 Peter Iredale Rd.; (800) 551-6949 or (503) 861-3170, (800) 452-5687 for reservations; www.oregonstateparks.org. Historic area open daily 10 a.m. to 6 p.m. in summer and 10 a.m. to 4 p.m. the rest of the year. Park hours vary. $ daily use fee or $$$$ annual permit for all state park day-use areas. Underground tours available in summer for a nominal fee; call (503) 861-2000.

Fort Stevens State Park and the adjacent Fort Stevens Historic Area, which stretch north to the mouth of the Columbia River at Clatsop Spit, are well worth a visit, especially in the summer months, when living history programs are offered.

Fort Stevens State Park encompasses sandy beaches, wetlands, forested areas of spruce and pine, and several shallow lakes. Follow a short trail to where the Columbia River meets the Pacific for an awe-inspiring view. The largest of these, Coffenbury Lake, is popular with sailboarders, hikers, swimmers, and anglers. You can circle the lake on a 2-mile trail. The park's 8-mile system of paved bicycle trails is a real treat for parents with active children.

Fort Stevens Historic Area is the only mainland military installation to receive enemy fire since the War of 1812. An interpretive center displays photographs of the fort's guns in action. Access to the still-visible 1906 shipwreck of the four-masted British ship *Peter Iredale* is through the park campground, at the end of a 1-mile road and a trail that both lead to the beach.

Fun Fact

On December 8, 1805, Captains Meriwether Lewis and William Clark set up their winter quarters at Fort Clatsop, where they began preparations for the trip home. On December 28 Lewis and Clark sent five men to find a site for mining salt along the seacoast. Five days later the men set up camp at a site 15 miles southwest of the fort. The stones they stacked to create a furnace are all that remain of the site, and their authenticity was documented by the Oregon Historical Society in 1900. To reach the saltworks site, turn west on Avenue G from US 101 and follow the green signs to South Beach Drive and Lewis & Clark Way. Find out more at www .lewisandclarktrail.com.

Astoria Riverfront Trolley (ages 3 and up)

On the Columbia riverfront between the Port of Astoria and the East End Mooring Basin; (503) 325-8790; www.oldoregon.com. Summer hours vary; generally 3 to 9 p.m. weekdays and noon to 9 p.m. weekends. $.

Old Number 300, built in 1913 and restored as part of a long-term loan from the San Antonio Museum of Art, now carries passengers along the riverfront. A sheltered deck at the end of Sixth Street and the dock at 17th Street provide views of the river and two Coast Guard cutters. The 14th Street ferry dock includes interpretive displays.

Columbia River Eco Tours (all ages)

Located at Slip D-7 at the west-end marina adjacent to the Red Lion Inn; (503) 325-8790; www.columbiariverecotours.com. Call or go online for required reservations. Tours of the lower estuary and Cape Disappointment "Graveyard of the Pacific" or of the upper estuary and Lewis & Clark Wildlife Refuge.

Captain Chris uses his love of the ocean and degree in oceanography to provide fully narrated tours exploring the rich local history and wildlife of the lower Columbia River estuary. Daily tours at 9 a.m., 3 p.m., or as requested. Sunset cruises at 7 p.m.

Seaside

Seaside has been a haven for families since pioneer settlers in the Tillamook Bay area stopped over for a rest on their way home from Portland. In 1920 Seaside built the **Promenade,** now a pedestrian walkway atop a concrete wall, paralleling an 8,000-foot stretch of beach. At the center of the Promenade, or Prom, the **Turnaround** marks the point where Lewis and Clark ended their westward journey.

From the Turnaround, Broadway is lined with amusements such as bumper cars, shooting galleries, and video arcades. Locals refer to this street as "Million Dollar Walk," no doubt because of the millions of quarters that kids have wheeled out of their parents over the years.

Seaside Aquarium (all ages)

200 N. Promenade; (503) 738-6211; www.seasideaquarium.com. Open daily at 9 a.m.; call or check the website for closing times. $$ adults, $ ages 6 to 13, $$$$ family (up to 6 people), under 6 free.

Established in 1937, the aquarium is one of the oldest on the West Coast and is home to a room full of rowdy harbor seals. You can buy a bag of fish to throw to the barking, baying bunch. Touch tanks give kids an opportunity to get close to the tide pool denizens. There's also a rubbing table and an interpretive center.

Top Seaside Events

January

Barbershop Cabaret Show. A festival of surprisingly hip and modern music, barbershop-quartet-style. (503) 738-3311; www.seasidechamber.com.

July

July 4th Celebration. Independence Day, coastal style. A parade, old-fashioned social, and fireworks on the beach. (503) 738-3311; www.seaside chamber.com.

Miss Oregon Pageant. This annual event charms many families who have never witnessed a beauty pageant live. (503) 738-9413.

Prom Walk & Beach Run. This midsummer event includes sand games and a Kids Downtown Bash.

August

Salt Makers Return. Experts in period costumes camp on the beach and re-create the salt-making efforts of Lewis and Clark's Corps of Discovery. They'll also answer your questions in character. (503) 738-7065; www.seasidemuseum.org.

September

Lewis & Clark Kite Exposition. Watch amazing stunt-kite demonstrations or try your hand at kite flying.

Seaside **Amusements** (ages 6 and up)

Amusement rides and arcades are found along Broadway—bumper cars, a carousel, and video arcades. A few miles south of town off US 101, you'll find miniature golf and go-karts. In addition, more fun can be found at these locations:

- **Outdoor Fun For All.** 407 S. Holladay Dr.; (503) 738-8447. Electric or standard bikes, lowriders, surreys, kayaks, and electric cars.

- **Interstate Amusement Co.** 110 Broadway; (503) 738-5540. Bumper cars, Tilt-A-Whirl, miniature golf, ice cream, and snacks. Non-summer hours vary widely.

- **Seaside Helicopters.** Just south of Seaside on US 101; (503) 738-7435; www .seaside-helicopters.com.

- **Funland Entertainment Center.** 201 Broadway; (503) 738-7361. Saltwater aquarium, video games, pinball, shooting gallery, air hockey, pizza restaurant, and big-screen TV.

- **Carousel Mall.** 300 Broadway; (503) 738-6728. Snacks and shops (such as Under the Big Top Toys) surround an indoor carousel.

- **Sunset Empire Park & Recreation.** 1140 Broadway; (503) 738-3311. Year-round swimming pool, spa, skate park and playground equipment.

- **Faraway Farms** (ages 10 and under). On Hamlet Road off US 101, immediately south of Seaside; (503) 738-6336. Call for appointments and prices.

The Seaside Museum and Historical Society (ages 5 and up)

570 Necanicum Dr. at Fifth Street; (503) 738-7065; www.seasidemuseum.org. Open Mon through Sat May through Sept 10 a.m. to 4 p.m., Oct through Apr 10 a.m. to 3 p.m. $ adults and kids, 6 and under free.

Lewis and Clark exhibits, along with Native American displays and depictions of the town's development as the ultimate family beach resort, charm parents and children alike. Kids love the photographs of Seaside's early bathing beauties. Butterfield Cottage depicts a rooming house from 1912.

Prom Bike Shop (all ages)

622 12th Ave.; (503) 738-8251; www.prombikeshop.com. Open daily 10:30 a.m. to 5:30 p.m. Rental prices vary.

Explore Seaside on wheels—bicycles or in-line skates. You'll be amazed at the variety of transportation modes available from this rental shop—bikes, tandems, adult two-seater trikes, infant seats, strollers, skates, Rollerblades, scooters, and surreys (four-person pedal carts).

Broadway Park (all ages)

Located off Broadway at the east end of town along the banks of Neawanna Creek; (800) 444-6740. Free.

You'll find covered picnic shelters and plenty of games for your family to play here. In summer, as part of Lewis and Clark historical reenactments, you can participate in the forgotten art of salt making on the beach (at the end of Avenue U).

Goodman Park (all ages)

(800) 444-6740. Free.

Next to the 12th Avenue bridge you'll find an entertaining space with swings, picnic area, and skate park, plus a locally famous salmon mural re-created from 34,000 tiles salvaged from its original 1960s location. Locals come here for easy crabbing access.

Cannon Beach

Cannon Beach, like Rockaway Beach to the south, developed as a resort community. The town combines quaint old-time charm with a thriving cultural community, good restaurants, and interesting shops—all within view of the most picturesque stretches of beach in the state.

Haystack Rock (ages 5 and up)

One-half mile south of Cannon Beach off US 101; (503) 436-2623; www.cannonbeach.org (click on "Haystack Rock"). Always open, though cut off from land at high tide. Free.

This ocean landmark has graced many a calendar and coffee-table book. A designated marine garden and bird sanctuary, the 235-foot Cannon Beach Haystack is one of the world's largest freestanding monoliths. Enjoy the tide pools around its base, which are accessible at low tide. In summer, interpretive guides are on hand to help identify the many marine species visible at low tide.

Ecola State Park (all ages)

Two miles north of Cannon Beach just off US 101; (800) 551-6949; www.oregonstateparks .org. Open until dusk. Summer day-use fee $ or $$$$ annual state park pass.

This day-use area provides an incredible view from the picnic tables, where brazen seagulls will beg your kids for handouts. Children love exploring **Indian Beach,** a tiny cove littered with driftwood and rocks.

Cannon Beach History Center and Museum (ages 5 and up)

387 S. Spruce St.; (503) 436-9301; www.cbhistory.org. Open daily except Tues 1 to 5 p.m. Free.

Relive the anxiety of the World War II blackouts or the terror of the 1964 tsunami that hit Cannon Beach. Learn about the history of the area through visual and hands-on exhibits including a Native American longhouse.

Sea Ranch Stables (ages 10 and up)

415 Fir St. at the back of Sea Ranch RV Park; (503) 436-2815; www.cannon-beach.net/sea ranch. Rides offered daily mid-June through Labor Day, 9 a.m. to 4:30 p.m. $$$$ (prices vary by length of ride, 45 minutes to multiple hours).

Reservations must be made in person at the stables. All rides are led by competent, experienced guides who strive to make each trip enjoyable and memorable. Horses are not available to take out on your own. Reservations are recommended, but walk-ins are welcome on a first-come, first-served basis. Rides vary from trips to Haystack Rock to special night excursions.

Top Cannon Beach **Events**

June

Cannon Beach Sand Castle Day. Bring your sand-carving tools to this international event that offers cash prizes. (503) 436-2623, ext. 3; www.cannon beach.org.

July through Labor Day

Sunday Concerts in the Park. Cannon Beach City Park, Second and Spruce Streets. Bring a picnic, spread out a blanket, and kick back and enjoy the music. (503) 436-0744; www.cannonbeach.org.

October

Annual Dog Show on the Beach. No Kennel Club credentials needed: with categories like "So Ugly You're Cute," Frisbee Catch, and Best Trick, it's a surefire family hit. (800) 547-6100; www.surfsand.com/pets.

All Year

Coaster Theatre. 108 N. Hemlock. This theater company hosts many productions with kids in mind. (503) 436-1242; www.coastertheatre.com.

Other Things to See & Do
in Cannon Beach

It's almost impossible to visit Cannon Beach without wandering through its many attractive stores. Kids can buy trinkets and treasures at **Geppetto's Toy Shoppe,** 200 N. Hemlock St. (503-436-2467), or experience some science fun at the **ExploraStore,** 1315 S. Hemlock St. (503-436-1844). You might even lure the children through some of the many art galleries in town with the promise of a stop at **Bruce's Candy Kitchen,** 256 N. Hemlock St, (503-436-2641), where watching the taffy-pulling machines is mouthwatering, or the **Picnic Basket,** 144 N. Hemlock St. (503-436-1470), where kids can enjoy ice cream cones while you get a lift from a shot of espresso.

Mike's Bike Shop (all ages)

West of City Park on Spruce Street; (503) 436-1266 or (800) 492-1266; www.mikesbike.com. $$ to $$$ per hour; $$$$ weekly rates. Open daily 9 a.m. to 6 p.m. mid-Mar through mid-Sept, 10 a.m. to 5 p.m. daily the rest of the year.

You can rent bikes for all ages (infant trailers or bike seats for kids under 3)—mountain bikes, tandems, and the classic whitewall "cruisers," as well as recumbent tricycles that are great for use on the beach (only available during low tide). Younger children pedal their own tagalong "bikes" attached behind Mom or Dad. Mike's even rents strollers for use around town when the little ones are worn out.

Fun Fact

Just a few miles north of Cannon Beach at the US 101 and Highway 26 junction is what used to be the world's tallest Sitka spruce: a 216-foot-high tree with a trunk 52 feet in circumference located in an old-growth fir and spruce forest in Klootchy Creek Park. A violent 2008 storm snapped the tree, which is believed to be more than seven centuries old, almost in half. The stump is still living and has retained the tree's designation as Oregon's first Heritage Tree, and fans still visit to watch its progress as new branches emerge and the top half, left lying on the ground, becomes a humongous nurse log.

Hug Point State Recreation Site (all ages)
Located 5 miles south of Cannon Beach off US 101; (800) 551-6949; www.oregonstateparks
.org. Always open. Free.

This park, named for the way pioneers traveling the beach "highway" had to hug the point
at low tide in order to pass, has caves and sections of the old road carved out of rock to
explore, though these are cut off when the tide comes in.

Manzanita

One of the most delightful beaches on this stretch of the north coast is the lesser-known
Manzanita, a small community that sits a few miles off US 101. Walk the beach in relative
solitude, or blend the sound of pounding horse hooves with the pounding surf on a horseback ride along the shore (call **Pearl Creek Stables** at 503-368-5267). The solitude makes
this a nice place to stay. Cafes, a few stores, and a small library are all nearby when you
want to wander away from the beach.

Neahkahnie Mountain (ages 8 and up)
The trailhead is ½ mile off US 101, 1½ miles north of Manzanita to hiker sign; turn east on
rocky access road ½ mile to trailhead. Neahkahnie Mountain is in Oswald West State Park,
which stretches to the north beyond Cape Falcon and Smuggler's Cove; (800) 551-6949;
www.oregonstateparks.org. Free.

To get a bird's-eye view of the beach and bay, walk to the top of Neahkahnie Mountain,
which rises 1,631 feet above the surf. The 1½-mile trail takes you through forest and, in

Fishing in Nehalem Bay

Nehalem Bay, according to locals, is one of the richest estuaries for both
clamming and crabbing. If you don't have your own equipment, the following
outlets can get you set up with buckets, shovels, and such.

Nehalem Bay fisheries (ages 10 and up). Rent crab rings or clam shovels as
well as boats and motors from either of these fisheries:

Brighton Marina. 29200 N. US 101, 3½ miles south of Wheeler; (503) 368-
5745. Call for hours. $$ for baited crab ring rentals to use on the dock. Boat
rentals $$$$ for 3 hours and 3 baited crab rings.

Wheeler Marina. 278 Marina Dr., 2 miles south of Nehalem off US 101;
(503) 368-5780. Call for hours. Boat rental $$$$ per hour; $ for crab rings; $
for bait. They also rent kayaks and will give you a short lesson on paddling
around Nehalem Bay estuary.

spring, beautiful wildflower meadows. Legend tells of buried treasure on the mountain, an enticing tidbit to entertain kids along the way. During World War II a Coast Guard sentry watched from the mountaintop for invaders. Allow an hour to get to the rocky summit, where children must use caution.

Oswald West State Park (ages 5 and up)
Located 10 miles south of Cannon Beach off US 101; (800) 551-6949; www.oregonstateparks .org. Free.

Strewn with red needles, the path through this enchanting rain forest is so peaceful that you can easily forget the ocean waves crashing on the cape just beyond. The trees form such a dense canopy that even if it's raining, you'll hardly notice. From the **Short Sand Beach** parking lot, follow a trail that parallels Short Sand Creek to where it merges with Necarney Creek at the ocean shore.

Rockaway Beach & Garibaldi

Rockaway and Garibaldi are small towns whose livelihoods depend on the sea, but in very different ways. Rockaway grew up as a resort community, while Garibaldi, one of the earliest settlements on the coast, is very much a working community.

Garibaldi Marina and Boat Rentals (ages 8 and up)
302 Mooring Basin Rd.; (800) 383-3828 or (503) 322-3312. Open daily 5 a.m. to 5 p.m. $ for crab ring rentals; $$$$ for 3-hour boat rentals, $$ each additional hour.

Rent crab rings at the Garibaldi Marina and catch your own appetizers. Boat rentals let you get out on the bay, and charters are available for deep-sea fishing.

Barview Jetty County Campground (ages 8 and up)
Located just north of Garibaldi off US 101; (503) 322-3522, (503) 322-0301 (chamber); www .co.tillamook.or.us/gov/parks/Campgrounds. Always open. Free for day use; $ camping.

This 160-acre park is a great place for surf fishing, and the beach to the north of the jetty gives the kids a place to roam. Campsites available year-round.

Fun Fact

Garibaldi was once the site of a Tillamook Indian whaling village. It was later explored by Captains Drake, Meares, and Cook and became a major lumber port and fishing village.

Oregon Coast Scenic Railroad (all ages)

403 American Way off US 101; (503) 842-7972; www.ocsr.net. Memorial Day through Sept, day trips leave weekends from Garibaldi at noon, 2 p.m., and 4 p.m. and from Rockaway Beach at 1 and 3 p.m.

Step back in time along the scenic Oregon coastline by riding the rail behind a 1910 Heisler steam locomotive. Call or check the website for sunset dinner trains (3 hours round-trip) and special excursions year-round.

Memorial Lumberman's Park (ages 5 and up)

**Third and American Streets, Garibaldi; (503) 322-0301. Always open.
Free.**

For a picnic and a bit of local industrial history, stop by this park.
Old logging donkeys and railroad equipment placed throughout the park invite children to climb.

Oregon **Coast Pass**

This multiagency pass covers entry, vehicle parking, and day-use fees at all state and federal fee sites along the entire Oregon coast. You can buy an annual pass valid for the calendar year for $35 or a 5-day pass for $10. For more information or to purchase your annual pass by phone, call the Oregon State Parks Information Center at (800) 551-6949.

The passport covers entry for the following locations:

- Fort Stevens State Park
- Ecola State Park
- Nehalem Bay State Park
- Cape Lookout State Park
- Fogarty Creek State Recreation Area
- Heceta Head Lighthouse Viewpoint
- Honeyman State Park
- Shore Acres State Park
- Fort Clatsop National Memorial

- Oregon Dunes National Recreation Area
- Sutton Recreation Area
- Cape Perpetua Scenic Area
- Sand Lake Recreation Area
- Marys Peak Recreation Area
- Drift Creek Falls Trail
- Yaquina Head Outstanding Natural Area
- Hebo Lake

Top Rockaway Beach & Garibaldi **Events**

May
Rockaway Kite Festival. During the day kids get help from the Oregon Kiters Association in making their own kites. A teddy bear drop and hobby horse races add to lots of family-oriented fun. When the weather's right, a lighted kite flight in the evening requires blankets for snuggling together on the beach.

July
Garibaldi Days Festival. Includes fishing derby, crabbing derby, antique car show, dancing in the street, parade, and children's games in the park. (503) 322-0301.

Tillamook

Most Oregonians know about Tillamook, if only because of the delicious cheddar cheese to be found in every grocery store cold case. Tillamook is a small community, well inland from the ocean but enjoying the generally mild climate associated with the coast.

Tillamook Cheese Factory (all ages)
4175 US 101 N; (503) 815-1300; www.tillamookcheese.com. Open daily 8 a.m. to 8 p.m. in summer; 8 a.m. to 6 p.m. the rest of the year. Free.

The Tillamook Cheese Factory is a favorite for all ages, with its free offerings of cheese samples. Be sure to take a quick tour to learn about the cheese-making process. Then stop by the deli to purchase a variety of packaged cheeses for vacation snacks or to send home, or choose from up to 40 flavors of Tillamook ice cream.

Blue Heron Cheese and Wine Company (all ages)
Located 1 mile north of Tillamook off US 101; (503) 842-8281 or (800) 275-0639; www.blue heronoregon.com. Summer hours 8 a.m. to 8 p.m.; winter hours 9 a.m. to 6 p.m. Free.

Blue Heron is a less well-known (and less crowded) cheese company in the area that offers delicious samples of creamy Bries as well as home-smoked sausages. Blue Heron sells its products at an on-site deli-restaurant. Have a snack, then head for the petting farm on the premises, filled with goats, emu, llamas, rabbits, cows, and sheep.

Tillamook County Pioneer Museum (ages 5 and up)
2106 Second St.; (503) 842-4553; www.tcpm.com. Open Tues through Sun 10 a.m. to 4 p.m. $ adults and kids 10 to 17, under 10 free.

Money-Saving **Travel Tips**

- Be sure to ask if a complimentary breakfast is included in the hotel rate. Enjoying a simple continental breakfast with the children in the room is often more relaxing than dining out first thing in the morning.

- A room with a small refrigerator saves money when you load it up with fruit, juice, and yogurt for the kids to snack on.

This large museum contains more than 35,000 artifacts of pioneers and Native Americans who lived in this area and features a replica of the original stump house where Tillamook's first settler lived.

Tillamook Air Museum (ages 5 and up)

6030 Hangar Rd., 2 miles south of Tillamook off US 101; (503) 842-1130; www.tillamookair
.com. Open daily year-round 9 a.m. to 5 p.m. Adults $$, children 6 to 17 $, under 6 free.

This museum is enclosed inside a World War II blimp hangar, with fighter planes and blimps that are fascinating for kids. The largest clear-span wood building in the world, the hangar is as wide as a football field is long and stretches 1,072 feet from end to end. The ceiling is 15 stories high—195 feet—making everything inside seem tiny by comparison. The hangar housed blimps that patrolled the ocean for enemy submarines during the war.

Cape Lookout State Park (all ages)

Located 12 miles southwest of Tillamook on Whiskey Creek Road; (800) 551-6949 or (503) 842-3182; (800) 452-5687 for camping reservations; www.oregonstateparks.org. Open daily year-round; $ day-use fee.

This is part of the **Three Capes Loop drive,** which takes you off US 101 for about 35 miles between Tillamook and Neskowin to view three outstanding natural areas. The park extends north along the Netarts Spit, which forms the boundary of Netarts Bay. Many campsites have ocean views or direct beach access. Yurts—canvas-walled circular build-ings—and tepees are available to campers who aren't traveling with their own tents, but weekend reservations fill up fast, so if you're planning to stay here, reserve early!

Cape Meares State Scenic Viewpoint (all ages)

Located 9 miles northwest of Tillamook via Whiskey Creek Road; (503) 842-7525 or (800) 551-6949; www.oregonstateparks.org or www.capemeareslighthouse.org. Open daily 7 a.m. to dusk; lighthouse usually open 11 a.m. to 4 p.m. Apr through Oct, weather permit-ting. Free.

The 1890 **Cape Meares Lighthouse** and the nearby giant spruce **Octopus Tree** are perennial favorites of kids. Oregon's largest seabird colonies thrive at **Three Arch Rocks**

National Wildlife Refuge offshore, where species include common murre, tufted puffin, storm petrel, and pigeon guillemot.

Cape Kiwanda State Natural Area (all ages)
Located south of Cape Lookout, 15 miles southwest of Tillamook on Whiskey Creek Road; (503) 842-7525 or (800) 551-6949; www.oregonstateparks.org. Day use only. Free.

You can watch Pacific City dories launch if you're here early in the morning, but it's even more fun to be standing on the beach just south of the park when they're on their way to shore. They head straight for the sand, riding to ground on high waves.

Munson Creek Falls (ages 3 and up)
Located about 6.5 miles south of Tillamook on US 101; (503) 842-7525 or (800) 551-6949; www.oregonstateparks.org. Always open. Free.

Here you'll find a trailhead that takes you through old-growth forest to the highest water-fall (319 feet) in the Oregon Coast Range. The 1½-mile road into the small parking area is pretty rough, but the ¼-mile walk to the falls is worth the ride. Another ½-mile trail leads to an upper viewpoint.

The Central Coast
Lincoln City

The largest of the coastal resort towns, Lincoln City has almost 8 miles of wide-open sands where families can walk, fly kites, jump over waves, and soak up the sun or—since this is, after all, the Oregon coast—the rain. With 15 beach access spots in town, you'll have no problem finding your way onto the sand.

Fun Fact

Lincoln City is the Kite Capital of the World, because kites are frequent sky decorations, especially along the beach around the D River. **Catch the Wind Kite Shop,** 266 SE US 101 (541-994-9500; www.catchthewind.com), south of the D River wayside, sells kites of all shapes and sizes for parents and kids who want to try their own hand at kite flying.

The D River is the world's shortest river, flowing from Devil's Lake a brief 120 feet to the ocean.

Devil's Lake has an interesting history, according to Indian folklore. Once known as Indian Bay, the lake was supposedly inhabited by an evil spirit, and sometimes Siletz warriors mysteriously disappeared in it. The legend remains that if a boat crosses the moon's reflection in the center of the lake, the passengers will feel a chill of fear rise up from the water.

Connie Hansen Gardens (ages 8 and up)

1931 NW 33rd St.; (541) 994-6338; www.conniehansengarden.com. Open daily dawn to dusk; hosted Tues and Sat 10 a.m. to 2 p.m. Mar through Nov. Free; donations appreciated.

Constance P. Hansen, a trained botanist, moved to Lincoln City in 1973 and developed a 1-acre plot with her own hybrid and exotic plants, converting an overgrown marshland meadow and creek into a showcase for more than 300 varieties of rare rhododendrons as well as azaleas, primroses, Siberian and Japanese irises, and hardy perennials. Today the Connie Hansen Garden Conservancy, a group of dedicated volunteers, continues to plant and tend the garden, guides visitors, and conducts horticulture classes.

Lincoln City Skateboard Park (ages 10 and up)

Behind Kirtsis Field on NE 22nd Street and US 101; (541) 994-8378 or (800) 452-2151. Always open. Free.

Lincoln City's skateboarders' oasis in Kirtsis Park has been named one of the "gnarliest" parks in the United States. The 8,000-square-foot facility has more than 100 lines and a unique 9-foot bowl to challenge boarders of all levels. It hosts the Board Games Skateboard Tournament, a competition for professionals, amateurs, and beginners held in September and October. The nearby Cradle, at 8,600 square feet, features 5,600 covered square feet for bad-weather boarding. It's named for its dome-shaped cradle that allows boarders to skate upside down—one of only a handful worldwide.

Pacific Northwest Surfing Museum (ages 12 and up)

Located inside the Lincoln City Surf Shop at 4792 SE US 101; (541) 996-7433. Free.

If your li'l dudes are into hanging ten, they'll enjoy a quick stop at this in-store museum, which has some 20 surfboards on display, along with newspaper articles, posters, books, videos, club jackets, and other paraphernalia from the history of surfing in the Northwest.

Fun Fact

Cascade Head is home to the Oregon silverspot butterfly, listed as a threatened species. It's known to only five other locations in the world.

Devil's Lake **Parks** (all ages)

Six parks offer recreation on Devil's Lake, from fishing and boating (in daylight, of course) to camping and picnicking. Call for hours and fees: (800) 551-6949, (541) 994-8378, or (541) 994-2131.

Blue Heron Landing, 4006 W. Devil's Lake Rd. (541-994-4708), has plenty of choices for water play. Canoes, paddleboats, bumper boats, and motorboats are available for rent by the day or by the hour.

Regatta Park is located on Devil's Lake, ¾ mile east off US 101 on Regatta Park Road. You can take advantage of a ½-mile exercise and jogging path while your kids try out the large castle-like wooden playground equipment, then visit the Interpretive Center or explore the walking trails.

Sand Point Park, located off East Devil's Lake Road on a point of land jutting into the lake, has a swimming beach and picnic tables.

Devil's Lake State Park, 1452 NE Sixth Dr., has camping facilities straddled between the lake and the ocean. It's open year-round, and you can make reservations in advance by calling (800) 452-5687. Check out the new wetland ecology trail.

Holmes Road Park, on Holmes Road, 8 blocks off US 101. A small dock allows access to the lake, and the picnic tables in this little park have a great view.

East Devil's Lake Park, located near the southern tip of the lake on East Devil's Lake Road near the Factory Stores at Lincoln City. There's a boat dock here, and a moderately difficult ½-mile hike takes you through natural forestland

North Lincoln County Historical Museum (ages 5 and up)

4907 SW US 101; (541) 996-6614; www.northlincolncountyhistoricalmuseum.org. Open Wed through Sat noon to 5 p.m., Sun in summer. Closed Dec 15 through Jan. $ family.

Housed in the old fire hall, the museum's rooms are set up as they would have looked in the early days of the pioneers. Displays include a variety of Native American baskets and beadwork as well as a hands-on table with pioneer and Native American artifacts that kids can handle, plus puppets and coloring activities. Most summer Thursday afternoons offer oral history or film archive presentations.

Top Lincoln City **Events**

March
Indoor Kite Festival & Kids Carnival. Think you need wind for kites? Think again. Kite experts perform and teach indoor kite flying. The nearby Kids Carnival at Taft High School is fashioned after the school carnivals of yesteryear.

June
Summer Kite Festival. Another kite extravaganza that offers prizes for the best children's kites, among other categories.

Late Summer
Sand Castle Competition. Fun in the sand for the whole family. If you aren't up to sculpting your own, you can watch the pros at work.

October
Fall Kite Festival. D River Wayside. The biggest and most spectacular of Lincoln City's annual events. Kids are thrilled by skydivers gliding on gigantic kitelike, colorful parachutes; kite battles and team choreography; and nighttime lighted kite flying.

October through May
Glass Float Search. From October through Memorial Day, handblown glass floats by local artisans are hidden above the high-tide level. If you find one, take it to the Visitor Center (801 SW US 101) for a certificate and description of the artist.

For information about Lincoln City events, call (800) 452-2151 or (541) 996-1274; www.oregoncoast.org.

Ocean Trails Riding Stables (ages 7 and up)

Located in Neskowin, 8 miles north of Lincoln City; (541) 994-4849 or (541) 921-1631. Beach rides June through Sept. $$$$ per hour.

Kids gain confidence and burn some of that seemingly endless energy handling the stable's well-trained horses on hour-long trail and beach rides. Call a few days ahead of time for reservations.

Super Shopping
Factory Stores at Lincoln City

US 101 at E. Devil's Lake Road; (541) 996-5000 or (866) 665-8680; www.tanger outlet.com. Open Mon through Sat 10 a.m. to 8 p.m., Sun 10 a.m. to 6 p.m.; daily 10 a.m. to 6 p.m. Jan and Feb. No discussion of activities in Lincoln City can ignore the presence of this mammoth shopping center. The collection of big-name factory stores includes at least a few to keep the kids happy: Go! Toys & Games, Stride Rite, Carter's Childrenswear, Children's Place Outlet, Gymboree Outlet, and the Book Warehouse. There's also an ice cream shop tucked in the mall, offering rewards for patience and good behavior!

Cascade Head (ages 5 and up)
Located 4 miles north of Lincoln City at the west end of Three Rocks Road (lower trailhead) or 3.3 miles west from US 101 on Cascade Head Road 1861; (503) 392-3161 or (541) 994-5564; www.oregon.com/hiking. Open dawn to dusk. No pets. Free.

An area of outstanding scenic beauty just 4 miles north of Lincoln City, Cascade Head is a haven for rare plants and the threatened Oregon silverspot butterfly and offers hiking trails to suit all ages. The two Nature Conservancy trails open up to a headland meadow that conjures the hilltop scene in the *Sound of Music* and has one of the best ocean views on the coast. The 1-mile upper trail is flat and easy but closed Jan 1 through mid-July. The 4⅕-mile lower trail, with a moderate incline, is open year-round.

Taft Waterfront Park (all ages)
Located at the mouth of the Siletz River, off 51st Street on the south side of town. Open dawn to dusk. Free.

Sea lions often congregate here and across the river on the northern edge of the Salishan Spit, which forms the south edge of the Siletz River mouth. A small parking area has restrooms. Crabbing is good at high tide October through February, off the public crabbing dock. Rent crab rings from **Eleanor's Undertow** (541-996-3800), a restaurant and take-out at 869 SW 51st St., for $10 for 24 hours, including bait, bucket, and gauge. While you're at Eleanor's, grab a delicious burger or crab cake to take with you, and top it off with one of Granny's Quarter-Pound Chocolate Chip Cookies, or what one local journalist deemed the best milk shake in the state.

Gleneden Beach

Here you'll find a small marketplace ideal for browsing or picking up picnic supplies, a golf course, and a resort that makes any trip to the coast very special. **Westin Salishan**

Lodge (800-452-2300; www.salishan.com), a well-known five-star resort, has something for the whole family: tennis courts, swimming pool, exercise room, large whirlpool spa, sauna, nature walks, jogging path, playground, and video arcade. Or head to **Gleneden Beach State Recreation Site** at milepost 122.5 and follow the short trail from the parking lot to a soft sand beach popular with both surfers and sea lions.

Depoe Bay

A little fishing village that claims the world's smallest harbor, Depoe Bay sits midway between the larger towns of Lincoln City and Newport. From the bridge it's fun to watch the boats navigate the narrow, rocky channel that leads into the tiny harbor. Your kids will be more fascinated by the spouting horns, a pair of ocean-driven geysers that spout plumes of water with the crashing of the waves, especially at high tide or after a storm. Watch out, though—if the waves are strong, you're in for a dousing!

Fogarty Creek State Recreation Area (all ages)

Two miles north of Depoe Bay on US 101; (800) 551-6949; www.oregonstateparks.com. Day use only. Free.

This is a beautiful spot to spend the day. You can walk on the path alongside the creek as it lazily winds through the park, crossing picturesque arched footbridges at several points. Spread out a picnic feast at the charming cove where Fogarty Creek meets the sea, and explore the tide pools at low tide.

Boiler Bay State Scenic Viewpoint (all ages)

One mile north of Depoe Bay on US 101; (800) 551-6949; www.oregonstateparks.com. Day use only. Free.

Between the bustling, commercial main drags of Lincoln City and Depoe Bay lies this stunning oasis of a viewpoint, with 180-degree views of the coastline, picnic tables,

Top Depoe Bay **Events**

September
Depoe Bay Annual Indian Style Salmon Bake. Sample delicious salmon prepared on alder stakes over open fire pits. The Siletz Dancers often perform traditional tribal dances for this event. (877) 485-8348 or (541) 765-2889.

May
Fleet of Flowers. Each Memorial Day, Depoe Bay's fishing fleet heads out to sea en masse, bedecked in flowers to honor those lost at sea. A truly moving tribute that helps families connect with the original intent of the holiday.

restrooms, and a large grassy area for little legs to stretch. It's also a great whale-watching spot.

Tradewinds Charters (all ages)
Located at north end of the bridge in Depoe Bay; (800) 445-8730 or (541) 765-2345; www .tradewindscharters.com. Whale-watching tour: $$$ adults and teens, $$ ages 5 to 12, under 5 free.

To experience the passage from the deck of a boat, try a whale-watching or fishing charter trip.

Whale Watching Center (ages 5 and up)
Located at north end of Depoe Bay Bridge; (541) 765-3304; www.oregonstateparks.org. Open daily 9 a.m. to 5 p.m. from Memorial Day to Labor Day, otherwise 10 a.m. to 4 p.m. Wed to Sat and noon to 4 p.m. Sun. Free.

The home of Oregon's "Whale Watching Spoken Here" winter and spring break whale-watching program, the center is not only a great spot from which to look for gray whales—including the area's resident pod that lives offshore March through December—but also a rich source of facts about them.

Otter Crest Loop (all ages)
Two miles south of the Depot Bay Bridge off Highway 101; (541) 574-2679. Always open. Free.

Take this 3-mile former section of the Coast Highway that's now a short alternate route. Kids will be fascinated by the first half-mile, where a single lane (one-way southbound) winds through the forested cliffs accompanied only by a bike lane. If you've brought bikes, older kids (it's a gradual uphill) could ride with one adult and meet the other and the car at **Cape Foulweather,** a charming reward at 500 feet above the ocean, where viewpoints share cliff space with **The Lookout** (541-765-2270), equal parts visitor center, museum, and gift shop.

Otter Rock & Devil's Punchbowl
State Natural Area (all ages)
Four and a half miles south of Depot Bay Bridge on US 101; (800) 551-6949; www.oregon stateparks.com. Day use only. Free.

Even young kids will be fascinated by the ocean roiling up through a bowl-shaped hole in the rocky cliffs below. A trail leads to an area of tide pools that is perfect for exploring during low or minus tides (indicated with a minus sign on the tide table). It can be hazardous during high tides, however, so keep an eye on the water level. This is also a popular whale-watching site. Restrooms, picnic sites, and a small cluster of nearby businesses make this a great lunch stop. **Mo's West** (541-765-2442) has been serving chowder and cheese bread to Punchbowl visitors since 1972. (Closed in winter, call for hours.) The **Flying Dutchman Winery** (541-765-2553) is the only winery on the Oregon coast, and its ice cream stand next door will entertain the kids while parents taste.

Whale-Watching Sites

Volunteers are usually stationed at the sites below to help you spot migrating whales during the peak migration seasons—the last two weeks in March and late December through early January. For specific dates and more information on the giants of the ocean, visit www.whalespoken.org or call (541) 765-3407 or (800) 551-6949.

- Ecola State Park
- Neahkahnie Mountain Historic Marker on US 101
- Cape Meares State Scenic Viewpoint
- Cape Lookout State Park (2½-mile hike to site at the tip of the cape)
- Inn at Spanish Head lobby on the 10th floor
- Boiler Bay State Scenic Viewpoint
- Depoe Bay Sea Wall
- Rocky Creek State Scenic Viewpoint
- Cape Foulweather
- Devil's Punchbowl (Otter Rock) State Natural Area
- Yaquina Head Lighthouse
- Yaquina Bay State Recreation Site
- Seal Rock State Recreation Site
- Yachats State Park
- Devil's Churn Viewpoint
- Cape Perpetua Overlook

- Cape Perpetua Interpretive Center
- Sea Lion Caves Turnout (large US 101 turnout south of tunnel)
- Umpqua Lighthouse, near Umpqua Lighthouse State Park
- Shore Acres State Park
- Face Rock Wayside State Scenic Viewpoint
- Cape Blanco Lighthouse, near Cape Blanco State Park
- Battle Rock Wayfinding Point, Port Orford
- Cape Sebastian
- Cape Ferrelo
- Harris Beach State Park, Brookings

Newport

This central Oregon coast community has developed a successful tourist industry that works hard to give people experiences worth coming back for. Visitors can easily spend a weekend exploring three main areas in town: the historic **Bayfront,** from which Newport's still-prominent fishing industry operates; **Nye Beach,** a beloved vacation spot at the turn of the 20th century that boasts a wide beach and several cafes and shops to explore; and **South Beach,** where families can go crabbing and visit the Marine Science Center and Oregon Coast Aquarium.

Oregon Coast Aquarium (ages 3 and up)

2820 SE Ferry Slip Rd.; (541) 867-3474; www.aquarium.org. Open daily 9 a.m. to 6 p.m. in summer and 10 a.m. to 5 p.m. in winter. $$$ ages 13 and older, $$ ages 3 to 12, children under 3 free.

The 29-acre state-of-the-art aquarium is an impressive complex nestled on the south shore of Yaquina Bay. Everything is geared to give your children an educational experience they'll only remember as fun. A favorite with kids of all ages is watching the otters float on their backs as they dine on crustaceans and other goodies at feeding time, or walking "through" an aquarium via the glass tunnel. On busy summer weekends it's a good idea to reserve tickets in advance or purchase them at the Lincoln City Visitors Center (801 US 101 S).

Mark O. Hatfield Marine Science Center (ages 5 and up)

2030 SE Marine Science Dr., south side of Yaquina Bay and east of US 101; (541) 867-0271; http://hmsc.orst.edu/visitor. Open daily 10 a.m. to 5 p.m. in summer and 10 a.m. to 4 p.m. Thurs through Mon the rest of the year. Free; donations appreciated.

This is a terrific, long-beloved option for coastal education. Your children will love the touching pool, where they can have close encounters with starfish, sea urchins, anemones, sculpins, and the deliciously yucky sea cucumber. The resident octopus is another favorite.

Super Shopping

Every Saturday May through October, you can pick up fresh organic produce, cut flowers, catch-of-the-day seafood, and local arts and crafts at the Newport Saturday Market. Open 9 a.m. to 1 p.m. in the Armory parking lot behind City Hall; park on Ninth Street. (541) 574-4040; http://newportfarmers market.org.

Top Newport **Events**

November to March
Oregon Coast Aquarium Family Sleepovers. Four weekends a year, the aquarium allows the public to reserve spots to "sleep with the sharks." Pitch your sleeping bags in the Passages of the Deep tunnels and fall asleep seemingly amid the fish. Pizza, a scavenger hunt, and a behind-the-scenes tour add to the kid appeal. Advance registration required. (541) 867-3474, ext. 5301.

May
Loyalty Days and Sea Fare. This gala 4-day event celebrates patriotism with a carnival, a parade, military ship tours, and lots of food and fun.

July
Rope in some good-old family fun at the annual **Lincoln County Fair and Rodeo.**

For information on these and other Newport events, call (800) 262-7844 or (541) 265-8801 or visit www.newportchamber.org.

Ripley's Believe It Or Not (ages 7 and up)

Wax Works (ages 7 and up)
Undersea Gardens (ages 4 and up)
Located at Mariner Square, 250 SW Bay Blvd.; (541) 265-2206; www.marinersquare.com. All open daily 9 a.m. to 8 p.m. July and Aug, 10 a.m. to 6 p.m. June and Sept, generally 10 a.m. to 5 p.m. the rest of the year. Admission to each center: $$ adults, $ ages 5 to 12, under 4 free. Combo rates for all three: $$$ adults, $$ children.

You can pay one admission price to enjoy all three Bayfront attractions or pick a favorite. Our family's favorite has always been the Undersea Gardens, located across the street. Call ahead to find out the schedule for the diver who adds an extra dimension to the show.

Bike Newport (ages 5 and up)

150 NW Sixth St.; (541) 265-9917; www.bikenewport.net. Hours are 10 a.m. to 6 p.m. year-round; closed Sun. Basic rental rates $$ per hour; daily and weekly rates available.

This bike shop is close to the beach access at Nye Beach and rents road bikes, mountain bikes, kids' bikes, trailers, and tag-alongs. Helmets included. They'll also provide maps and directions for all types of riding in the Newport area, from family trips to road, mountain, trail, or sightseeing.

Yaquina Head Outstanding Natural Area (all ages)

Two miles north of Newport off US 101; (541) 574-3129; www.yaquinalights.org. Open dawn to dusk daily. Lighthouse and Interpretive Center open daily; call for hours. $$ day-use pass.

Visitors are in for a real treat here. During whale migrations there's often a park ranger on hand with strong binoculars or a spotting scope to help you see them. During summer some resident gray whales have taken to feeding offshore. You can also get a look at a wandering sea lion or, on the rocks below, some offshore bird species, such as the elusive tufted puffin or the endangered guillemot. Kids will love the clacking sound of the waves rolling the smooth, volcanic cobblestones at Cobble Beach or the king-of-the-mountain feel at the top of short but steep Salal Hill. Wheelchair-accessible trails and an interpretive center make this a place for everyone to enjoy. The **Yaquina Head Lighthouse** is a 93-foot-high tower that stands 162 feet above sea level, making it Oregon's tallest lighthouse. You can tour the authentically refurbished 1873 lighthouse year-round, weather permitting.

Free Things to Do in Newport

Clamming (ages 8 and up)

South Beach Marina. Under the bridge adjacent to the marina. Clamming is popular in the Yaquina Bay's tide flats during spring and summer minus tides (check the tide tables). This spot gives the best access to gaper clams. Grab a shovel and bucket, roll up your jeans, and get ready to have a ball and make a mess. Be sure to check that there isn't a red tide, a rare occurrence in Oregon but potentially fatal.

Beachcombing (ages 5 and up)

Agate Beach. Located on the north edge of town off Ocean View Road. Agates are commonly found among the loose gravel on top of the sand, especially in off-season months, from October to April. From Agate Beach you've got a clear stretch of beach leading north to Yaquina Head or south to Yaquina Bay.

Yaquina Bay State Park. Located at the north end of Yaquina Bay, just west of US 101. Park on the bluff below the historic lighthouse, then enjoy a picnic, walk the trail down to the beach, or throw a fishing line into the surf off the north jetty (be very watchful of children on the jetty—sneaker waves can be dangerous).

Marine Discovery Tours (all ages)

345 SW Bay Blvd.; (541) 265-6200 or (800) 903-2628; www.marinediscovery.com. Call for hours. (The Chamber of Commerce can provide a list of other charter services; call 800-262-7844 or visit www.coastvisitor.com.) Two-hour Sea Life cruise $$$$ adults, $$$ ages 4 to 13, under 4 free.

To see the whales up close, a number of tour operators take charter trips into the ocean for whale watching and offer both a 1-hour bay tour and a 2-hour whale-watching cruise. Marine Discovery Tours has a naturalist on board who leads the kids in fun learning activities during the 2-hour ride.

Newport Marina Store and Charters (ages 4 and up)

2128 SE Marine Science Dr.; (541) 867-4470. Open daily 7 a.m. to 6 p.m. $$ per day for crab rings; $$$$ for 4-hour boat rental with three crab rings, $$$$ for full day. Whale-watching tours $$$ kids 5 to 12, $$$$ adults, kids under 5 free.

This South Beach marina rents crab rings at its store and at the fuel dock. The long public pier adjacent to the marina is a perfect place to toss your rings into the water and wait for those delicious Dungeness crabs to take the bait.

Oregon Coast History Center (ages 5 and up)

545 SW Ninth St.; (541) 265-7509. Open Tues through Sat 11 a.m. to 4 p.m. Free; donations appreciated.

The Lincoln County Historical Society operates both the Log Cabin Museum and the Burrows House. The 1895 Victorian Burrows House includes Native American, maritime, and coastal settlement exhibits. The professionally designed exhibits draw from some 40,000 artifacts in the center's collection.

US Coast Guard Station (ages 8 and up)

Located on the east end of Bay Boulevard on the Newport waterfront; (541) 265-5381. Open daily 1 to 4 p.m. Free.

You will get a strong sense of the Coast Guard's role on the Oregon coast here, both past and present. It's also a great chance for your kids to learn about ocean safety as well as the Coast Guard's dramatic rescue capabilities.

Yaquina Bay Lighthouse/State Park (all ages)

8465 SW Government St. at the north end of the bay bridge; (541) 867-7451, (541) 574-3129, or (800) 551-6949; www.yaquinalights.org. Lighthouse open 11 a.m. to 5 p.m. daily in summer and on weekends, otherwise noon to 4 p.m. Day use. Free, but donations are welcome for the lighthouse.

Built in 1871, the lighthouse is Newport's oldest building. It operated for only three years before giving way to the more powerful lighthouse at Yaquina Head. Your kids will appreciate the tale of the lighthouse "ghost"; look for a pamphlet at the museum that tells the story.

Seal Rock State Recreation Site (all ages)

Located 10 miles south of Newport on US 101; (800) 551-6949 or (888) 628-2101. Free.

This lovely park sits atop a bluff next to Seal Rock, a large basalt sea stack just offshore. Picnic tables are nestled along narrow forest paths that lead to the beach below.

Waldport

Waldport means "port of the woods" in German. The early settlers in this Alsea River basin were Germans who came for the brief gold rush and then stayed to develop the timber industry.

Alsea Bay Bridge Interpretive Center (ages 8 and up)

620 NW Spring St., on US 101 just south of the Alsea Bay Bridge; (541) 563-2002 or (800) 551-6949; www.oregonstateparks.org. Open daily in summer, Wed through Sun the rest of the year, 9 a.m. to 5 p.m. Daily bridge tours at 2 p.m. Free.

In the center you'll learn the old bridge's story through photographs and a short video. Once the longest cement-poured bridge in the world, it was torn down in 1992 and rebuilt to be more structurally sound.

Attractions kids will appreciate include a model replica of the old bridge, displays on the history of transportation, a powerful viewing scope trained on the new bridge, and exhibits about the Alsi Indians who once lived in this area. You can also participate in clamming and crabbing demonstrations; times and locations vary with the tides.

Beachside State Park (all ages)

Three miles south of Waldport on US 101; (541) 563-3220, (800) 551-6949 (information), or (800) 452-5687 (reservations); www.oregonstateparks.org. Campground open Mar 15 through Oct; day-use area open year-round 6 a.m. to 9 p.m.

This small campground lives up to its name with very close and easy access to a pleasant and uncrowded expanse of beach.

Top Waldport **Events**

June
Beachcomber Days. These fun-filled days include a sand castle contest, a treasure hunt, slug races, and a parade. www.beachcomberdays.com.

September
Cruzin' for Crab Festival. This event features a crab-ring toss, a crab-catching contest, crab races, and, of course, a crab feed.

For information call (541) 563-2133 or visit www.waldport.org.

Fantastic Facts about Oregon

- Nearly half of Oregon's 97,073 square miles is forested.

- Oregon's campgrounds have more than 5,800 registered campsites and more than 159 circular, domed tents, called yurts. located in 19 parks. (Call 800-551-6949 for a copy of the state campground guide.)

- Oregon is one of the very few states that still has no sales tax—it's a shopper's paradise for visitors.

- Oregon is one of only two states (New Jersey is the other one) that don't allow motorists to pump their own gasoline—so sit back, relax, and let someone else do the work!

Yachats

Practice pronouncing the name of this tiny coastal town before you venture any questions to the locals. It's "YAH-hots," and it comes from the local tribe of Chinook Indians and is said to mean "dark waters at the foot of the mountain."

Smelt Sands State Recreation Site (all ages)
Located at the north end of Yachats; (800) 551-6949. Day-use area. Free.

Both a whale-watching viewpoint and a great kid-oriented hiking trail, this area is located about ½ mile north of town along the oceanfront. From the parking area you can walk to oceanside picnic spots or take the Yachats 804 Trail, ¾ mile one way. The trail is wheelchair accessible, so even your youngest will manage the easy, level terrain. It leads along a cliff top above odd-shaped rocks that eroded from the 25 million-year-old Yaquina Formation.

Little Log Church Museum (ages 5 and up)
Corner of Third and Pontiac Streets; (541) 547-3976. Open daily except Thurs, noon to 3 p.m. Free; donations welcome.

This tiny museum houses an interesting collection of Native American artifacts as well as pioneer tools and household items, such as a 100-year-old crazy quilt, teddy bears, fossils, and a molar from a wooly mammoth.

Yachats Ocean Road State Natural Site (ages 5 and up)
Located immediately south of Yachats, 500 feet off US 101; (800) 551-6949; www.oregon stateparks.org. Day-use area. Free.

Access to a wide sandy beach begins here along a 1-mile loop road. Tide-pooling is great on the rocks that edge the ocean shore. But be very careful, and venture onto these rocks only when the tide is well out. Sneaker waves—especially during winter months—can be deadly, and the rocks can be slippery.

Cape Perpetua Scenic Area (ages 5 and up)

Three miles south of Yachats; (541) 547-3289; www.fs.fed.us/r6/siuslaw. Visitor center open daily 10 a.m. to 5:30 p.m. in summer. Call for winter hours and whale-watching information. Day-use fee is $ per vehicle; covers Oregon Dunes National Recreation Area and all of Cape Perpetua.

One of the most beautiful areas on the coast—and the highest point along the Oregon coast—Cape Perpetua winds along coastal cliffs that jut straight up from the ocean. Stop by the **visitor center,** which contains exhibits that explain local geological features, give whale-watching tips, present local history, and describe Native American culture. Maps are available for the area's 23 miles of hiking trails. The **Giant Spruce Trail** leads for 1 mile to a massive 500-year-old Sitka spruce.

Devil's Churn Viewpoint, just north of the junction at Cape Perpetua Road and US 101, is a day-use area with trails near the viewpoint that take you down to the rocks below, where the surf at high tide churns in the deep chasm and crashes onto the rocks, throwing sea spray onto everything around—including tourists who get too close! Enjoy the view at high tide from above, which is now a wheelchair-accessible viewpoint. Several other scenic overlooks and turnoffs in this area give you access to sandy beaches, picnic spots, tide pools, and hiking trails.

Family Favorites
on the North & Central Coasts

1. Astoria Aquatics Center

2. Fort Clatsop National Memorial, Astoria

3. Haystack Rock Marine Garden, Cannon Beach

4. Tillamook Cheese Factory

5. Tillamook County Pioneer Museum

6. Cascade Head, near Lincoln City

7. Oregon Coast Aquarium, Newport

8. Yaquina Bay Lighthouse, near Newport

9. Cape Perpetua Scenic Area, near Yachats

10. Devil's Churn Viewpoint, near Yachats

Where to Eat

IN ASTORIA

Mr. Fultano's Pizza. 201 Broadway; (503) 738-5612. Fultano's has old-fashioned pizzas, Italian and Mexican dishes, hamburgers, and a salad bar. They'll even deliver to your hotel room. $$

Pier 11 Restaurant & Lounge. 77 11th St.; (503) 325-1775; www.pier11steakhouse.com. Almost all tables here offer a view of the river and frolicking sea lions and seals. Seafood specialties; breakfast, lunch, and dinner; children's menu. $–$$$

IN CANNON BEACH

Cannon Beach Bakery. 240 N. Hemlock St.; (503) 436-0399. Danish family traditions are kept alive and featured at this bakery. Try the eight-grain and crusty Haystack breads. There is also a daily offering of sweet treats. $–$$

Dooger's Seafood & Grill. 1371 S. Hemlock St.; (503) 436-2225. Casual dining well-suited for families with young children. Pick up a clam chowder kit to take the tastes of Cannon Beach home with you. $–$$

Lazy Susan Cafe. 126 N. Hemlock St.; (503) 436-2816. A cheerful cafe in a brick courtyard off the main street in downtown Cannon Beach. Highly recommended for breakfast waffles and omelettes. $–$$

IN & AROUND LINCOLN CITY

Blackfish Café. 2733 NW US 101; (541) 996-1007; www.blackfishcafe.com. Some of the best clam chowder in the area and well-prepared fresh local ingredients make this one of our family's favorites. Lunch is more affordable for families and less crowded, but the kids' menu and the staff make children welcome at any time. $$ lunch, $$$$ dinner. Dinner reservations recommended.

Eleanor's Undertow. 869 SW 51st St.; (541) 996-3800; near Taft Waterfront Park.

Homemade burgers, halibut sandwiches, and other hearty delights plus sweets and unbeatable ice cream treats. $–$$

McMenamin's Lighthouse Brewery Pub and Restaurant. Located in the Roads End shopping center, 4157 N. US 101; (541) 994-7238. The Lighthouse Brewery has burgers, fish and chips, and other kid-oriented fare on the children's menu as well as local ales for Mom and Dad to try. $–$$$

Tidal Raves. 279 NW US 101 in Depot Bay, south of Lincoln City; (541) 765-2995; www.tidalraves.com. Incredible views combined with fresh and lively chowders, shellfish, and fish make this a great choice for families who eat seafood. $$–$$$

IN MANZANITA

Big Wave Café. US 101 and Laneda Avenue; (503) 368-9283. The Wave offers a wide variety of tasty favorites. It's favored by locals, who especially appreciate the meat loaf served each Wednesday. $–$$

Bread and Ocean Bakery. 154 Laneda Ave.; (503) 368-5823; www.breadandocean.com. This moderately priced bakery, deli, and cafe features locally sourced, fresh, and delicious food. It's a great spot for breakfast, lunch ($–$$), or dinner ($$$) or to pick up pastries or picnic lunches to go. Cash or checks only.

Marzano's Pizza Pie. 60 Laneda Ave.; (503) 368-3663. Gourmet fresh pizzas featuring house-made Italian sausage and dough made fresh daily. $–$$

IN NEWPORT

April's at Nye Beach. 749 NW Third; (541) 265-6855. Fresh ingredients and great home-made desserts are a plus for this casual restaurant with an ocean view. $$–$$$

Chowder Bowl at Nye Beach. 728 NW Beach Dr.; (541) 265-7477. Heaping bowls of chowder make this the perfect stop for lunch. $–$$

Georgie's Beachside Grill. 744 SW
Elizabeth St.; (541) 265-9800; www.georgies beachsidegrill.com. The grill offers great oceanfront views, and its tasty breakfast menu ranges from the traditional to surprises. $–$$

Kam Meng Chinese Restaurant. 4424
N. Coast Highway; (541) 574-9450. You can't miss the bright green exterior of this local favorite on the north end of town. Try one of four clay pot entrees or go for satisfying standards or the buffet. Lots of vegan options. $$–$$$

Local Ocean Seafoods. 213 SE Bay Blvd.;
(541) 574-7959. Fresh, sustainably harvested seafood tops the menu at this Bayfront hot spot. Don't miss the fish tacos or roasted garlic crab soup. Kids' menu is seafood heavy, but burgers are available. $$–$$$

Rogue Ales Public House. 748 SW Bay
Blvd.; (541) 265-3188. Although technically a pub, Rogue Ales welcomes families during meal hours with a special menu for kids, and local microbrew tastings for adults. The brewery and another restaurant are located under the bridge on the south side of the bay. $–$$

IN SEASIDE

Dooger's Seafood & Grill. 505 Broadway;
(503) 738-3773. Famous for its rich clam chowder. Wonderful desserts might extend the dinner hour for your family. Breakfast, lunch, and dinner. Children's menu available. $$–$$$

Norma's Ocean Diner. 20 N. Columbia;
(503) 738-4331; www.normasoceandiner .com. Voted tops by *Oregon Coast* and *Sunset* magazines, this is soup central, particularly clam chowder and oyster stew. A kids' menu and other choices, both surf- and turf-based, give families lots of lunch and dinner options. After a long day playing on the

beach, head here before 4:30 p.m. for a late lunch or early dinner to take advantage of early-bird specials. $$–$$$

IN YACHATS

The Drift Inn Historic Pub & Café. 124
US 101; (541) 547-4477. Choose from an eclectic mix of seafood, burgers, and entrees featuring Northwest and world cuisine. The large menu features lots of gluten-free and vegan options, and you'll enjoy reading the charming story of the restaurant's place in Yachats lore.

Green Salmon Bakery, Coffee & Tea
Shoppe. 220 US 101; (541) 547-4409. Organic, fair-trade coffee roasting, individually brewed coffee and tea, baked treats, and light breakfast and lunch make this a popular gathering place for locals and visitors alike. $–$$

Luna Sea Fish House. 53 US 101; (541)
547-4794. Owner Robert Anthony is also a full-time fisherman, so all of the seasonal seafood Luna Sea serves came off of his boats. This small, friendly place has some of the best chowder on the coast plus non-seafood options like organic eggs for breakfast and grass-fed beef for lunch and dinner. $–$$$

Where to Stay
IN & AROUND ASTORIA

Crest Motel. 5366 Leif Erickson Dr.; (503)
325-3141 or (800) 421-3141 (for reservations only); www.crestmotelastoria.com. Forty rooms on a picturesque hilltop overlooking the Columbia River. Continental breakfast, spa, coin laundry. $$–$$$

Fort Stevens Campground. Ten miles
west of Astoria off US 101; (800) 452-5687; www.oregonstateparks.org. Oregon's third-largest campground. $–$$

Shilo Inn. 1609 E. Harbor Dr., Warrenton;
(800) 222-2244 or (503) 861-2181; www .shiloinns.com. Despite tired carpet and

Vacation Rentals:
An Alternative to Motels

All along the Oregon coast, you can find a home away from home through a variety of vacation rental agencies. You'll be amazed at the options—from small beach cottages and condos to oceanfront luxury homes. These privately owned homes are furnished, have well-stocked kitchens so you don't have to eat all your meals in restaurants, and are often equipped with family fun extras, such as games, bicycles, hot tubs, and barbecues. Here are several agencies, organized from north to south.

- **Vacation Rentals by Owner.** Entire coastline (and rest of Oregon, too). View rentals, availability, and rates online. Book either online or directly with each owner. www.vrbo.com.

- **Oceanside Vacation Rentals.** 43 N. Holladay, Seaside; (800) 840-7764; www.oceanside1.com; e-mail: oceanside@freedomnw.com.

- **Cannon Beach Vacation Rentals.** 3363 S. Hemlock St., Cannon Beach; (866) 436-0940 or (503) 436-0940; www.visitcb.com; e-mail: info@visitcb.com.

- **Manzanita Rental Company.** 686 Manzanita Ave., Manzanita; (800) 579-9801 or (503) 368-6797; www.manzanitarentals.com; e-mail: mrc@nehalemtel.net.

- **Seahaven Rentals.** 2110 NE 36th Ave., Lincoln City; (877) 315-1138 or (541) 996-8800; www.seahavenrentals.com.

- **Dolphin Real Estate.** 547 SW Seventh St., Newport; (800) 365-6638 or (541) 265-6638; www.dolphinrealtynewport.com.

- **Bayshore Rentals Inc.** P.O. Box 879, Waldport 97394; (800) 752-6321 or (541) 563-3162; www.bayshore-rentals.com.

- **Ocean Odyssey Vacation Rentals.** 261 N. US 101, Yachats; (800) 800-1915 or (541) 547-3637; www.ocean-odyssey.com.

furniture, the service, cleanliness, and cost make this a reasonable choice for families. Restaurant, some kitchenettes, indoor swimming pool, hot tub, sauna, and fitness center. $$–$$$$

IN CANNON BEACH

Blue Gull Inn. 632 S. Hemlock St.; (800) 507-2714 or (503) 436-2714; www.bluegullinn.com. Just a few steps away from the beach. Two-bedroom suites and cottages are ideal for families. $$$–$$$$

McBee Motel Cottages. Check in at the Sandtrap Inn at 539 S. Hemlock St.; (866) 262-2336 or (503) 436-2569; www.mcbeecottages.com. Cottages a block from the beach and a short walk to downtown. Some kitchens and fireplaces. Well-mannered pets are welcome. $$–$$$

RV Resort at Cannon Beach. 345 Elk Creek Rd.; (800) 847-2231 or (503) 436-2231; www.cbrvresort.com; e-mail: info@cbrvresort.com. This facility offers the closest camping in the Cannon Beach area and has a kids' playground, indoor pool, and spa. $

Schooner's Cove Inn. 188 N. Larch St.; (800) 843-0128 or (503) 436-2300; www.schoonerscove.com. Minimum two-night stay on weekends. Beach access and ocean views from private decks. A variety of rooms and suites with fireplaces and fully equipped kitchens. Oceanfront lawn features gas barbecues, picnic tables, and chaise lounges. $$$–$$$$

The Waves Motel. 188 W. Second SL.; (800) 822-2468 or (503) 436-2205; www.the waves motel.com. Above the beach in the heart of town. Kitchens, fireplaces, and views. $$$$

IN GARIBALDI

Garibaldi House Inn & Suites. 502 Garibaldi Ave.; (877) 322-6489; www.garibaldi houseinn.com. A heated indoor pool and whirlpool, laundry, **free** hot breakfast, and afternoon popcorn are just a few amenities that make this comfortable and clean hotel a favorite. $$–$$$$

IN LINCOLN CITY

Oceanfront Inn. 2855 NW Inlet; (541) 994-8901 or (800) 889-7037. Oceanfront lodging on miles of walking beach with low access. Budget-priced rooms and apartments. Balconies, fireplaces, kitchenettes. Walking distance to restaurants, casinos, shops. Pets allowed. $$–$$$$

Pelican Shores Inn. 2645 NW Inlet; (541) 994-2134; www.pelicanshores.com. Oceanfront with well-laid-out rooms with refrigerators, microwaves, and DVD players for a cozy night in after a day at the beach. Large, clean, indoor heated pool. $$–$$$$

Seagull Motel. 1511 NW Harbor; (541) 994-2948 or (800) 422-0219; www.seagull moteloregon.com; e-mail: seagullmotel@charterinternet.com. Oceanfront motel with low beach access. Large variety of rooms with kitchens and private spas. Small pets welcome. $$–$$$$

IN MANZANITA

Nehalem Bay State Park. Nehalem Bay; (800) 452-5687; www.oregonstateparks.org. A children's playground, showers, and a boat ramp into the bay are among Nehalem Bay State Park's amenities. On the beach you can walk 6 miles to the end of the spit at the mouth of the river, where you might see Roosevelt elk, migrating whistler swans, or harbor seals. $

Spindrift. 114 Laneda; (877) 368-1001 or (503) 368-1001; www.spindrift-inn.com. This charming inn is just a block from the beach. Some kitchenettes; pets welcome. Cafe has varied menu. $$–$$$

IN NEWPORT

Beverly Beach State Park. Located 7 miles north of Newport on the landward side of US 101; (800) 452-5687 for reservations; (541) 265-9278 or (800) 551-6949 for information; www.oregonstateparks.org. Primitive campsites and facilities for electrical or full hookup. Yurt camping available. Open year-round. $

Little Creek Cove. 3641 NW Oceanview Dr. just off US 101 before you arrive in Newport; (800) 294-8025 or (541) 265-8587; www.little creekcove.com. All rooms have an ocean view and access to a nearly private beach. Parents will love the 1- and 2-bedroom options and kitchens in these condo-style rooms. $$$$ summer, $$$–$$$$ Sept to mid-June. Weekly rate discounts.

South Beach State Park. About 2 miles south of Newport; (800) 452-5687 or (541) 867-4715; www.oregonstateparks.org.

Hiker/biker sites and facilities for electrical or full hookup. Yurt camping also available. $

Viking's Condominiums and Cottages. 729 NW Coast St.; (800) 480-2477 or (541) 265-2477; www.vikingsoregoncoast.com. There are 24 condominiums and 14 cottages. Kitchenettes, oceanfront rooms, family units. Stairs to beach, heated outdoor pool, and spa. $$$–$$$$

The Waves of Newport Motel and Vacation Rental Houses. 820 NW Coast St.; (800) 282-6993 or (541) 265-4661; www .wavesofnewport.com; e-mail: info@wavesof newport.com. Some kitchens, ocean view, close beach access, skateboard park across the street, and free continental breakfast, coffee/tea, fruit, and popcorn. $$–$$$

IN ROCKAWAY BEACH

Jetty Fishery RV Park & Marina. 27550 US 101 N; (800) 821-7697 or (503) 368-5746; www.jettyfishery.com; e-mail: jettyfishery@ nehalemtel.net. Riverside park at the mouth of the Nehalem River. Boat and canoe rentals year-round. $

Tradewinds Motel. 523 N. Pacific St.; (503) 355-2112 or (800) 824-0938; www .tradewinds-motel.com. Fifty feet from edge of the beach. Children's playground on beach side of motel. Oceanfront rooms have fireplaces, refrigerators, and coffeemakers. Pets allowed. $$–$$$

IN WALDPORT

Beachside State Recreation Site. Located about 3 miles south of Waldport off US 101; (800) 452-5687 for reservations; (800) 551-6949 or (541) 563-3220 for information; www.oregonstateparks.org. Open mid-Mar through Oct, this park provides sheltered campsites with a measure of privacy not always found in coastal campgrounds. A separate day-use picnic area lies across a small stream. A section of the Oregon Coast Trail, connecting Yachats and Waldport,

passes through the campground. Yurts also available. $

Cliff House Bed and Breakfast. 1450 Adahi St.; (541) 563-2506; www.cliffhouse oregon.com; e-mail: innkeeper@cliffhouse oregon.com. Located south of Waldport just off US 101, this beautiful little house sits atop the cliff, with decks and a sunroom and even an all-glass gazebo, where you can enjoy your morning coffee with an incredible view without being buffeted by the coastal winds. $$$–$$$$

IN YACHATS

Fireside Resort Motel. P.O. Box 313, 1881 US 101 N; (800) 336-3573 or (541) 547-3636; www.firesidemotel.com. Kitchenettes; coffeemaker and fridge in all rooms. Oceanfront rooms. $$–$$$

Ocean Haven. 94770 US 101; (541) 547-3583; www.oceanhaven.com. This ecologically minded hotel has family friendly rooms with organic coffee and tea and no televisions. The guest library has books from authors who have stayed, plus hiking and nature guides. $$$$

Wayside Lodge. 5773 US 101 N; (541) 547-3450; www.waysidelodge.com. All units a stone's throw from the beach. Kitchenettes. Swings and large lawn area make this inexpensive spot ideal for families with young kids. $$–$$$

For More Information

Astoria-Warrenton Area Chamber of Commerce. P.O. Box 176, 111 W. Marine Dr., Astoria, OR 97103; (800) 875-6807 or (503) 325-6311; www.oldoregon.com; e-mail: info@oldoregon.com.

Astoria-Warrenton Highway 101 Visitor Center. 143 S. US 101, Warrenton, OR 97146; (503) 861-1031.

Cannon Beach Chamber of Commerce. P.O. Box 64, Second and Spruce Streets,

Cannon Beach, OR 97110; (503) 436-2623; www.cannonbeach.org; e-mail: chamber@cannonbeach.org.

Central Oregon Coast Association. 137 NE First St., Newport, OR 97365; (800) 767-2064 or (541) 265-2064; www.coastvisitor.com; e-mail: coca@coastvisitor.com.

The Confederated Tribes of Siletz Indians. 201 SE Swan Ave., Siletz, OR 97380; (541) 444-2532; www.ctsi.nsn.us.

Depoe Bay Chamber of Commerce. P.O. Box 21, 70 NW US 101, Depoe Bay, OR 97341; (541) 765-2836 or (877) 485-8348; www.depoebaychamber.org; e-mail: info@depoebaychamber.org.

Garibaldi Chamber of Commerce. P.O. Box 915, 235 Garibaldi Ave., Garibaldi, OR 97118; (503) 322-0301; www.garibaldichamber.com; e-mail: info@garibaldichamber.com.

Greater Newport Chamber of Commerce. 555 SW Coast Hwy., Newport, OR 97365; (800) 262-7844 or (541) 265-8801; www.newportchamber.org; e-mail: chamber@newportnet.com.

Lincoln City Visitor & Convention Bureau. 540 NE US 101, Lincoln City, OR 97367; (800) 452-2151 or (541) 996-1274; www.oregoncoast.org; e-mail: info@newportchamber.org.

Nehalem Bay Area Chamber of Commerce. P.O. Box 601, Wheeler, OR 97147; (877) 368-5100 or (503) 368-5100; www.nehalembaychamber.com; e-mail: nahelem@nehalem@nahalemtel.net.

Oregon Coast Visitors Association. P.O. Box 74, 137 NE First St., Newport, OR 97365; (888) 628-2101 or (541) 574-2679; www.visittheoregoncoast.com; e-mail: info@visittheoregoncoast.com.

Rockaway Beach Chamber of Commerce. P.O. Box 198, 103 S. First St., Rockaway Beach, OR 97136; (503) 355-8108; www.rockawaybeach.net; e-mail: answers@rockawaybeach.net.

Seaside Visitors Bureau. 7 N. Roosevelt, Seaside, OR 97138-6825; (888) 306-2326 or (503) 738-3097; www.seasideor.com; e-mail: visit@seasideor.com.

Tillamook Chamber of Commerce. 3705 US 101 N, Tillamook, OR 97141; (503) 842-7525; www.tillamookchamber.org; e-mail: tillchamber@oregoncoast.com.

Waldport Chamber of Commerce and Visitors Center. P.O. Box 669, 620 NE Spring St., Waldport, OR 97394; (541) 563-2133; www.waldport-chamber.com; e-mail: chamber@peak.org.

Yachats Area Chamber of Commerce and Visitors Center. P.O. Box 728, 241 US 101, Yachats, OR 97498; (800) 929-0477 or (541) 547-3530; www.yachats.org; e-mail: info@yachats.org.

The South Coast

T he dramatic scenery of Oregon's south coast is markedly different from that of the north and central coasts. In fact, it's hard to believe they're on the same stretch of ocean. The vast dunes around Florence, the sandstone cliffs south of Coos Bay, and the myriad sea stacks dotting the shore from Bandon to Brookings will surprise first-time travelers and are what keep people coming back. Weather can also be a little more dramatic on the south coast, where winds near Bandon make for dramatic storm watching and the sunny shores of Brookings, the state's "Banana Belt," can fool you—even in winter—into thinking you're somewhere farther south.

Florence

In the past several years, Florence's Old Town has been revitalized with an influx of boutiques, cafes, restaurants, and other attractions. Around Florence you can enjoy all kinds of recreation on more than a dozen lakes covering some 10,000 acres and on several hiking trails.

Sea Lion Caves (ages 3 and up)

Located 11 miles north of Florence at 91560 US 101 N; (541) 547-3111; www.sealioncaves .com. Open daily 9 a.m. to 5:30 p.m. $$$ ages 13 and older, $$ ages 3 to 12, under 3 free.

After walking down stairs and a ramp to the elevator, you'll descend nearly 200 feet to the largest sea cave in North America, with a 2-acre base and a 125-foot vaulted ceiling. Depending on the time of year, you might see 100 or more Steller (northern) sea lions in the cave—or just a few. The strong stench is worth it for this loud and raucous glimpse into sea lion life.

THE SOUTH COAST

Florence

Winchester Bay • Reedsport

Charleston • North Bend
Coos Bay

Bandon

Port Orford

Gold Beach

Brookings

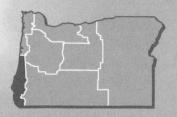

Fun Fact

Florence marks the exact north–south center of the Oregon coast. It is also the start of the largest expanse of sand dunes in the United States, stretching 50 miles south to Coos Bay.

C & M Stables (ages 6 and up)

Located 8 miles north of Florence at 90241 US 101 N; (541) 997-7540; www.oregonhorse backriding.com. Call ahead for reservations. Open daily year-round 10 a.m. to 5 p.m. $$$$

Guided rides on the beach (ages 8 and up), the dunes (ages 6 and up), or both. For a true summer adventure, take a 2-hour sunset beach ride followed by an outdoor barbecue dinner.

Darlingtonia State Natural Site (ages 5 and up)

Located 5 miles north of Florence, ¼ mile off US 101 on Mercer Lake Road; (541) 997-3128 or (800) 551-6949; www.oregonstateparks.org/park_115.php. Day use. Free.

Here's something to delight the gore-loving imagination of many a youth. A loop trail overlooks thousands of carnivorous plants that flourish in the marshy area of this 18-acre park. *Darlingtonia californica,* better known as the cobra lily or pitcher plant, lures insects with a sticky, sweet-smelling nectar, then traps and eats them.

Siuslaw Pioneer Museum (ages 5 and up)

Corner of Maple and Second Streets at the edge of Old Town Florence in the old Florence Schoolhouse; (541) 997-7884. Open daily noon to 4 p.m. July to Sept, otherwise closed Mon; closed Christmas through Jan. $ adults, children under 16 free.

The museum displays trace the area's past, including exhibits on home life, a general store, and the fishing, farming, logging, and shipbuilding industries. A large dugout canoe found at the mouth of the river is a central feature in the museum's collection. The Siuslaw and Siletz trading baskets are beautiful in their simplicity and utility.

Super Shopping

Old Town Florence, located at the waterfront below the Siuslaw River Bridge (US 101), is a charming, quiet spot to explore antiques stores, art galleries, and gift and specialty shops. Kids will love the variety at Funky Monkey Toys and the homemade ice cream and fudge at BJ's.

Top Florence **Events**

May
Rhododendron Festival. Florence's yearly event draws thousands who enjoy arts and crafts, floral displays, 5K and 10K runs, parades, and more. (541) 997-3128; www.florencechamber.com.

September
Chowder Blues and Brews Festival. This event welcomes fall with a chowder cook-off, live music, arts and crafts, and microbrew tasting. A carnival in Old Town is just the ticket for the kids. (541) 997-3128 or (541) 997-1994.

Old Town Gazebo Park (all ages)
Located on Bay Street at the end of Laurel Street; (541) 997-3128. Always open. Free.

This small public park has a boat dock that's fenced to keep kids from falling into the Siuslaw River. Take the opportunity to throw a fishing line or a crab ring in here.

Siltcoos Lake (all ages)
Located 6 miles south of Florence on the east side of US 101; (541) 997-3128; www.siltcooslake.com. Always open. Free.

The largest lake in Florence, it covers more than 3,000 acres. You can rent watercraft from pedal boats to motorboats, canoes to Jet Skis.

Woahink Lake (all ages)
Located just north of Siltcoos Lake; (541) 997-3128. Always open. Free.

Woahink is the first lake south of town and offers swimming, waterskiing, and fishing.

Fun Fact

Dave Barry made Florence famous with his report of an actual—he was not making this up—exploding whale. When confronted with what to do about a 45-foot-long, 8-ton beached whale, the Oregon Highway Department decided the situation called for a half ton of dynamite. Pieces of whale carcass landed everywhere—including on the many spectators who'd gathered to watch! View a video at www.theexplodingwhale.com.

Jessie L. Honeyman State Park (all ages)

Located 3 miles south of Florence; (541) 997-3641 or (800) 551-6949 for information; (800) 452-5687 for campground reservations; www.oregonstateparks.org. $ day-use fee.

This park spans a diverse natural landscape, from ocean and sand dunes to lake and forest. On the east side it's bordered by 350-acre Woahink Lake. Cleawox Lake, which covers a mere 87 acres, is the perfect size for paddling around in; you can rent boats at the lodge. Both lakes have dedicated swimming areas, and the west side of Cleawox Lake is a big sand dune that's ideal for kids to run down and into the water. Six miles of hiking trails wind through the 522-acre park.

Honeyman Lodge (ages 5 and up)

(541) 997-2118 or (541) 997-3641. Open Memorial Day to Labor Day 10:30 a.m. to 5:30 p.m.

Built by the Civilian Conservation Corps in the 1930s, this historic lodge is the place to rent canoes, rowboats, kayaks, or pedal boats for Cleawox Lake and to purchase snacks.

Oregon Dunes National Recreation Area (ages 5 and up)

Begins in Florence and continues south on the coast to Coos Bay Visitor Center at the junction of US 101 and Highway 38; (541) 271-6000; www.fs.fed.us/r6/siuslaw/recreation /trippplanning/oregondunes. Visitor center open 8 a.m. to 4:30 p.m. daily in summer. The $ day-use fee also covers the Cape Perpetua National Scenic Area.

Oregon Dunes National Recreation Area (ODNRA) will make your kids gape with wonder at this seemingly endless sandbox containing 30-plus lakes, 13 campgrounds, and more than

Hiking/Cycling around Florence

You can enjoy miles of off-road hiking or cycling trails around Florence. Here are four trails that you can explore by foot or on wheels.

- **Threemile Lake Trail,** 14 miles south of Florence on the west side of US 101. This 7-mile round-trip trail offers great scenery with some hills to climb on the way.

- **Siltcoos Lake Trail,** 7 miles south of Florence on the highway's east side. The trail takes you 2¼ miles through a 60-year-old forest to the lake.

- **Sutton Creek Trail,** 3 miles north of Florence on the west side of the highway. You'll find at least 5 miles of assorted, mostly flat trails.

- **China Creek Trail,** 13½ miles north of Florence on the east side of the highway. This area offers great photo opportunities on about 2 miles of flat trail with a picnic area about 1 mile in at the site of an old homestead.

Family Favorites
on the South Coast

1. Oregon Dunes National Recreation Area, Florence to Coos Bay

2. Jessie L. Honeyman State Park, near Florence

3. Dean Creek Elk Viewing Area, Reedsport

4. South Slough National Estuarine Research Reserve, Charleston

5. Shore Acres State Park, near Charleston

6. Coquille River Museum, Bandon

7. Umpqua Discovery Center, Reedsport

8. Bandon State Park–Face Rock Wayside

9. Cape Blanco State Park, near Port Orford

10. Samuel H. Boardman State Scenic Corridor, Brookings

10,000 acres of sand. ODNRA stretches from Florence to Coos Bay, with a number of dune access roads, campgrounds, and day-use picnic areas along the way. Ten miles south of Florence is the **Oregon Dunes Overlook,** a nicely constructed series of viewpoints overlooking the dunes. In summer guided tours are offered. The area is crisscrossed by 14 hiking trails; maps are available at the visitor center.

Sandland Adventures Family Fun Center (ages 8 and up)
85366 US 101, located less than 1 mile south of Florence; (541) 997-8087; www.sandland .com. Open daily 9 a.m. to 5 p.m. in summer; closing hours vary in the off-season. Reservations recommended year-round. Dune-buggy tours $$–$$$$; self-driven rentals $$$$ per hour.

While the older members of the family hit the beach in a mini-rail buggy, parents can take turns staying behind with younger ones to play miniature golf or ride in bumper boats, go-karts, or the newest addition, the Cloverline 24-inch railroad. The whole family can take a tour in open-air dune buggies that seat a driver and four or five passengers or in the giant dune buggy for large groups.

Reedsport

Home to the Oregon Dunes National Recreation Area headquarters, Reedsport is close to several freshwater lakes and often-overlooked campgrounds that are filled with wax myrtle and huckleberry bushes. It might be one of the few areas along the coast that offer a measure of outdoor privacy in the summer.

Umpqua Discovery Center (ages 5 and up)

409 Riverfront Way, off US 101; (541) 271-4816; www.umpquadiscoverycenter.com; e-mail: info@umpquadiscoverycenter.com. Open daily 9 a.m. to 5 p.m. in summer, 10 a.m. to 4 p.m. rest of year. $$ adults, $ children ages 6 to 15, under 6 free. Family ticket $$$ for two adults and up to three children.

The center has an impressive exhibit area designed to educate visitors about the local geography, geology, and relationships between people and the environment. Listen to stories from the early pioneers and watch videos of early logging. Next, take a hike on the indoor trail, Pathways to Discovery, with interactive exhibits about the plants and animals

Top Reedsport **Events**

June through September

Riverfront Rhythm Summer Concerts. Held on the grounds of the Umpqua Discovery Center some Friday evenings from mid-June through mid-September, starting at 6:30 p.m.

July

Reedsport Ocean Festival. Kite-flying contests, old-time games, arts and crafts booths, and live music in a beer garden are all part of this oceanside community's summer celebration. A parade on Saturday and a salmon dinner Sunday evening at Winchester Bay round out the festivities.

August

Dune Fest. Dune-buggy races and all kinds of fun in the sand.

September

Tsalila Education Days and Umpqua River Festival. Pronounced "sa-lee-la," this cross-cultural event features entertaining and educational activities that are free and open to the public. Visitors can walk through the salmon maze, enjoy Native American drumming and dancing performances, listen to top musical acts and storytelling by Pacific Northwest entertainers, or participate in hands-on watershed education programs. Held at the Umpqua Discovery Center in Reedsport.

For more information on Reedsport events, visit www.reedsportcc.org or call (800) 247-2155 or (541) 271-3495.

The Great Oregon **Beach Cleanup**

SOLV is a nonprofit organization that brings together government agencies, businesses, and individual volunteers to enhance the livability of Oregon. Twice a year, in spring and fall, SOLV sponsors the Great Oregon Beach Cleanup. Thousands of people go to their favorite spots on the coastline to pick up litter and debris that have washed ashore. It's like an upside-down treasure hunt, searching for trash instead of treasure, but who knows what you'll find along the way—and it's a great feeling to help contribute to the beauty of the Oregon coast. For more information, call (541) 844-9571 or visit www.solv.org.

of tidewater country, and slide into the "bear cave." Kids love to look through the 35-foot periscope and inspect the working weather station.

Loon Lake Recreation Area (all ages)

Located east on Highway 38, about 20 miles east of Reedsport; (541) 599-2254 for information; (888) 242-4256 for campground reservations; www.blm.gov. Call for hours and fees. Campground open mid-Mar through Nov; day use and lodge open year-round. $ day-use fee per vehicle or walk-in; $ boat launch.

Created by a major landslide about 1,400 years ago, the area is now a popular summertime spot for swimming, camping, waterskiing, and fishing. When it's foggy on the coast in the summer, locals often head here to find the sun. Throughout the summer park rangers offer interpretive programs and nature walks. **Loon Lake Lodge** (541-599-2244) offers boat rentals, campsites and RV spots, cabin, yurt, and room rentals, and a boat dock.

Umpqua Lighthouse State Park (ages 5 and up)

Located 6 miles south of Reedsport, less than 1 mile off US 101; (541) 271-4631 or (800) 551-6949; (800) 452-5687 for campground reservations; (541) 271-4118 for yurt or cabin reservations; www.oregonstateparks.org. $, children under 12 free.

Here's a gem tucked in a rolling coastal hillside covered with fir, Sitka spruce, and hemlock, with huckleberry and rhododendron creating a lush understory. At the center of the park is tiny Lake Marie, with a sandy beach near a picnic area. Hiking trails circle the lake and lead to the beach, passing a viewpoint overlooking the large Punch Bowl area of the Oregon Dunes. Yurts and log cabins are available to rent, in addition to RV and tent camping spaces.

Umpqua River Lighthouse (ages 5 and up)

Located 6 miles south of Reedsport, less than 1 mile off US 101; (800) 247-2155 or (541) 271-4631; www.oregonstateparks.org or www.umpqualighthouse.org. Open daily except Tues for tours, May through Sept, 9 to 11:30 a.m. and 1 to 3:30 p.m., Sun 1 to 4 p.m.; off-season tours by appointment. $, children under 12 free.

Inside is a museum that tells the story of this 1894 lighthouse and of Fort Umpqua, built to protect the lighthouse and settlers from the Umpqua Indians, who didn't welcome either intrusion. The 67-foot tower contains the light, which still shines out on the sea.

Dean Creek Elk Viewing Area (ages 5 and up)
Located 3 miles upriver on Highway 38; (541) 756-0100; www.co.douglas.or.us/countyinfo /elk.html. Always open. Free.

The excellent interpretive panels at the O. H. Hinsdale Interpretive Center describe the resident herd of more than a hundred elk and some of the other wildlife you might see. If you don't find any elk here, drive on a bit. They're often sighted next to the road in the early morning or evening hours. Bring your binoculars.

Winchester Bay

This small town at the mouth of Winchester Bay provides the nearest access to the Oregon Dunes National Recreation Area. Restless children will appreciate the chance to walk along the docks that moor mammoth fishing boats. A cannery offers information about local oyster farming and oysters to eat fresh on the premises or to take home.

Dune buggies are a fun way to explore the area. Rentals are available from a variety of sources, including:

Winchester Bay Dune Buggy Adventures. 881 US 101, Winchester Bay; (541) 271-6972; www.dunebuggyadventure.com. Sandboard, ATV rentals, and tours.

Dune Country ATV. Located on Salmon Harbor Boulevard, Winchester Bay; (541) 271-9357; www.discoverypointresort.com. Direct access to the dunes.

William M. Tugman State Park (all ages)
Located next to Eel Lake, 9 miles south of Reedsport; (800) 551-6949 or (541) 759-3604 for information; (800) 452-5687 for reservations; www.oregonstateparks.org. Open year-round. Day-use area free.

On the land side of the highway, the lake has a campground where privacy is protected with wax myrtle and huckleberry bushes. It's closed in winter, but the day-use area remains open year-round. Yurt camping as well as walk-in campsites are available. Kids will appreciate the playground and designated swimming area.

Oregon's Bay Area

Welcome to Oregon's Bay Area. That's how signs greet you as you enter this region of three towns—Coos Bay, Charleston, and North Bend—bordering Oregon's largest natural deepwater port.

North Bend

This community marks the southern edge of the Oregon Dunes National Recreation Area, that giant sandbox stretching 45 miles north to Florence. There are a variety of options for exploring this popular recreation area, including cars, boats, dune buggies, and hiking trails.

Spinreel Dunebuggy Rentals (ages 8 and up)
67045 Spinreel Rd., 10 miles north on US 101; (541) 759-3313; www.ridetheoregondunes.com. Open in summer at 9 a.m., winter at 10 a.m., closes at sunset year-round; call ahead in winter. Four-wheeler rental $$$$ per hour; dune-buggy tour $$$$ per hour.

Children can take out four-wheelers with parental supervision.

Coos County Historical and Maritime Museum (ages 5 and up)
1220 Sherman Ave. (US 101); (541) 756-6320; www.cooshistory.org. Open Tues through Sat 10 a.m. to 4 p.m. $, children under 12 free.

A vintage boxcar rests outside, while inside your kids will appreciate the miniature boat model and learn about several area shipwrecks. Efforts are under way to renovate and

Top Bay Area **Events**

July
Oregon Coast Music Festival. These concerts, which are held in Shore Acres State Park in Coos Bay, run the gamut from classical to jazz and folk. A number of events during the festival weeks are geared to introducing children to classical music. (877) 897-9350 or (541) 267-0938; www.oregoncoast music.com.

August
Blackberry Arts Festival. This annual fair in Coos Bay features handmade arts and crafts along with food booths and live entertainment. (541) 888-5005.

September
Bay Area Fun Festival. Held in downtown Coos Bay, this midmonth weekend starts with a parade and includes live entertainment and family-oriented activities. (800) 752-9153; www.oregonsbayareachamber.com.

An Adventure to Remember

South Slough National Estuarine Research Reserve (ages 5 and up). P.O. Box 5417, Charleston, OR 97420; located on Seven Devils Road, south of Charleston; (541) 888-5558; www.southsloughestuary.org. Trails open daily dawn to dusk; interpretive center open Tues through Sat 10 a.m. to 4:30 p.m. **Free.**

This slightly out-of-the-way oasis provides a wonderful environmental learning adventure for the entire family. The 4,400-acre South Slough, reserved for the study of estuarine life and ecosystems, is one of only a few remaining sloughs in the United States that do not have a city or town built on their shores. An estuary marks the junction where the river meets the sea, mixing fresh and salt water to create a complex environment that supports a unique variety of plants and animals. This South Slough is the southwestern arm of the larger Coos estuary. There's a dramatic shift in temperature as you begin your hike to the marshes. At the trailhead are deciduous trees, which suddenly give way to fragrant, moist ferns and a much cooler terrain—an instant lesson for children about the ways flora and fauna impact climate. At the end of the trail, you're rewarded with a viewing deck from which to marvel at the expanse of fresh- and saltwater marshes and mudflats. Be sure to stop by the Interpretive Center at the top of the hill above the estuary, where you will find detailed trail maps and can view exhibits on the wildlife found in the estuary. An informational video is available at the center for those unable to walk the trail. Write or call ahead for a list of summer educational programs or visit the website.

move to the Old Marshfield Historic District and integrate the museum and the waterfront boardwalk.

Simpson Park (all ages)

On Sherman Avenue, adjacent to North Bend Visitors Center and Coos County Historical County Museum; (541) 756-2656. Always open. **Free.**

The park has picnic tables and a Frisbee golf course that will have your whole family stepping up to the "tee" to meet the challenge of landing the Frisbee in basket "holes" atop bright poles. Pick up a free scorecard from the Visitor Center next to the museum. If you left your Frisbee at home, **Moe's Bike Shop** (1397 Sherman Ave.; 541-756-7536) across the street has several varieties for sale. The North Bend Visitors Center is a wealth of information staffed by decades-long residents. A hands-on coastal exploration area and book nook for kids gives them a break while you plan your visit.

Coos Bay

Bayfront Boardwalk and Interpretive Structures
(ages 5 and up)
Located at the Coos Bay waterfront; (541) 269-8918. Always open. Free.

The new Coos Bay waterfront project and paved trail is an easy ⅓-mile walk where the kids can view a tiny tug and colorful flag display. Huge ships from all over the world dock here. Several cafes and eateries line nearby avenues.

Egyptian Theatre (ages 5 and up)
229 S. Broadway; (541) 269-8650; www.egyptian-theatre.com. Call for showtimes. $.

If the weather turns foul, you can warm up inside this old theater. It's a classic remnant of the elegant 1920s era.

Coos Art Museum (ages 8 and up)
235 Anderson Ave.; (541) 267-3901; www.coosart.org. Open Tues through Fri 10 a.m. to 4 p.m., Sat 1 to 4 p.m. Free, but donations accepted.

Here you'll find an impressive collection of both contemporary and historic art. Call ahead to find out about the many children's educational programs offered throughout the year.

Other Things to See and Do
in the Bay Area

Rockhounding (all ages). Best spot is 8 miles south of Charleston at Seven Devils Wayside State Park and Whiskey Run Beach. Day-use area. Free. Agates, agatized myrtle, jasper, and other woods can be gathered here. (800) 551-6949.

Clamming (ages 5 and up). Best locations are the tiny seafront community of Charleston and the Coos Bay estuary. Always open. Free when you bring your own buckets and digging tools. Abundant in this area are mussels and soft-shell, bay, butter, littleneck, cockle, and gaper clams. All local waters are open for clamming. Although clams may be removed without a license, it's unlawful to remove them from their shells before leaving the clamming area.

For more information, call the **Bay Area Chamber of Commerce** at (541) 266-0868; www.oregonsbayarea.com.

Fun Fact

The Doerner Fir in Coos Bay is the largest-known Douglas fir in the world. You can reach it by driving south on US 101, then heading east on Highway 42. The kids will be awestruck by the 329-foot-tall, 11½-foot-wide tree. A self-guided tour map is available from the local Bureau of Land Management office (541-756-0100). Coos Bay sits at the midpoint between Seattle, Washington, and San Francisco, California.

Mingus Park (ages 5 and up)

725 N. 10th Ave.; arboretum at 500 Central Ave.; skate park at 10th and Commercial; (541) 267-1360. Always open. Free.

The community swimming pool, open during summer months, will occupy the kids while you walk the trails in the adjacent arboretum and rhododendron gardens. A playground sits next to a pond where ducks and geese clamor for crumbs. The skateboard park is a destination spot for older kids, and the park also offers an 18-hole Frisbee golf course (on East Park Roadway behind Milner Crest School).

Empire Lakes at John Topits Park (ages 5 and up)

Located on Hull Street next to Southwest Oregon Community College, north of Newmark Avenue; (541) 269-8918. Always open. Free.

Two lakes reserved for nonmotorized boating and rimmed with 5½ miles of walking and cycling trails make this a nice retreat for the day. A paved walking and biking path circles Lower Empire Lake, which also boasts a swimming beach.

The Legendary Pre

Famed runner Steve Prefontaine was born in Coos Bay in 1951. During his senior year, he broke the national 2-mile record (running it in 8 minutes and 41.5 seconds) and caught the attention of Bill Bowerman, the future Nike co-founder who was then track coach at the University of Oregon. Bowerman recruited "Pre," who went on to win an amazing seven NCAA National Championships for the school. He was aiming for gold at the 1976 Montreal Olympics but tragically died in a car accident the year before. Pre is buried at Sunset Memorial Park just south of Coos Bay.

Millicoma Marsh Interpretive Trail (ages 5 and up)

Located on Blossom Gulch, near Blossom Gulch School in Coos Bay; (541) 269-0215. Always open. **Free.**

This self-guided 1-mile trail at Coos Bay leads to an estuary and freshwater marshes and offers a great spot for bird watching.

Cranberry Sweets Candy Factory (all ages)

1005 Newmark Ave.; (800) 527-5748; www.cranberrysweetsandmore.com. Open Mon through Sat 9 a.m. to 5 p.m.

Your children will enjoy the **free** samples from this factory and store where scrumptious chocolate and cranberry confections are made and sold.

Charleston Area

Shore Acres State Park (ages 5 and up)

Located on Cape Arago Highway 4 miles southwest of Charleston; (800) 551-6949 or (541) 888-3732. Open daily 8 a.m. to dusk. $ day-use fee.

The dramatic tilt of the layered rock formations, with waves crashing over them, lures artists and photographers to the cliff tops. The botanical and Japanese gardens are not, perhaps, your child's idea of a great time, but there are plenty of places for kids to run while the grown-ups appreciate the beauty of the exquisitely landscaped gardens. Once the home of lumber baron Louis J. Simpson, the park is open throughout the year. Part of the Oregon Coast Trail winds through the park. During the winter, storm watching is awe-inspiring from the large, glass-enclosed gazebo above the cliffs. Thanksgiving weekend through December visit the park for Holiday Lights from 4 to 10 p.m., when the garden is transformed with thousands of colored lights.

Cape Arago State Park and Lighthouse (ages 5 and up)

Located 5 miles southwest of Charleston off US 101; (541) 888-3778, ext.26; www.oregon stateparks.org. Call for hours. **Free.**

The victim of erosion and harsh weather, the lighthouse is not open to the public, but tremendous views are available just south of it. Take the North Cove trail to view Shell Island, a year-round hangout for seals and sea lions (closed Mar through June for seal pup birthing). For tide-pooling, head down the steep trail to South Cove, where the rocky shoreline is bursting with sea life. Watch out for slippery rocks.

Bandon

Bandon-by-the-Sea is such a popular spot, you'll want to make plans well in advance, particularly now that it's home to three world-class golf courses. The local beach, renowned

Free Thing to Do in Bandon

Tide Pools (all ages)

Face Rock Wayside. Located in Bandon State Natural Area, along Beach Loop Road just south of Bandon; (800) 551-6949; www.oregonstateparks .org. Day use only. Call for hours. Free. The sea stacks along this stretch of beach all have names. Face Rock, the most distinctive of these, is named for Ewauna, the beautiful daughter of Chief Siskiyou. She swam alone in the sea and was caught by the evil ocean spirit Seatka, who threw Ewauna's cat and kittens into the sea with her and turned them all to stone. Ewauna's chin points toward Cat and Kittens Rocks to the north.

for its majestic rock formations, is also the perfect spot for bird watching, exploring tide pools, and building sand castles. Rock hounds often find agate, jasper, and petrified wood here.

Bullards Beach State Park and Coquille River Lighthouse (all ages)

Located 2 miles north of Bandon; (800) 551-6949 or (541) 347-3501 for information; (800) 452-5687 for campground reservations; www.oregonstateparks.org. Park open daily year-round. Lighthouse open daily May through mid-Oct 11 a.m. to 5 p.m. Free.

This large park is home to the 1896 Coquille River Lighthouse, a unique octagonal structure situated alongside the river. In the summer, park staffers offer daily interpretive tours leading to the lantern room. Camping among the shore pines is available year-round, with yurts, hiker/biker campsites, RV hookups, and a horse camp. You can hike on a variety of trails (including a 1-mile paved trail from the campground booth to the beach), try your hand at the exceptional fishing or crabbing in the Coquille River, or just wander along 4½ miles of broad beach.

Fun Fact

In the 1930s, Bandon's population was more than 1,500 and growing, until the Great Fire of 1936 destroyed all but 16 of the town's 500 buildings. A tavern was the first to reopen, followed by City Hall. The city's population, which dropped to just over 1,000, didn't reach 1,500 again until the 1960s.

Bandon Historical Society Museum (ages 5 and up)

270 Fillmore St. and US 101; (541) 347-2164. Open Mon through Sat 10 a.m. to 4 p.m. $ adults, children free.

A nice array of exhibits that includes local history, pioneer and maritime life, Native American culture, the Bandon fire, and cranberry industry memorabilia. Kids will gravitate toward the newer school-life, scouting, and historic clothing exhibits, and the scale model of a Coast Guard lifeboat.

Bandon's Old Town District (ages 5 and up)

Located between US 101 and the Bandon Boat Basin; (541) 347-9616. Most shops are open daily year-round 9 a.m. to 6 p.m.

Take your time strolling in and out of this colorful blend of curio, book, and arts and crafts shops. The boardwalk features a totem, glass-enclosed picnic area, and marine sculptures your kids will want to investigate.

Big Wheel General Store (ages 5 and up)

Baltimore between First and Second Streets; (541) 347-3719. Open 9 a.m. to 5:30 p.m. daily, 10 a.m. to 5 p.m. Sun.

After your fresh shrimp or crab salad, buy a sweet treat at the store's fudge factory. Check out the free "driftwood museum" while you're there.

Cranberry Sweets (all ages)

Chicago Avenue and First Street; (541) 347-9475. Mon through Sat 10 a.m. to 6 p.m.

If the fudge wasn't quite enough, satisfy your sweet tooth at this sweet shop.

Top Bandon **Events**

July
Old-fashioned July Fourth Celebration. Join the residents of this charming coastal community in their Independence Day celebration, complete with a parade, old-fashioned fireworks, annual fish fry, and crafts fair.

September
Cranberry Festival. This lively local event features a street fair, parade, food booths, dances, and, of course, cranberries.

For information on Bandon events, call (541) 347-9616; www.bandon.com; e-mail: bandoncc@harborside.com.

The Boat Basin (all ages)
Located on First Street at the Old Town dock; (541) 347-9616. Free.

This is a great place to watch the boats or head out on the pier for fishing or crabbing.

Port o' Call and Tony's Crab Shack (all ages)
On the dock in Old Town at 155 First St.; (541) 347-2875; www.tonyscrabshack.com. Open daily sunrise to sunset. Clamming and crabbing $–$$; fishing $$ (includes bait, rod, and hooks).

Rent crab rings, fishing rods, clamming shovels, and boats here. They'll tell you the best spots for jetty fishing or clamming, and they'll even cook your crabs. If you don't feel like catching your own, they sell freshly caught seafood. At Tony's Crab Shack next door, you can get fresh clam chowder, seafood cocktails, and fish tacos for about $5 or less.

Oregon Islands National Wildlife Refuge (ages 5 and up)
Located on 11th Street SW; 541-347-1470; www.fws.gov/oregoncoast/oregonislands. Always open, but best time to view wildlife is early morning or late afternoon. Free.

The "islands" are actually large offshore rocks that provide habitat for a great number of seabirds and mammals. The Coquille Point area presents one of the most spectacular places for viewing puffins, murres, oystercatchers, seals, and other animals that congregate on these offshore rocks. A group called Shoreline Education for Awareness (SEA) often has volunteers here and elsewhere along the coast with spotting scopes to enhance your viewing.

Bandon Marsh National Wildlife Refuge (ages 5 and up)
Located at the mouth of the Coquille River off Riverside Drive; (541) 347-1470; www.fws .gov/oregoncoast/bandonmarsh. Day-use area. Always open. Free.

This estuary at the river mouth contains nearly 300 acres of salt marsh. Some 115 species of migratory birds, 8 species of mammals, 45 species of fish, and other forms of sea life can be found within the refuge. Bring your binoculars for a closer look. SEA (Shoreline Education for Awareness) volunteers are often here with spotting scopes and to show visitors the legal access routes.

Fun Fact

Oregon is one of the five states in the country where tart and tangy cranberries are grown. Buy them in candy form in several of the local shops, celebrate them at the community's fall festival, or view them along the highway in late September and October.

Fun Fact

In 1990, about 60,000 pairs of Nike shoes were dumped into the Pacific Ocean from a storm-tossed freighter. Six months later, shoes began washing up on the coasts of Oregon, Washington, and British Columbia. Over the years, shoes have turned up in Hawaii, Japan, and the Philippines.

Free Flight Bird and Marine Mammal Rehabilitation (ages 5 and up)
1185 Portland Ave.; (541) 347-3882. Call for reservations. Free, but donations welcome.

Bandon's bird and mammal rescue and rehabilitation volunteers are happy to talk to visitors about local efforts to return wildlife to their natural habitats. Tours are available by appointment.

Bandon Beach Riding Stables (ages 5 and up)
Along Beach Loop Road; (541) 347-3423 or (541) 260-1437; www.bandon.com. Rides depart every 2 hours beginning at 10 a.m. year-round. Call for reservations. $$$$.

Guided rides with gentle horses are available for all ages, but children under 5 must ride double. Ask about 1½- to-2-hour sunset rides.

West Coast Game Park (all ages)
Located 7 miles south of Bandon on US 101; (541) 347-3106; www.gameparksafari.com. Open daily (weather permitting) except Jan and Feb, when the game park is open weekends only. Hours vary seasonally but open at least 10:30 a.m. to 4:30 p.m. $$$ ages 13 and older; $$ ages 2 to 12; under 2 free.

If your kids are fond of animals, this will be a sure winner. A walk-through safari covering 10 acres of the 21-acre preserve brings you up close and personal with 75 species of wildlife. Children might pet bear cubs, tiger cubs, or baby leopards. The many hoofed animals—deer, goats, caribou, and others—swarm around you as you feed them from ice cream cones filled with animal ambrosia.

Port Orford

The westernmost town in the lower forty-eight states, Port Orford is perched on the headland in the shadow of Humbug Mountain. The picturesque commercial harbor is unique in that it opens directly to the sea, without a river bar.

Berry Interesting

In late September and throughout October, you will see farmers harvesting cranberries along US 101 in Port Orford. Watch them gathering these round, red berries with a "beater" that churns the bog water and loosens them from their vines.

Battle Rock City Park (all ages)

Located on the shore adjacent to US 101 at the south end of Port Orford. Visitor center next to park is open daily; (541) 332-8055. Free.

This is a good place for picnicking or letting the kids play in the sand. After lunch take advantage of an obliging hiking trail. It was the scene of a fierce Native American battle in 1851. For an in-depth account of the battle, visit www.discoverportorford.com.

Buffington Park (all ages)

Located off 14th Street and Lakeshore Drive; Dreamland Skate Park at 13th and Arizona; (541) 332-8055 or (541) 332-3681. Always open. Free.

Sit in the shade while your kids run off energy, swing from the playground equipment, or try out the curves and cradle at Dreamland Skate Park. The park provides picnic facilities, tennis and handball courts, basketball courts, and a nature jogging trail.

Cape Blanco State Park and Lighthouse (ages 5 and up)

Located 9 miles north off US 101; (541) 756-0100; www.oregonstateparks.org. Lighthouse and Hughes House tours Apr through Oct Tues through Sun 10 a.m. to 3:30 p.m. Park and campground open year-round. $.

The renovated 1870 Cape Blanco Lighthouse, the oldest continuously operating lighthouse in Oregon, is located on the westernmost point of the 48 contiguous states. The campground, on a bluff adjacent to the lighthouse area, provides electrical sites with picnic tables, fire rings, and water. Bushes of huckleberry, salal, salmonberry, and thimbleberry lend privacy to the individual campsites. Several trails take off from the campground.

Fun Fact

Port Orford's port is the only natural open-water port for 600 miles, and it's one of only a half-dozen "dolly" ports left in the world. A dolly, or giant hoist, is used to lift boats into and out of the water. Rough seas prevent boats from mooring in the ocean, so they must be kept on land.

Top Port Orford **Events**

July

Fourth of July Jubilee. On top of the standards like parades and fireworks, this multi-day event features the annual Dingy Race, where teams of two build a boat and row a short course close to shore.

December

Hughes House Christmas Tours. The whole community gets involved in decorating this resplendent 1898 Victorian house, which is nestled in Cape Blanco State Park. (541) 332-0248; www.portorfordoregon.com/Friends.

For more information on Port Orford events, call (541) 332-8055 or visit www .portorfordoregon.com or www.discoverportorford.com.

Within the park is the 1898 **Hughes House** (www.hugheshouse.org), a 3,000-square-foot Victorian ranch house built in 1898.

Humbug Mountain State Park (ages 5 and up)

Six miles south of Port Orford on US 101; (541) 332-6774 or (800) 551-6949; www.oregon stateparks.org. Open daily year-round. Free.

From the campground, a fairly strenuous trail leads 3 miles to the summit of Humbug Mountain where, if the weather is clear, you'll enjoy an amazing 360-degree view. If the children are not up for climbing, try the lesser-known 2⅗-mile hike north from the campground along the old coast highway. The trail ends at the highway just south of Rocky Point, which is a terrific spot for exploring tide pools.

Port Orford Lifeboat Station (ages 6 and up)

92331 Coast Guard Hill Rd.; head west on Ninth Street (at mile marker 301) and up Coast Guard Hill to the park; (541) 332-0521; www.portorfordlifeboatstation.org. Open Apr through Oct 10 a.m. to 3:30 p.m. Thurs through Mon; by appointment other times of the year. Free.

The 1934 lifeboat station is located on what is known as "the Heads" or "Coast Guard Hill" and now houses a museum in the main barracks building. Listed on the National Register of Historic Places, the site also features the original officers' quarters as well as other outbuildings. Museum exhibits include a Lyle gun (line-throwing cannon), information on the Japanese attacks on Curry County during World War II, the Dog Tag Maker, local shipwrecks and rescues, and signaling systems (semaphore flags and flares). Hiking trails surround the station, providing spectacular ocean views, and lead to the lookout and Nellie's Cove, where lifeboats were once launched for rescues.

Prehistoric Gardens (ages 5 and up)

About 12 miles south of Port Orford; (541) 332-4463; www.theprehistoricgardens.com; e-mail: info@prehistoricgardens.com. Open in summer 9 a.m. to dusk; call for winter hours. $$ adults and children ages 11 to 18; $ ages 3 to 10; 2 and under free.

Wander through a dense coastal rain forest where life-size models of prehistoric dinosaurs and other creatures lurk. Jurassic Park? Well, no, but young children will be captivated by the huge, brightly colored creatures they've read about. Parents will appreciate the luxuriant foliage of ferns and mosses that keep the forest looking green and lush year-round. The giant *Tyrannosaurus rex* standing alongside the highway lets you know you've arrived. Some visitors say winter is the best time to visit the gardens because Oregon's misty weather provides just the right prehistoric ambience.

Elk River Fish Hatchery (ages 3 and up)

Three miles north of Port Orford and 8 miles east of US 101 on Elk River Road; (541) 332-7025; www.dfw.state.or.us/resources/visitors. Call for hours. Free.

Interpretive signs describe how the Oregon Department of Fish and Wildlife hatchery raises salmon and steelhead smolts that are released to return as spawning adults. The hatchery produces 475,000 fall chinook salmon smolts for the Elk and Chetco Rivers and other area waterways and some 50,000 winter steelhead smolts. About 700 rainbow trout are raised for the "lunkers" program, a special project to release large trout (3 to 6 pounds each) into Floras Lake, Garrison Lake, and Libby Pond. Each spring the hatchery sponsors a free fishing day for children. Staff and volunteers teach kids about fishing and let them fish in a rearing pond stocked with trout—some of which have been fed all year by visitors and have become enormous—until they have caught their limit of three fish. There's also swimming at the Elk River boat launch for older children.

Gold Beach

Nestled on the shores of the Rogue River is Gold Beach, where early prospectors literally scooped up gold off the beaches. Later the area attracted sport fishermen. It was here that Zane Grey wrote his novel *The Rogue River Feud*. Now Gold Beach is the launching spot for a variety of jet boat tours.

Rogue Wilderness Whitewater Trips (ages 8 and up)

P.O. Box 1110, 325 Galice Rd., Merlin, OR 97532; (800) 336-1647 or (541) 479-9554; www .wildrogue.com. Operates May through Oct; trips begin at 9 a.m. and noon. Advance reservations required. $$$$.

Rafting presents another way for the family to take in river sites. This company offers full-, half-, and multi-day whitewater trips and a wide variety of fly-fishing, wilderness lodge, and hiking trips. You can also rent rafts and inflatable kayaks and all the gear you'll need for a self-guided adventure, plus shuttle service to get you and your gear to the river and back.

Fun Fact

Gold was discovered in the sands of Curry County in the 1850s, and hundreds of placer miners set up operations near the mouth of the Rogue River. The settlement here was originally called Ellensburg after the daughter of Captain William Tichenor, an early area explorer, but was later renamed Gold Beach to avoid confusion with a town in Washington Territory.

Hawk's Rest Ranch Stables and Trail Rides (all ages 8)

94667 N. Bank Pistol River Rd.; located 11 miles south of Gold Beach at the Siskiyou West Day Lodge, east at Pistol River junction; (541) 247-6423; www.siskiyouwest.com. Open daily year-round. In spring and summer, 60- to 90-minute rides are offered every 2 hours starting at 8 a.m.; last ride is before sunset. Fall and winter rides available with 2-day advance reservation. Half- and full-day rides also available. All ages can join ranch and rain forest rides (younger than 5 must share the saddle with an adult); beach riders must be at least 8 years old. $$$$.

Experience the old-fashioned way of exploration, beginning your day with a ride up an alder-lined creek or ending it with a sunset ride on the beach. The Hawk's Rest Day Lodge has a gallery, pioneer museum, and gift store.

Jerry's Rogue River Museum (ages 6 and up)

Port of Gold Beach off Port Drive Mail; (541) 247-4571 or (800) 451-3645. Open daily year-round. Free.

Top Gold Beach **Events**

June

Pistol River Wave Bash. The whole family will be awestruck by the sight of professional and amateur windsurfers riding and "bashing" the waves of the rough spring Pacific shoreline. www.americanwindsurfingtour.com.

July

Curry County Fair. One of Oregon's largest flower shows plus a parade, rodeo, wildlife exhibitions, truck pull, and a lamb barbecue are featured at this annual county-sponsored event. (541) 247-4541; www.curryfair.com.

Jet Boating the Rogue River

One of the most popular experiences in Gold Beach is a jet boat trip up the wild and scenic Rogue River. Several tour companies operate full- and half-day trips on the river, stopping for lunch at one of several resort lodges upriver. Tours start the first of May and usually end in late October. There's no age limit for either of the following trips.

Jerry's Jet Boats. Port of Gold Beach off Port Drive Mail; (800) 451-3645 or (541) 247-4571; www.jerrysroguejets.com. Open May 1 through Labor Day. Tours depart daily starting at 8 a.m. Call for departure schedules. $$$$ adults, $$$ ages 4 to 11, under 4 free. Jerry's offers two traditional trips of 104 and 80 miles, and now also runs the "Mail Boat" hydro jets offering, on which you follow the 64-mile Original Postman's Run and learn how the area's first postmen delivered mail to the remote community of Agness. Expect to get splashed a bit on the 80- and 104-mile trips, which surge through river rapids.

This family-run jet boat tour company has collected river memorabilia and geological exhibits that follow the formation of the Rogue River Canyon.

Curry County Historical Museum (ages 5 and up)
Located at the Curry County Fairgrounds, 29419 Ellensburg Ave.; (541) 247-6396; www .curryhistory.com. Open Tues through Sat 10 a.m. to 4 p.m.; closed in Jan. $.

You'll see exhibits of old-time logging equipment and Native American arrowheads, petroglyphs, baskets, and other artifacts, including a canoe. A maritime display shows old photographs of shipwrecks that occurred along the Pacific coast.

Brookings

Brookings is known as Oregon's "Banana Belt," where the weather is warm and sunny more often than anywhere else on the Oregon coast—and sometimes in the entire state! Coming into Brookings from Gold Beach, you'll cross Thomas Creek Bridge, which, at 345 feet high, is the highest bridge in Oregon. Less than 10 minutes from the California border, Brookings is within easy reach of northern California's majestic redwoods.

Tidewind Sportfishing (ages 8 and up)
16368 Lower Harbor Rd., Brookings-Harbor; (541) 469-0337. Call for hours and prices.

Tidewind offers fishing and scenic tour charters as well as whale-watching trips. Costs include tackle and gear. Just bring a lunch.

Fun Fact

Named for the lumber baron John E. Brookings, president of the Brookings Lumber & Box Company, Brookings was founded as a company town in 1908. A cousin, Robert S. Brookings, provided financial support and hired a San Francisco architect to design the town site—the only early plat in Oregon to receive such professional attention, according to *Oregon Geographic Names* by Lewis L. McArthur.

Bud Cross Park (all ages)

Third Street and Ransom Avenue; (541) 469-2163 or (541) 469-3181; www.brookings.or.us. Open daily sunrise to sunset year-round. Free. Swimming pool open in summer; call (541) 469-4711 for days and hours. $, children under 7 free (must be accompanied by an adult at all times).

Bud Cross Park was named for a longtime chief of police and is the major recreational park in Brookings. It offers baseball fields, tennis and basketball courts, and the municipal swimming pool. The Skate Park, located within the park at Third and Hassett Streets, was designed and built by Dreamland Team and has a huge doughnut shape, a triple bowl in the middle, and walls 4 to 10 feet high.

Kidtown in Azalea Park (all ages)

Follow the signs at the north end of Harbor Bridge; park entrance is on the right on North Bank Chetco River Road. (541) 469-2163 or (541) 469-3181; www.brookings.or.us. Day use only. Free.

Younger children love it here. It's a child-size fortress, complete with turrets and towers, slides and tunnels. Parents will enjoy wandering among the park's many azalea bushes—some 300 years old—when the spring bloom is on.

Fun Fact

The name Chetco comes from the Indians who were the original inhabitants of this area. The last member of the tribe, a woman who went by the name Lucky Dick, died in the 1940s.

Fun Fact

Sam Boardman is known for planting trees along treeless areas of the Old Oregon Trail and the Columbia River Highway. Later his plantings were taken over by the state highway department.

Samuel H. Boardman State Scenic Corridor
(all ages)

Located 4 miles north on US 101; (800) 551-6949; www.oregonstateparks.org. Closes at dusk; open year-round. Free.

Named for the state's first parks superintendent, who believed Oregon's shining coastline should be saved for the public, the park covers 12 miles of coastline, beginning 4 miles north of Brookings. All along this stretch are fascinating and picturesque rock formations and tide pools to explore. You can gain access to the beach at both Whalehead Cove Viewpoint, overlooking Whalehead Island, and at Indian Sands Wayside. At the south end of Indian Sands beach, look for the Indian midden, an area with huge piles of shells and bones left behind after many feasts. This is a look-but-don't-touch situation—disturbing the midden is against federal law. The park offers several interpretive events and nature programs in the summer.

Natural Bridge Viewpoint (ages 5 and up)

Located about 9 miles north of Brookings near the beach access point at Miner Creek; (800) 535-9469; www.traveloregon.com. Always open. Free.

From the parking area, walk south along the trail to a viewing platform to see the remains of ancient sea caves that collapsed eons ago. It's a short but often steep walk to the beach. For trail maps, log on to the Oregon State Parks Trail Maps website at www .oregon.gov.

Alfred A. Loeb State Park (all ages)

North Chetco River Road, 8 miles northeast of Brookings; (541) 469-2021 or (800) 551-6949 (information); (800) 452-5687 (cabin reservations); www.oregonstateparks.org. Open daily year-round. Free.

Loeb State Park sits in a grove of old-growth myrtlewood. You can camp and picnic here, take a swim in the Chetco River, throw a fishing line into one of the best salmon streams in the area (Emily Creek), or walk a 1¼-mile nature loop trail through a redwood forest. Yes, redwoods in Oregon! The most impressive of the trees you'll pass are between 300 and 800 years old. A self-guiding brochure with a map is available at the trailhead in the day-use area of the park along the Chetco River. In addition to campsites, log cabins are available to rent.

Top Brookings **Events**

May

Azalea Festival. This week of special events celebrates the glories of spring-time on the coast. (800) 877-9741 or (541) 469-3181.

May through September

American Music Festival. Concerts are held in Azalea Park every other Sunday from the end of May through mid-September. (541) 469-3181.

August

Brookings-Harbor Festival of the Arts. Named the best fine arts festival in Oregon more than once, this 2-day event has arts and crafts exhibits and demonstrations, plus entertainment and children's art activities. (541) 469-3181

December

Nature's Coastal Holiday. A brilliantly festive light show and sculpture display, plus refreshments, in Azalea Park nightly. (541) 469-3181.

Chetco Valley Historical Society Museum (ages 6 and up)

15461 Museum Rd.; (541) 469-6651; www.brookingsharbororegon.com. Open weekends noon to 4 p.m.; extended days and hours in the summer. Free, but donations welcome.

This pioneer museum is housed in the historic Blacke House. The largest Monterey cypress tree in the United States is on the grounds.

Where to Eat

IN BANDON

Bandon Baking Co. & Deli. 160 Second St.; (541) 347-9440. An Old Town favorite with a delicious selection of cookies, pastries, croissants, and breads, plus breakfast and, for lunch, homemade soup and sandwiches. $–$$

The Station Restaurant. US 101, just east of Old Town; (541) 347-9615. In the gift shop next door, kids enjoy watching the German-made LGB model trains and the glass hive full of live honeybees. Breakfast, lunch, and dinner. $$–$$$

Thai Thai Restaurant. 160 Baltimore St.; (541) 329-0160. Fantastic Thai to eat in the Old Town location or take back to your room. $$

2 Loons Café. 120 Second St. SE in Old Town; (541) 347-3750. A small menu of breakfast and lunch favorites attracts locals and repeat visitors alike. $–$$

IN BROOKINGS

Mattie's Pancake & Omelette. 15975 US 101 S. Traditional breakfast and lunch fare with a great family atmosphere. The French toast is a must. $–$$

One Love. 623 Memory Lane; (541) 469-6100. Made-from-scratch, gourmet pizzas, pasta dishes, and fish on limited but very good menu. Reggae music and a pleasant atmosphere make this a family fave. $$–$$$

Rancho Viejo Family Restaurant. 1025 Chetco Ave.; (541) 412-0184; www.rancho viejobrookings.com. Authentic Mexican food the kids will love and delicious margaritas for frazzled parents! $$–$$$

Slugs and Stones and Ice Cream Cones. 97950 Holly Lane, Port of Brookings-Harbor; (541) 469-7584. You can bribe your children to let you peacefully enjoy the stunning viewpoints along the way with a promise of an ice cream cone. The "For Kids Only" menu offers Slyme Sundae and Baby Pickles Gummy Worm Sundae. $

IN COOS BAY

Benetti's Italian Restaurant. 260 S. Broadway; (541) 267-6066. Home-style Italian food with a downstairs area for family dining. $–$$

Sharkbites. 240 S. Broadway; (541) 269-7475. Fresh seafood and traditional American fare is a hit at this fun spot. $

IN FLORENCE

Bridgewater Restaurant. 1297 Bay St.; (541) 997-9405; www.oldtownflorence.com. Seafood entrees are offered in a tropical-like setting that supplies crayons and colorable children's menus. $$–$$$

Nature's Corner Café and Market. 185 US 101; (541) 997-0900. Healthy options and lots of gluten-free choices provide a welcome spot for those who have specific diets or just want fresh, well-prepared food. $–$$

IN GOLD BEACH

Nor'Wester Seafood. Port of Gold Beach; (541) 247-2333. Seafood, steaks, and other American food with a great view of the harbor. $$$–$$$$

Playa del Sol. 29455 Ellensburg Ave. (US 101); (541) 247-0314. Family-run Mexican restaurant offering specialty shrimp and crab enchiladas. $–$$

IN REEDSPORT

Bedrock's Pizzeria. 2165 Winchester Ave.; (541) 271-4100. A pizza place with other options for dough-weary parents. $–$$

Where to Stay

IN BANDON

Bullards Beach State Park. Located 2 miles north of Bandon; (800) 452-5687 for reservations; www.oregonstateparks.org.

Campsites and yurt camping are available here year-round. Beach access. In the summer state rangers provide educational activities for children. $

Sunset Oceanfront Lodging. 1865 Beach Loop Dr.; (800) 842-2407 or (541) 347-2453; www.sunsetmotel.com. Kitchenettes, pets allowed, spa and pool, and easy access to Bandon's famous beach. $$–$$$

Table Rock Motel. 840 Beach Loop Dr.; (541) 347-2700 or (800) 457-9141; www .tablerockmotel.com; e-mail: tablerock@ harborside.com. Simple but clean rooms. Kitchenettes; pets allowed. Just behind the building is the Oregon Island Bird Sanctuary. Vacation rentals also available. $–$$$

IN THE BAY AREA

Best Western Holiday Motel. 411 N. Bayshore Dr., Coos Bay; (541) 269-5111 or (800) 228-8655; e-mail: 0063@hotel.bestwestern .com. Complimentary continental breakfast, kitchenettes, spa, pool, fitness center. Pets allowed; kids under 12 stay free. $$–$$$

Red Lion Hotel. 1313 North Bayshore Drive, Coos Bay; (541) 267-4141 or (800) 733-5466. Dining room, swimming pool, spa, large rooms, and central location. $$–$$$

Sunset Bay State Park. Located 3 miles south of Charleston on Cape Arago Highway; (800) 452-5687; www.oregonstateparks .org. One of the most beautiful state parks in Oregon, nestled in a snug cove at the base of coastal hills with easy access to the beach and hiking trails. $

IN BROOKINGS

Best Western Beachfront Inn. 16008 Boat Basin Rd.; (800) 468-4081 or (541) 469-7779. Many of the guest rooms are within 50 feet of the ocean. Kitchenettes, heated pool, spa. All rooms have an ocean view with microwave, fridge, and coffeemaker. Easy beach access. Small pets allowed. $$$–$$$$

Harris Beach State Park. 1655 US 101 N, 2 miles north of Brookings; (541) 469-2021; (800) 452-5687 for reservations; www.oregon stateparks.org. Tent and yurt camping. Five RV spaces. $

Westward Inn. 1026 Chetco Ave.; (541) 469-7471 or (888) 521-6020. Small pets OK, downtown location, walking distance to shops. $$–$$$

IN FLORENCE

Driftwood Shores Resort. 88416 First Ave.; (800) 422-5091 or (541) 997-8263; www .driftwoodshores.com. Restaurant, indoor pool, spa. All rooms have ocean views. $$$$

Fish Mill Lodge and RV Park. Located 5.5 miles south of Florence off US 101 at 4484 Fish Mill Way; (541) 997-2511; http://fishmill .tripod.com/homepage.html. Fully equipped kitchen rooms overlooking Siltcoos Lake. $$

Lighthouse Inn. 155 US 101; (866-) 997-3221; www.lighthouseinn.tripod.com; A traditional motel with recently refurbished family units and a large suite that accommodates families of 6, it sits a block off the river near Old Town. Pets allowed. $$–$$$

IN GOLD BEACH

Azalea Lodge. 29481 Ellensburg Ave. (US 101); (800) 381-6635 or (541) 247-6635. Small, clean, and centrally located. Free limited breakfast; in-room coffeemaker, fridge; cable TV; laundry facilities. $$

Gold Beach Resort and Condominiums. 29232 S. Ellensburg Ave. (US 101); (541) 247-7066 or (800) 541-0947; www.gbresort.com. One of the only beachfront accommodations in the area, offering rooms and condos. Indoor swimming pool, hot tub. Microwave, refrigerator, coffeemaker in each room. All rooms have ocean view. Restaurant just across the parking lot. $$$–$$$$

Inn of the Beachcomber. 29266 Ellensburg Ave. (US 101); (800) 690-2378 or (541)

247-6691; www.innofthebeachcomber.com. Ocean views, beach access, fireplaces, kitchenettes, pool, and spa. $$–$$$$

Ireland's Rustic Lodges. 1220 S. Ellensburg Ave. (US 101); (541) 247-7718; www .irelandsrusticlodges.com. Lots of options for log cabins and lodge rooms near the ocean, some with kitchens, fireplaces, and oceanfront real-estate. Shaded parklike setting. $–$$$$

IN REEDSPORT

Best Western Plus Salbasgeon Inn. 1400 US 101; (541) 271-4831; www.bestwest ernoregon.com. Large, clean rooms and a heated indoor pool. Kitchen and family suites available. Dog-friendly. $$–$$$$

Winchester Bay Inn. 390 Broadway, Winchester Bay; (541) 271-4871 or (800) 246-1462; www.winbayinn.com. Free continental breakfast, cable TV, and HBO. Some harbor-view rooms, kitchens, kitchenettes, in-room spas, suites. Kids under 18 stay free.

For More Information

Bandon Chamber of Commerce. P.O. Box 1515, 300 SE Second St., Bandon, OR 97411; (541) 347-9616; www.bandon.com.

Bay Area Chamber of Commerce/Coos Bay–North Bend Visitor Bureau. 50 E. Central Ave., Coos Bay, OR 97420; (800) 824-8486 or (541) 269-0215; www.oregons bayarea.com or www.oregonsadventure coast.com; e-mail: info@oregonsbayarea .com.

Brookings-Harbor Chamber of Commerce. P.O. Box 940, 16330 Lower Harbor Rd., Brookings, OR 97415; (800) 535-9469 or (541) 469-3181; www.brookingsor.com.

Charleston Information Center. P.O. Box 5735, Charleston, OR 97420; (800) 824-8486 or (541) 888-2311 (May through Sept).

Coquille Chamber of Commerce. 119 N. Birch St., Coquille, OR 97423; (541) 396-3414; www.coquillechamber.net; e-mail: coquille chamber@mycomspan.com.

Florence Area Chamber of Commerce. 290 US 101, Florence, OR 97439; (541) 997-3128 or (800) 524-4864; www.florence chamber.com.

Gold Beach Chamber of Commerce Visitor Center. 29692 Ellensburg Ave., #6, Gold Beach, OR 97444; (800) 525-2334 or (541) 247-7526; www.goldbeach.org; e-mail: visit@ goldbeach.org.

Oregon Dunes National Recreation Area Visitor Center. 855 Highway Ave., Reedsport, OR 97467; (541) 271-6000; www .fs.fed.us/r6/siuslaw/recreation/tripplanning /oregondunes.

Port Orford Chamber of Commerce. P.O. Box 637, 520 Jefferson St. in Battle Rock Park, US 101 S, Port Orford, OR 97465; (541) 332-8055; www.portorfordoregon.com; e-mail: chamber@portorfordoregon.com. See also: www.discoverportorford.com.

Reedsport–Winchester Bay Chamber of Commerce. 855 Highway Ave., Reedsport, OR 97467; (800) 247-2155 or (541) 271-3495; www.reedsportcc.org.

Portland
& the
Columbia
Gorge

P ortland, named after Portland, Maine, on the toss of a coin, has a population of more than 500,000 in the city and more than 2 million in the larger metropolitan area.

Now known as the City of Roses, Portland grew from the pioneer spirit that brought hundreds of thousands of settlers along the Oregon Trail despite often heartbreaking hardships.

Today people still flock to Portland from points east and south, whether to visit or to make a permanent move, and it is consistently named as one of the nation's "greenest" and most liveable cities. Famous for biking, bridges, beer, cuisine, and its progressive yet laid-back attitude, there is no better launch point for an Oregon vacation than the Portland and Columbia Gorge region.

Portland

Portland is organized on a quadrant that makes it easy to get around from day one. The Willamette River divides the city into the east and west sides, and Burnside Street marks the boundary between north and south. The result is four distinctive regions (North/Northeast, Southeast, Northwest, and Southwest) that each have their own personality and offerings for visitors and local travelers alike.

The city also benefits from award-winning urban planning. In the late '70s, former mayor Neil Goldschmidt and other leaders revitalized the downtown area and installed the beginnings of a mass transit system that has become a model for those around the world. A combination of buses, light-rail trains, and trolleys makes it easy to get almost anywhere in the city quickly. For the most part, all paths lead through downtown to ensure easy access from all corners and a constantly vibrant, happening city center.

PORTLAND & THE COLUMBIA GORGE

Downtown

Pioneer Courthouse Square (all ages)

Located in the block between Broadway and Sixth, and SW Morrison and Yamhill; (800) 962-3700, (503) 823-2223, or (503) 275-8355; www.travelportland.com or www.parks.ci .portland.or.us. Open 5 a.m. to midnight. Free.

Billed as "Portland's Living Room," the square is a great place to people-watch or just take a break while you eat lunch or a snack from one of the nearby food carts. Kids enjoy splashing in the fountain or trying to get a smile from the "umbrella man"—a lifelike bronze sculpture. The **Weather Machine** is another kid favorite. At noon each day the machine plays a musical fanfare and sprays mist, out of which comes the symbol for the day's weather—a stylized sun, a dragon for storms, or a great blue heron for Oregon's perennial drizzle. In summertime the square comes alive with concerts, some planned and some impromptu, from sometimes very talented buskers (street musicians). The square is also home to the Portland Visitors Association and the Tri-Met offices, where you can get information on bus and light-rail services in the city.

Portland Art Museum (ages 5 and up)

1219 SW Park Ave.; (503) 226-2811; www.pam.org. Open Tues through Sat 10 a.m. to 5 p.m.; Thurs and Fri until 8 p.m.; Sun noon to 5 p.m. $$, children under 18 free.

The kids will love seeing one of the premier collections of Northwest Indian art in the country, especially the ceremonial masks used in dances and potlatch celebrations. The museum also hosts many distinguished traveling exhibits that have included such artists as M. C. Escher, Gauguin, and Monet.

Oregon Historical Society (ages 5 and up)

1200 SW Park Ave.; (503) 222-1741; www.ohs.org. Open Tues through Sat 10 a.m. to 5 p.m., Sun noon to 5 p.m. $$$ adults; $ seniors, students 19 and older, and children ages 6 to 18; 5 and under free.

The covered wagon and other pioneer displays of Oregon My Oregon are just a piece of the many permanent, and traveling exhibits and programs kids love in this lively museum. Children also enjoy the larger-than-life-size murals outside, bordering the Portland Park Blocks.

Fun Fact

The *Portlandia* statue on the Portland Building (SW Fifth Avenue between Main and Madison Streets) is the world's second-largest hammered copper sculpture, smaller only than the Statue of Liberty.

Lan Su Chinese Garden (ages 5 and up)

NW Third Avenue and Everett Street; (503) 228-8131; www.lansugarden.org. Open daily Nov through Mar 10 a.m. to 5 p.m., Apr through Oct until 6 p.m. Tours offered daily at noon and 1 p.m. $$, children under 5 free.

Created to mimic a Ming dynasty garden, Portland's authentic Suzhou-style garden was designed by architects and artisans from China to convey artistic beauty and symbolic meaning, embodying the balance and harmony of nature. The 40,000-square-foot walled garden encloses a full city block and includes an 8,000-square-foot lake, a teahouse, 9 restful pavilions, and nearly 100 specimen trees, water plants, bamboo, and orchids. The standing Taihu rocks were mined from Lake Tai, a freshwater lake near Suzhou in China. More than 500 tons of rocks were shipped to Portland along with the fir, gingko, and nanmu woods used for columns and beams in the pavilions. This is an amazing oasis of tranquility in the heart of Portland's bustling downtown.

Portland Police Museum (ages 6 and up)

1111 SW Second Ave., 16th Floor; (503) 823-0019; www.portlandpolicebureau.com. Open Tues through Fri 10 a.m. to 3 p.m. Free.

Get a look at police uniforms, handcuffs, and weapons from a century of policing in Portland.

Powell's City of Books (all ages)

1005 W. Burnside; (800) 878-7323 or (503) 228-4651; www.powells.com. Open daily 9 a.m. to 11 p.m.

Here's a bookstore that's very close to being a city within a city—it takes a map to find your way through the stacks and stacks of new and used books in room after room. Families will want to head to the "rose" room for children's books. There's a coffeehouse-style cafe upstairs that serves espresso drinks for weary moms and dads and cookies and pastries for kids. Powell's is the largest new and used bookstore in the world, with more than a million books.

The Sternwheeler *Rose* (all ages)

6211 N. Ensign St., docks at RiverPlace Marina; (503) 286-7673. Call for hours, prices, and reservations.

The 130-passenger sternwheeler offers brunch, lunch, and dinner cruises that let you experience the Willamette River from the water.

Willamette Shore Trolley (all ages)

North terminal at RiverPlace, off SW Clay; south terminal at 311 N. State St. in Lake Oswego; (503) 697-7436; www.trainweb.org/oerhs/wst.htm. Call for hours, fares, and departure times.

This antique trolley line operates May through Oct between Portland's RiverPlace and Lake Oswego, passing through a warehouse district to the river's shore, then past Willamette

Get **Carted Away**

Portland's entrepreneurial spirit and funky, do-things-differently ethos have produced one of the city's newest dining crazes that's garnering national attention: the food cart. Originally started in high-traffic business locales, a few of these trailer-based, portable restaurants turned into hundreds that have taken seemingly permanent roost in spots around the city. The happy result at each "pod" is a huge variety of unique and sometimes wacky specialties within less than a city block. Families can find something affordable for every member's tastes. Some of the best pods are listed below, but "independents" and smaller pods are sprinkled throughout the city—keep your eyes peeled as you travel around. Visit www.foodcartsportland.com for maps and cart listings.

SE Hawthorne and Twelfth

N. Mississippi and Skidmore

N. Greeley and Killingsworth

SW Alder between Ninth and 11th

SW Fifth between Oak and Stark

Park and through the 1,400-foot S-shaped Elk Rock Tunnel. At Lake Oswego the **Tillamook Ice-Creamery,** about a block from the train stop at 37 SW Λ St., sells the delectable ice cream cones usually found only at the coastal factory in Tillamook.

Gov. Tom McCall Waterfront Park (all ages) and the Eastbank Esplanade

Located in downtown Portland, stretching 2 miles along the Willamette River; (800) 962-3700 or (503) 823-2223; www.portlandonline.com/parks. Open 5 a.m. to midnight. Free.

This is a terrific place for walking, jogging, cycling, and roller-skating. These parks line the river on the east and west sides, between the Steel Bridge to the north past the Hawthorne Bridge to the south. Tom McCall Waterfront Park is on the west (downtown) side. From the Saturday Market under the Burnside Bridge, you can stroll south through the park, hang out around the Salmon Street Springs fountain, then cross under the Hawthorne Bridge along the river to the **RiverPlace Promenade,** where you can get ice cream cones or espresso from sidewalk vendors or grab a curbside cafe table for a bite of lunch. Walk across the Hawthorne or Steel Bridges for great views of downtown and to link with the Eastbank Esplanade. The mile-long esplanade features a 1,200-foot floating walkway—the longest in the United States—public boat docks, river overlooks and cantilevered walkways, plazas, urban markers and interpretive panels, public art, and access to the Steel Bridge Walkway, built for bicyclists and pedestrians on the lower deck of the

Fun Fact

The Steel Bridge is on the National Register of Historic Places and is the only telescoping vertical lift span truss bridge in operation in America.

Steel Bridge. Fully accessible, the walkway gives pedestrians a safe connection to the Convention Center, Lloyd District, and Old Town/Downtown.

The entire loop across one bridge and back on the other is about 2¼ miles. Rent bikes or pedal-powered surreys by the hour at **Kerr Bikes** (503-808-9955), and get some exercise while you enjoy the sights of the loop or venture into downtown.

Oregon Maritime Museum (ages 5 and up)

Located aboard the steamer *Portland*, moored at Waterfront Park at the foot of Pine Street; (503) 224-7724; www.oregonmaritimemuseum.org. Open Wed through Sat 11 a.m. to 4 p.m., Sun 12:30 to 4:30 p.m. Last tour 30 minutes before closing. $, children under 6 free.

Young and old alike are intrigued by the many scale-model ships and nautical artifacts on display. The most fascinating part of the museum is listening to the "watch-standers," volunteer docents who provide living-history programs—each one an "old salt" with many years at sea. You'll also tour the historic steam sternwheeler *Portland*.

Portland Saturday Market (all ages)

SW Ankeny and Naito Parkway just south of the Burnside Bridge; (503) 222-6072; www .portlandsaturdaymarket.com. Rain or shine, open Sat 10 a.m. to 5 p.m., Sun 11 a.m. to 4:30 p.m., Mar through Dec 24. Free entry.

About 450 crafts and food booths transform this asphalt area from Apr through Dec every Sat and Sun. Most weekends there's nonstop entertainment that aims to please the whole family. Clowns with balloons and vendors who paint faces attract kids like magnets.

Ira Keller Fountain (all ages)

At Third Avenue between Clay and Market Streets, across from the Keller Auditorium; (503) 823-7529.

You'll see this fountain alive with kids and families cooling off in the summer or just enjoying the sound of cascading water in this city-block-size water park.

Southwest

Southwest is best known for the West Hills that house Washington Park and the zoo. Farther out, Portland's western hills are a popular spot in the summer and fall for appreciating the bounty of the harvest. U-pick farms abound, for everything from Oregon's own marionberries (grown in very few places in the country), delicious peaches, and tasty hazelnuts to bright orange pumpkins and juicy wine grapes. For a display of fall colors, take a drive from Beaverton along Farmington Road.

Oregon Zoo (all ages)

4001 SW Canyon Rd., 2 miles west of Portland off US 26; (503) 226-1561; www.oregonzoo .org. Open daily except Christmas. Summer hours 8 a.m. to 6 p.m. May 15 through Sept 15; winter hours 9 a.m. to 4 p.m. $$ adults, $ children ages 3 to 11, ages 2 and under free. Discounts for riding MAX line there and on the second Tues of every month.

From a thunder-and-lightning storm in the West African rain forest to the underwater viewing areas in the Penguinarium and the Arctic tundra where the polar bears roam, the zoo takes your family into strange and wonderful new worlds. Visit Packy, the "baby" elephant that made international headlines on April 14, 1962, as the first elephant born in captivity. Ride the zoo train for a tour of the grounds, and don't miss the predatory bird shows on the great lawn in summer—your kids will love ducking as the great birds swoop low over the crowd.

CM2: Children's Museum—Second Generation

(ages 6 months and up)

4015 SW Canyon Rd.; (503) 223-6500; www.portlandcm.org. Open Tues through Sun 9 a.m. to 5 p.m., Thurs until 8 p.m. $$, children under 1 free.

Plan on spending an afternoon in this wonderland for kids, which has 3 floors of exploratory hands-on exhibits, art activities, and fun centers. The Clay Shop gives budding sculptors a chance to create, and the carpeted Baby's Garden challenges little ones from infancy to 2 years with all kinds of visual and physical stimuli. Other perennial favorites are the Dig Pit, Water Works, Play It Again Theatre, and the Treehouse Adventure. Traveling exhibits keep it fresh for repeat visitors. One warning: Weekends can be very crowded and the divided rooms can make it difficult for one adult to track multiple kids.

International Rose Test Gardens (ages 5 and up)

400 SW Kingston Ave.; (503) 823-3636. Open daily 7 a.m. to 10 p.m. Free.

Roses begin blooming in late May and continue through Sept in this 4½-acre sanctuary. The many rhododendrons and azaleas start the blazing show off early in Mar or Apr. In the summer free concerts are held in the amphitheater, and you can spread out a picnic lunch just about anywhere. This is one of the largest and oldest rose test gardens in the United States, and it also has one of the best views of downtown Portland. Proceeds from the gift shop support the gardens.

Fun Facts

- Matt Groening, creator of the popular TV show *The Simpsons*, got his start in Portland.

- Mill Ends Park is 24 inches in diameter and the world's smallest dedicated park. Portland also has Forest Park, the largest forested municipal park in the nation.

- Powell's City of Books is the largest new and used bookstore in the world, with more than 1 million books in a store that takes up a full city block.

Hoyt Arboretum (ages 5 and up)

4000 Fairview Blvd., adjacent to the Oregon Zoo and International Rose Test Gardens; (503) 865-8733; www.hoytarboretum.org; e-mail: info@hoytarboretum.org. Open 9 a.m. to 4 p.m. Mon through Fri, 9 a.m. to 3 p.m. Sat. Free.

Laced with 10 miles of trails that wind through the largest selection of conifer species in the United States, as well as a huge variety of deciduous trees and shrubs, the arboretum is a quiet respite from the lively zoo. Markers identify the various species. In the fall take a self-guided "autumn color" walk through 1½ miles of vibrant maple, persimmon, dogwood, and photinia. New plantings include a bamboo garden, a magnolia area that blooms Apr through June, and a holly area with specimens from all over the world.

Japanese Garden (ages 5 and up)

611 SW Kingston Ave., just up the hill from the International Rose Test Gardens; (503) 223-1321; www.japanesegarden.com. In summer, open Tues through Sun 10 a.m. to 7 p.m., Mon noon to 7 p.m. From Oct to Mar, closing time is 4 p.m. Last entry 30 minutes before closing. $$ adults, children 5 and under free.

Take a breather from the busier pace at the zoo and stroll through these five different soothing and peaceful gardens. In May there's a special Children's Day.

World Forestry Center (ages 4 and up)

4033 SW Canyon Rd., across the large parking lot from the zoo; (503) 228-1367; www.world forestry.org. Open daily 10 a.m. to 5 p.m. $$ adults, $ kids 3 to 18, 2 and under free.

Pretend to ride a raft through the forest, drive heavy equipment, or venture into the tree canopy. Educational exhibits on old-growth and rain forests will enlighten and excite both children and adults.

Tryon Creek State Natural Area (ages 5 and up)
11321 SW Terwilliger Blvd.; (503) 636-4398, (503) 636-9886, or (800) 551-6949; www.oregon stateparks.org. Open dawn to dusk. Free.

More than a dozen miles of walking and cycling trails are available here, including the **Trillium Trail,** which is fully accessible. In early morning or evening, listen for the sounds of resident owls, coyotes, and foxes. The **Nature Center** presents exhibits and programs for kids and adults throughout the year.

Jenkins Estate (all ages)
Grabhorn Road, off Farmington and 209th; continue along Grabhorn to its junction with Scholls Ferry Road, then return on the loop to Beaverton; (503) 642-3855; www.thprd.org. Grounds open daily 8 a.m. to 8 p.m. in summer, 8 a.m. to 5 p.m. Oct through May. Call for information about touring building. Free.

Once a private residence and now a public park, the estate has lovely gardens for a walk or a picnic. You'll pass a number of farms before you get there, many of which produce, in Sept and Oct, the most spicily refreshing apple cider you've ever tasted. You will also find U-pick walnut and hazelnut farms. For adults, a stop at one of several wineries along the way is especially fun.

Jackson Bottom Wetlands (all ages)
Trailhead is located off Highway 219 south of Hillsboro; (503) 681-6206; www.jackson bottom.org. Open dawn to dusk. Education Center open daily 10 a.m. to 4 p.m. No dogs or bicycles. Free.

The preserve has developed a number of educational programs that you and your kids can appreciate together. One of the simplest ways to get a sense of the wetlands environment is to walk the Kingfisher Marsh Interpretive Trail, which takes you on a 3-mile walk along the Tualatin River and into the Kingfisher Marsh.

Recommended **Reading**

Wild in the City is a comprehensive guide to Portland's natural areas. Published by the Oregon Historical Society Press in collaboration with the Audubon Society's Urban Naturalist program, *Wild in the City* guides you to nearly 100 sites and provides detailed maps to natural spaces, trails, waterways, parks, golf courses, and even cemeteries, where wildlife habitat or natural-history features can be viewed. It also includes "must see" nature events throughout the year, such as the return of bald eagles to their winter roost, the gathering of Vaux's swifts in the fall, and spring wildflowers. The $22.95 book is available at the Audubon Society Nature Store and bookstores throughout Portland.

Top Portland **Events**

May

Cinco de Mayo. Sample authentic, award–winning food, from tortas to tamales to the latest in southwestern and Mexican cuisine. Dance to merengue, cumbias, and the modern rhythms of Tejano music or simply enjoy peaceful music from the Andes. Enjoy Mexican performances and peruse arts and crafts hand-made by artisans—or make your own! Held in Gov. Tom McCall Waterfront Park; (503) 222-9807; www.cincodemayo.org.

Summer

Summer Concerts at the Zoo. Concerts by regional and national musicians are held on the lawn outside the Africafe at the Oregon Zoo throughout the summer. Bring your own picnic or buy food and drinks on-site. Tickets required. (503) 226-1561; www.oregonzoo.org/concerts.

Sunday Parkways. In 2010, its second year, Sunday Parkways attracted more than 91,000 people over 5 Sundays. Miles of streets are closed off so you can safely walk, bike, or skateboard through the heart of some of Portland's most interesting and lively neighborhoods. Food, music, and the mist from household hoses add to the fun. www.facebook.com/PortlandSundayParkways.

June

Festival of Balloons. Head to Cook Park in Tigard to see the sky filled with colorful hot-air balloons during 3 days of festivities, carnivals, and other family activities. (503) 612-8213; www.tigardballoon.org.

Good in the (Neighbor)Hood Festival. A 3-day celebration of multicultural food, music, games and art showcases the rich culture in North and Northeast Portland. (503) 282-1288; www.goodintheneighborhood.org.

Portland Rose Festival. This yearly mega-event includes carnivals, concerts, dragon-boat and Indy-car races, an air show, and fireworks. Favorite family

Northwest

Shoppers and foodies have long loved the neighborhoods around 21st and 23rd Avenues. Since the late 1990s the Pearl District (mainly between Burnside and Kearney Streets and Ninth and 14th Avenues) has exploded as the area's trendiest urban center. Nestled against these asphalt jungles is the biggest urban forest in the country, making the area a draw for both city and country mice.

events include the Junior Rose Festival Parade, the nation's largest and oldest children's parade, and the nighttime Starlight Parade through downtown. Fleet Week brings in big military ships you can tour. (503) 227-2681; www .rosefestival.org.

July

Portland Highland Games. For more than 50 years this event has brought bagpipers, drummers, Highland dancers, Scottish food and wares, clan tents, and an evening *ceilidh* (traditional Highland music party) to Gresham's Mt. Hood Community College campus. (503) 293-8501; www.phga.org.

August

India Festival. The India Cultural Association hosts a celebration of Indian culture, with authentic food and performances, in Pioneer Courthouse Square. (503) 645-7902.

September

Oregon Symphony Waterfront Concert. A free concert at Gov. Tom McCall Waterfront Park starts with the Portland Youth Philharmonic and ends with the symphony's traditional performance of Tchaikovsky's 1812 Overture, complete with an elaborate fireworks show and cannons from the Oregon Army National Guard.

Oregon Polish Festival. The swirling colors of Eastern European folk dancers and the savory scents of rich ethnic foods entice crowds to the St. Stanislaus Polish Catholic Church. (503) 287-4077; http://portlandpolonia.org /festival.

Forest Park (ages 5 and up)

Stretches 8 miles through the hills of northwest Portland; (800) 962-3700 or (503) 823-2223; www.portlandonline.com/parks or www.forestparkconservancy.org. Open daily 5 a.m. to 10 p.m. Free.

With more than 5,100 acres, this is the largest forested municipal park in the nation. Its amazing network of more than 70 miles of hiking and biking trails through tall timber allows city dwellers to escape into a wilderness experience right in their backyard. Elk, black bears, and deer live in this virtually untouched municipal park. You can go online to download a map of 30-mile **Wildwood Trail** and others in Forest Park, or stop at **Hoyt Arboretum Visitor Center,** 4000 Fairview Blvd.

Audubon House (ages 5 and up)

Located next to Forest Park, 5151 NW Cornell Rd.; (503) 292-9453 or (503) 292-6855; www .audubonportland.org. Park open dawn to dusk (no pets); house and nature store open 10 a.m. to 6 p.m. Mon through Sat, 10 a.m. to 5 p.m. Sun. Free.

Audubon House rests at the edge of its own extensive park. Your kids can stroll in search of the many bird species attracted by the nesting and feeding stations. The Audubon Society frequently offers nature walks, birdhouse–building workshops, and other events to entertain and educate your youngsters.

Portland's Pittock Mansion (ages 8 and up)

3229 NW Pittock Dr.; (503) 823-3623; www.pittockmansion.org. House open daily 11 a.m. to 4 p.m., 10 a.m. to 4 p.m. in summer; park open 7 a.m. to 9 p.m. year-round. Closed major holidays and the month of Jan. $$ adults, $ ages 6 to 18, children 5 and under free.

Take a guided tour of this 1914 mansion and grounds, which are open to the public. You can picnic on the lawn of this 46-acre park, which connects with Forest Park and its many walking trails.

Sauvie Island (all ages)

18330 NW Sauvie Island Rd. (for trail maps), about 10 miles north of downtown Portland off US 30; (503) 621-3488; www.sauvieisland.org. Call for hours. Parking $ per day, $$$ annually.

If you are looking for a wonderful retreat, whether it be a beach picnic and swim in August, a trip to island farms to select jack-o'-lanterns, or bird watching for sandhill cranes in March, Sauvie Island has it all. It's home to farmers as well as to the **Sauvie Island Wildlife Area,** which is open daily. However, during waterfowl season much of the area is closed to protect migrating geese, ducks, and swans. Hiking trails wind through the 12,000-acre wildlife area, which covers half of the island. Wheelchair-accessible fishing docks are available at the Big Eddy and Gilbert River boat ramps in the wildlife area. **Walton Beach,** located about 10 miles north of the Sauvie Island Wildlife Office off Reeder Road, is a 3-mile stretch of sandy beach along the Columbia River. It's a favorite spot for swimming, fishing, and picnicking (no tables, but you can spread your blanket on the sand). On summer weekends visit the historic **Bybee Howell House** (13901 NW Howell Road; 503-797-1850; www .ohs.org) for a look at farm life in the 19th century. Stop by the **Cracker Barrel Grocery Store** (15005 NW Sauvie Island Rd.; 503-621-3960) for provisions on the way.

Southeast

When I was growing up, much of Southeast was considered the wrong side of the tracks; but since the 1990s its bohemian neighborhoods, like Sellwood and the Hawthorne and Belmont districts, with their funky shops and cutting-edge restaurants, have been attracting west-siders in droves.

Oregon Museum of Science and Industry (OMSI) (all ages)

1945 SE Water Ave.; (800) 955-6674 or (503) 797-4000; www.omsi.edu. Summer hours 9:30 a.m. to 7 p.m., winter hours 9:30 a.m. to 5:30 p.m., closed Mon except when Portland Public Schools are closed. $$$ adults, $$ 3 to 13, children 2 and under free. OMNIMAX shows $$, submarine tours, planetarium, and laser shows $ each. Combination tickets $$$$ and include museum entrance plus one OMNIMAX show and either the planetarium show or submarine tour.

Let your kids experience interactive exhibits that teach as well as entertain. Hands-on fun ranges from computer games to earthquake and tornado simulations. OMSI is a staple for Portland families because it offers something to engage all ages (even a baby area). The **OMNIMAX Theater** here was the first of its kind in Oregon, with a 5-story domed screen and complete surround sound, light, and motion that let you experience changing exhibitions, from earthquakes to volcanic eruptions, or journeys, such as exploring the Grand Canyon from top to bottom. The **Murdock Sky Theater** presents

An Adventure to Remember

We've been to the Oregon Museum of Science and Industry (OMSI) a number of times, both as a family and with out-of-town visitors. Situated in a gorgeous waterfront location, the museum is a bit out of the main traffic stream now but well worth a visit. There's an extensive gift shop, restaurant, OMNIMAX Theater, and numerous hands-on exhibit rooms; you will find that several hours pass with nary a "When are we leaving?" inquiry from the little ones. Send away for a brochure, because the museum schedules well in advance classes and exhibits that not only educate but intrigue. You can spend hours interacting with exhibits that explore human body systems; dioramas that depict the evolution of man; and look-and-touch displays that examine, through superheroes such as Superman, Wonder Woman, and Batman, the marvels of movement, speed, and space. The OMNIMAX Theater blends the wonders of nature and technology with explorations of the most intrepid human adventures, such as a climb up Mt. Everest, a river-rafting trip along the Colorado, and an airplane ride over the Grand Canyon. The images on the massive screen quite literally envelop the viewer and force the squeamish of stomach to hold onto their seats.

amazing laser-light and astronomy shows. The OMNIMAX shows change periodically, and hours vary, so call first.

Willamette Jet Boat Excursions (ages 6 and up)

1945 SE Water Ave., adjacent to the Oregon Museum of Science and Industry (OMSI); (888) 538-2628 or (503) 231-1532; www.willamettejet.com. Reservations recommended; arrive at least 15 minutes before departure. Daily departures for 2-hour city and falls tour May through Sept and 1-hour tours mid-June through Labor Day. Call for seasonal tour times. One-hour tours $$$$ adults, $$$ ages 4 to 11, children 3 and under free. Two-hour tours $$$$ adults and kids, 3 and under free. $ to park in OMSI's lot, which you pay (in cash) at the Jet Boat office.

This is an exciting way to view the Portland skyline, waterfront activity, and bird life on a 37-mile round-trip excursion from the docks next to OMSI to the base of Willamette Falls in Oregon City.

Oaks Amusement Park (ages 3 and up)

Located alongside the Willamette River, just east of the Sellwood Bridge; (503) 233-5777; www.oakspark.com. Rides open mid-Mar through Sept; call for times. Free entry; charge for individual rides or ride bracelets ($$$). Rink open year-round (after-school and evening sessions in winter). $.

Considered the oldest continuously running amusement park in the country, this park has been delighting kids of all ages since 1904. The fun includes a roller-skating rink complete with 1923 Wurlitzer organ and "wavy" floor, amusement rides that range from toddler swings and an antique carousel to the Looping Thunder roller coaster and the Screaming Eagle ride. There's also a vintage train that circles the grounds, a large, shady picnic area, and a sandy beach. On summer Tues and Wed mornings, the park is open only to kids 6 and under, who get discounted tickets (and their adults get in free) and a free story time, complete with treats.

Literary **Link**

Families who've enjoyed **Beverly Cleary**'s Ramona and Henry Huggins books will be eager to learn that Portland is home to the real Klickitat Street, and Ramona's house does exist—as do the streets and homes of the rest of the characters from the series. They're all off of NE Broadway and 33rd, in the area in which Cleary grew up (take the #10 bus to Grant Park and go from there). Grant Park contains the Beverly Cleary Sculpture Garden, while the Multnomah County Library's Hollywood Branch (4040 NE Tillamook St., 503-988-5391; www.multcolib.org/agcy/hwd.html) has a tiled wall map of Ramona's neighborhood. Ask for a walking-tour brochure.

To the **Theater!**

Portland boasts a number of theater companies that cater to kids or regularly include kids' plays in their lineups. A few of our favorites are:

Ladybug Theater (ages 2 and up). Located at Smile Station, 8210 SE 13th, at the foot of SE Spokane Street; (503) 232-2346; www.ladybugtheater.org. Call for show schedule, hours, and prices. Oregon's oldest surviving children's theater offers a wonderful introduction to live performing arts, with weekly interactive performances and classes. A great place for kids to learn how to act at live performances.

Northwest Children's Theater and School. Located at 1819 NW Everett St.; (503) 222-4480 (tickets) or (503) 222-2190 (office); www.nwcts.org. Five family-oriented, thought-provoking shows featuring adult actors working beside talented young actors. The intimate yet substantial 450-seat theater has few bad seats. The school offers year-round instruction for ages 4½ through 18.

Oregon Children's Theatre. Performances at Hatfield Hall, 1111 SW Broadway; classes at 600 SW 10th Ave., Suite 313. (503) 228-9571; www.oct.org. Produces 5 shows per season for a variety of ages. Acting Academy offers classes for ages 4 to 17.

Penny's Puppet Productions. (503) 282-9207; www.pennyspuppets.com. A one-woman, dynamic puppet theater that performs at local venues, schools, and birthday parties. Penny has a master's degree in education and the shows usually have a few hidden lessons that young kids can laugh at and relate to. Call or go online for a schedule of upcoming performances.

Do Jump! At the historic Echo Theatre, 1515 SE 37th Ave. off of Hawthorne Boulevard; (503) 231-1232; www.dojump.org. Acrobatic theater with trapezes and more. Classes and day camps are popular with kids.

Laurelhurst Park (all ages)

SE 39th and Stark; (503) 823-2223; www.portlandonline.com/parks. Open daily dawn to dusk. Free.

When I was a child, this was my favorite Portland park. Its natural beauty, towering trees, lush rhododendrons, and noisy ducks who clamored for crumbs on Laurelhurst Lake all reside vividly in my memory. Therefore, it's truly enchanting to return here and find little changed, except for the addition of lighted tennis courts, volleyball courts, and a bigger playground.

Swimming in the City

Sometimes kids just need to get wet! When the water beckons, here are several choices in the Portland area for taking a dip. Most offer swimming lessons, lap swims, water exercise classes, and recreational play swims, plus extended hours during holiday breaks and school closure days. Call for hours and pricing.

Indoor Pools

- **Buckman Pool.** 320 SE 16th Ave.; (503) 823-3668. Twenty-yard heated swimming pool.

- **Columbia Pool.** 7701 N. Chautauqua Blvd.; (503) 823-3669. Twenty-five-yard heated swimming pool ranging from 1.5 feet to 8 feet deep.

- **Dishman Pool.** 77 NE Knott; (503) 823-3673. Twenty five-yard, L-shaped heated pool with whirlpool spa and diving boards. Water depths are 2 feet to 12 feet.

- **Mt. Scott Pool.** 5530 SE 72nd Ave. at Harold; (503) 823-3183. Leisure pool with slide, current channel, vortex, and interactive toys. Lap pool with water basketball and rope swing, plus a spa pool.

- **Southwest Community Center Pool.** 6820 SW 45th Ave.; (503) 823-2840. Leisure pool with slide, rope swing, and interactive toys. Spa pool and lap pool.

Mt. Tabor Park (all ages)

SE Salmon and Sixtieth; (800) 962-3700 or (503) 823-7529; www. portlandonline.com/parks. Call for hours. **Free.**

This 195-acre park frames the only extinct volcano within the limits of any US metropolitan area. The park contains a permanent exhibit of the volcanic cone. Hiking trails take you to the top, where you'll find a small playground and a terrific view of Portland. An exhibit displays volcanic cinders found in the park and outlines its geologic history.

North/Northeast

North and Northeast Portland is a mixture of stately neighborhoods like Irvington and Alameda, tons of fantastic parks, and lively urban areas like Alberta and North Missisippi. In the past decade North and Northeast Portland have experienced a renaissance and now house some of the hippest spots in the city.

Outdoor Pools

All are heated and open summer only. Call for season information.

- **Creston Pool.** SE 44th Avenue and Powell Boulevard; (503) 823-3672. Shallow and deep pools with kiddie slide and drop slide.

- **Grant Pool.** 2300 NE 33rd Ave.; (503) 823-3674. Shallow and deep pools with kiddie slide.

- **Montavilla Pool.** 8219 NE Glisan; (503) 823-3675. Shallow and deep pools with kiddie slide and drop slide.

- **Peninsula Pool.** 700 N. Rosa Parks Way; (503) 823-3620. Large pool with shallow and deep ends.

- **Pier Pool.** N. Seneca and St. Johns; (503) 823-3678. Shallow and deep pools with kiddie slide.

- **Sellwood Pool.** 7951 SE Seventh Ave.; (503) 823-3679. One large pool with shallow and deep ends, kiddie slide, drop slide, and interactive toys.

- **Wilson Pool.** 1151 SW Vermont St.; (503) 823-3680. Large, shallow pool with kiddie slide, slide, current channel, vortex, play structures, and shade umbrella. Leisure and lap pool with diving board and water basketball.

Lloyd Center Mall and Ice Rink (all ages)
2201 Lloyd Center; (503) 288-6073; www.lloydcenter.com. Call for hours.

The completely refurbished mall is a favorite teen spot, but kids of all ages love the Lloyd Center Ice Rink, which has been entertaining families for nearly 40 years. Lloyd Center was one of the first large shopping malls in the country. There's also a movie theater on the top floor, near the food court.

The Grotto (all ages)
NE Sandy Boulevard at 85th Street; (503) 245-7371; www.thegrotto.org. Gardens and gift shop are open daily year-round. Call for hours and admission price.

You will find respite at this 62-acre garden that includes a natural stone grotto in the side of a cliff. The lands of this meditative setting are owned by the Roman Catholic Church, but people of all faiths are welcome. Regular church services are held outdoors at the Grotto during spring and summer, weather permitting. Two annual events, the Christmas Festival of Lights and Gallery in the Woods, are held here in Dec and June, respectively.

Candy Basket (ages 6 and up)

1924 NE 181st; (800) 864-1924 or (503) 666-2000. Store open 9 a.m. to 6 p.m. Mon through Fri, 10 a.m. to 5 p.m. Sat. Tours Tues through Thurs morning at 9:30 a.m.; 6 and up only; advance reservations required. $.

A stream of warm, luscious chocolate cascades over 20 feet 3 inches of sculpted marble and bronze in this will-bending store. The fountain circulates 2,700 pounds of chocolate, and the aroma is scrumptious. The one-of-a-kind cascade is part of an hour-long tour through the candy factory.

Troutdale

Troutdale is the home of a large factory outlet shopping center and **Lewis & Clark State Park** on the Sandy River, just south of where it empties into the Columbia. Just before you leave the main area of town, you'll see the small but fascinating rail museum.

Troutdale Rail Museum (ages 5 and up)

473 E. Historic Columbia River Hwy., located at the edge of town toward the Sandy River; (503) 661-2164. Open Tues through Fri 10 a.m. to 4 p.m. and the third Sat of each month from 10 a.m. to 2 p.m. $, children under 12 free.

It's an original 1882 rail depot and one of the earliest stations along the Columbia. On the third Saturday, ask at the depot gift store for directions to the Harlow House and the Barn Museum, which both have rotating exhibits of country life and the history of the area.

McMenamin's Edgefield (all ages)

2126 Southwest Halsey St.; (503) 669-8610; www.mcmenamins.com.

Portland's McMenamin Brothers are famous for converting forgotten old buildings into colorful and quirky hotels, brewpubs, and restaurants that are always casual, affordable, and festive. Edgefield, housed in a former insane/poor asylum, is one of McMenamin's most successful efforts, featuring lodging, restaurants, a cigar bar, movie-theater pub, and a 9-hole, par-3 golf course where the conversations are likely to focus more on what kind of pint you're sipping than whether you'll use your wedge or putter. In the summer an amphitheater hosts some of the country's biggest music acts in an intimate outdoor venue. Families can easily spend a day here playing golf, lawn croquet, or board games or spelunking for whimsical art in the hotel's many nooks and crannies.

Blue Lake Park (ages 5 and up)

Located on Marine Drive, off 205th Avenue; (800) 962-3700; www.travelportland.com. Call for hours. Free entry; $ swimming fee; $–$$ boat rentals.

Concrete-bordered swimming areas line the sandy north shore, and the "sprayground" will delight even the smallest non-swimmer. The inventive dragon slide and other playground equipment keep kids busy between stops at the snack bar. In summer you can rent paddleboats, canoes, and rowboats.

Family Favorites
in Portland & the Columbia Gorge

1. Waterfront Park and Eastbank Esplanade

2. Oregon Zoo

3. Japanese Garden

4. Oregon Museum of Science and Industry

5. CM2: Children's Museum

6. Oaks Amusement Park

7. Powell's City of Books

8. Columbia River Gorge National Scenic Area

9. Scenic Mt. Hood Railroad

10. Fruit Loop, Hood River

Oregon City

Oregon City was founded by the Hudson's Bay Company, which had been launched by the fur trade and had its western headquarters at Fort Vancouver, Washington, just across the Columbia River. This community is considered by many to be the end of the Oregon Trail and was the first seat of government for the Oregon Territory.

Museum of the Oregon Territory (ages 5 and up)

211 Tumwater Dr., located on the bluff above the river; (503) 655-5574; www.orcity.com /museum. Call for hours. $, family admission (up to 5 persons) $$, children under 5 free.

One of the treasures among small-town history museums, the exhibits cover the course of local history, from Native American life and culture to the fur-trading days of the Hudson's Bay Company and the settlement of early pioneers.

Stevens Crawford Heritage House

Located at the corner of Sixth and Washington Streets in Oregon City; (503) 655-2866; http://clackamashistory.org. Open Thurs through Sat noon to 4 p.m. (last tour at 3:30 p.m.). Closed mid-Dec through Jan. $, children under 5 free.

Adults will appreciate the period furniture and the incredible craftsmanship of this classic 1908 foursquare, with its beveled, leaded windows and intricate woodwork. Kids will

Fun Fact

Willamette Falls, in Oregon City, is considered the second-largest waterfall in the United States by volume, second only to Niagara Falls.

migrate to the sights in the fully equipped kitchen—complete with stocked pantry—plus the old Victrola (a wonder to those raised on digital music files) and the vintage toy collection.

McLoughlin House (ages 5 and up)

713 Center St.; (503) 656-5146; www.mcloughlinhouse.org. Open Wed through Sat 10 a.m. to 4 p.m., Sun 1 to 4 p.m., closed in Jan. Free.

Take a guided tour of the home in which Dr. John McLoughlin, called the "Father of Oregon" for his work helping settle and govern the area, retired in 1846. The furnishings have been fully restored and are authentic to the mid-19th century.The house is now part of the Oregon National Historic Trail, run by the National Park Service.

Oregon City Elevator (ages 5 and up)

Located near the McLoughlin House; (800) 962-3700 or (503) 657-8241. Call for hours. Free.

Take the elevator or stairs from the top of the bluff down to river level; from the observation deck at the top you have a great view of the Oregon City Falls.

George Rogers Park (ages 5 and up)

Located at the south end of State Street in Lake Oswego; (503) 697-6500; www.ci.oswego .or.us/parksrec. Call for hours. Free.

One of the most complete family-fun parks in the metro area, George Rogers Park offers swimming areas, sandy beaches, a wading stream for kids to splash around in, a waterfall that adds a lilting cascade of sound, great playground structures, and a walking trail that connects with **Mary Young State Park,** about 5 miles upriver. More trails take you to

Fun Fact

The Oregon City Elevator is officially platted in city documents as "Elevator Street"—the only vertical "street" in the country.

Oswego Creek, and there's even a bit of intriguing local history left in the park—a large chimney that's the last remnant of Oregon's first iron smelter.

Molalla

To reach Molalla, take Highway 213 south from Oregon City. Signs in town point to Feyrer Park and Shady Dell; both are highly recommended locations.

Feyrer Park (all ages)

Located on the Molalla River; (503) 829-6941. Open 6 a.m. to 10 p.m. May through Sept, 6 a.m. to 6 p.m. Oct through Apr. $ day-use fee on weekends and holidays; weekdays free.

Swimming holes, picnic tables, and playground equipment make a summertime visit worthwhile for families with energetic kids who have been in the car all day. Camping is available for a fee.

Shady Dell Pacific Northwest Live Steamers (all ages)

Follow signs in town toward Feyrer Park; turn onto Shady Dell Drive; (503) 829-6866. Open Sun noon to 5 p.m. May through Oct, weather permitting. Private parties available.

Train rides are free, although donations are gratefully received. The kids will love the electric, steam, and diesel trains this group runs on small-scale tracks along a placid stream, around a pond, over trestles, and through the forest in the Molalla Train Park. Bring a picnic to eat at any of several sites on the property.

Canby Ferry (all ages)

To reach the ferry, drive along the Willamette River on Highway 99E; (503) 650-3030 or (503) 557-6391. Open daily 6:45 a.m. to 9:15 p.m. $ per car.

Top Molalla **Events**

July

Mollala Buckeroo Rodeo. Since 1913, when firemen sponsored a rodeo to raise money for firefighting equipment, cowpokes, rodeo queens, and the animals they ride and rope have been kicking up their heels to the delight of locals. (503) 829-6941; www.mollallabuckeroo.com.

October

Apple Festival. Enjoy entertainment, apple pie, and homemade ice cream while celebrating Molalla's pioneering heritage with tours of the historic Dibble and Von der Ahe houses. (800) 424-3002.

The ferry has operated since 1914 and is one of only three car ferries still operating in Oregon. The ride across the river takes only 5 minutes, and you can either continue your journey on the opposite side or just ride the ferry back across the river. Kids will delight at how the road just ends at the river, then picks up again on the other side.

Molalla River State Park (all ages)

Located downriver from the Canby Ferry; (800) 551-6949; www.oregonstateparks.org. Day-use area. Free.

A gem of a park, this beautiful spot has paved walking trails; lots of ducks, frogs, great blue herons, and other marsh-loving critters. In summer locals often bring radio-controlled planes to fly in the open field between the two picnic areas.

Sandy

A quiet community in the foothills, Sandy is the gateway to Mt. Hood from the west. Here you'll find a variety of restaurants and lodging options, often less expensive than those on the mountain.

Rainbow Trout Farm (all ages)

Located 7.5 miles east of Sandy off Sylvan Drive; (503) 622-5223; www.rainbowtroutfarm .com. Open daily 8 a.m. to dusk Mar 1 through Oct 15. Price based on size of fish caught.

Kids will have fun reeling in their very own fish at this U-catch pond.

Lost Lake (all ages)

Located 40 miles northeast of Sandy, 20 miles southwest of Hood River on Lost Lake Road; (541) 352-6002 (Forest Service) or (541) 386-6366 (resort); www.lostlakeresort.org. Call for hours and campground fees.

This is one of the most photographed lakes in the nation because of the snowcapped peak of Mt. Hood, which rises above and often casts its reflection upon the lake's pristine waters. Rent a rowboat, drop a line in the water to catch one of the brown or rainbow trout lurking beneath the surface of this 231-acre lake, or hike the trail surrounding the

Top Sandy **Event**

July

Sandy Mountain Festival. The 4-day festival starts with a pet show and continues with a parade, live music, a carnival, 5-generation queen and court, food, microbrews and wine from the local winery, and arts and crafts to make this a fun event for the whole family. (503) 668-5900; www.sandymountain festival.org.

lake. Native Americans called the lake E-e-kwahl-a-mat-yan-ishkt, which means "heart of the mountains." It was a favored camping ground, and according to legend, during a potlatch wolves pursued a snow-white doe that jumped into the lake, swam to the middle, and disappeared. Medicine men called this a bad omen, and the Native Americans left the camp immediately and never returned.

Ramona Falls (all ages)

65000 US 26 in Welches, located off Lolo Pass Road and FR 1825; (503) 622-7674 or (800) 622-4822; www.fs.fed.us/r6. Call for hours. $.

During the summer take the 4½-mile loop trail (Trail #797) leading to the falls. It's one of the most popular day hikes on the mountain, both because it's easy enough for young children and because of the stunningly beautiful falls awaiting you.

Columbia Gorge

This area is so intensely beautiful it's been designated a National Scenic Area. You can explore its westernmost gateway from the old road, US 30, leading out of Troutdale past a score of waterfalls and stunning viewpoints. Or take I-84 east from Portland for a water-level view of highlights such as Multnomah Falls and Bonneville Dam. In the east the gorge extends to Hood River and The Dalles.

Historic Columbia River Scenic Highway (all ages)

Crossing the bridge from Troutdale over the Sandy River leads you along the Columbia River Scenic Highway (US 30); (888) 275-6368 (ODOT) or (541) 308-1700 (USFS); www.byways .org/explore/byways/214 or www.fs.fed.us/r6/columbia. Always open. Free.

An engineering feat when it was built between 1913 and 1922, this 70-plus-mile highway winds through rich agricultural land and deep forests and cuts through the sides of steep basalt cliffs to a series of waterfalls that pour over the edge on their way to the Columbia. Designated a National Historic Landmark, it was the first modern highway in the Northwest. Several waterfalls here are worth driving many miles to see. Hiking trails take you between falls or to the points where the falls cascade over the cliff tops. Paths at Latourel Falls, Bridal Veil Falls, Wahkeena Falls, Multnomah Falls, Oneonta Gorge, Horsetail Falls, and Elowah Falls are all under a mile. **Tad's Chicken 'n Dumplings** (503-666-5337), at the Troutdale end of the highway, is a great place for dinner after a day in the gorge. Nestled in the banks along the Sandy River, Tad's is an old-school restaurant with large windows and a warm interior that harkens back to earlier times. Indeed, Tad's has been serving its famous dumplings and delicious pan-fried chicken since the '20s. Call-ahead seating is recommended; it's usually busy here.

Crown Point Vista House (ages 5 and up)

Located 5 miles east of Troutdale on the Columbia River Scenic Highway; (503) 695-2230; www.vistahouse.com. Open daily to the public mid-Apr through mid-Oct 8:30 a.m. to

6 p.m., mid-Oct through mid-Apr weekends only 10 a.m. to 4 p.m. (weather permitting). **Free,** but donations welcome.

One of the first stops along the way on the Columbia River Scenic Highway, the recently renovated 1917 house gives you an outstanding viewpoint from which to see the rugged gorge and the river that carved it. A small gallery and interpretive center, open mid-Apr through mid-Oct, offer information on the area. On Saturday during the summer months, the whole family can enjoy folk-art demonstrations or historical and cultural programs.

Multnomah Falls (ages 4 and up)
Located in the Columbia Gorge on I-84; (503) 695-2372 (visitor center); www.fs.fed.us/r6
/columbia. Visitor center open daily year-round 9 a.m. to 5 p.m., until 7 p.m. in summer.
Free.

At 620 feet high, Multnomah Falls is the tallest and most famous of the more than 75 falls along the Oregon side of the gorge. If you have the time and your kids have the energy, walk the trail to the top of the upper falls, about 1 mile of fairly steep climbing on a paved path. At the top, follow the creek upstream to some beautiful shaded dells where children can dabble their feet in the water or search for crawdads. The Multnomah Falls Lodge has snacks and historical photographs.

Oneonta Falls (ages 10 and up)
Located on the Columbia River Scenic Highway (US 30) east of Multnomah Falls; (800) 984-6743; www.fs.fed.us/r6/columbia. **Free.**

Oneonta Falls isn't the tallest or most beautiful of the falls, but it is a favorite because it's the most fun to get to. Not appropriate for very young children, Oneonta Falls is at the end of a tall, narrow slit carved by Oneonta Creek. The walls rise a sheer 150 feet above the creek bed. The most kid-satisfying and most direct route to the falls is ¼ mile and gives the kids a chance to hop rocks in the creek and get delightfully damp in the process. Oneonta means "place of peace," and that sense of peace pervades this gorge.

Benson State Recreation Area (all ages)
On the Columbia River 30 miles east of Portland off I-84 (eastbound access only); (800) 551-6949; www.oregonstateparks.org. Open year-round. $ day-use fee.

Benson Lake is a non-motorboat lake, making it a great spot for swimming. There's even a Frisbee golf course. The first weekend in June brings kids out for a free fishing day on the lake.

Rooster Rock State Park (all ages)
Accessible only from I-84; (800) 551-6949 or (503) 695-2261. Open daily 7 a.m. to dusk. $ day-use fee.

You won't have a hard time finding this park, because the large basalt "rooster tail" rock that rises above it makes the site easy to spot. The park has shaded picnic groves, a protected moorage area, and sandy beaches. You may want to be forewarned that at the far east end of the park, a stairway leads to secluded beaches where nude sunbathing is allowed beyond a point 100 yards farther east.

Bonneville Locks and Dam and Fish Hatchery
(ages 5 and up)

From Portland take I-84 east to exit 40; (541) 374-8820; http://traveloregon.com. Call for hours. **Free.**

The visitor center at the dam has some very impressive educational exhibits on river history, the production of electricity, and a Native American sacred burial ground. The viewing windows looking into the fish ladder in the Underwater Observatory give you an up-close look at fish that are bigger than some children. The sturgeon pond, where these ancient giants cruise through water rimmed with lily pads, always was my favorite part of the fish hatchery. These prehistoric fish, which thrive in the Columbia River, have been around for 200 million years and grow to lengths of 10 feet and more. Your kids get the whole picture of the salmon life cycle in several areas of the hatchery, and depending on the time of year, they can view fish culturists removing eggs from spawning females, the incubation room where millions of bright red eggs in trays become tiny salmon fry, or the outdoor pools where the fry grow big enough to be released into Tanner Creek.

   Grounds at the hatchery. (541) 374-8393. Open daily 7:30 a.m. to dusk. Enjoy a picnic dinner on the attractive grounds while your kids enjoy feeding the brooder rainbow trout or climbing on the playground equipment.

Eagle Creek (ages 10 and up)

Just east of Bonneville Dam on the north side of I-84 off exit 41; (800) 984-6743; www.fs.fed .us/r6/columbia. Open year-round. $ day-use fee (National Forest Day Pass).

At Eagle Creek Park you'll find a picnic area, walking trails, and some nice swimming holes on the creek. Eagle Creek Scenic Trail, #440, takes you past Metlako, Punchbowl, Loowit, and Tunnel Falls in just 6 miles on the way into the Columbia Wilderness Area. With kids you'll probably want to walk only the 2 miles to Punchbowl Falls, truly one of the most impressive around. Because there are some sheer cliffs with no guardrails, this hike may not be suitable for some children.

Hood River

The Hood River Valley is Oregon's largest producer of fruit, yielding apples and pears that are valued across the United States. A loop drive, best in late Aug and early Sept, takes you past a number of fruit stands where you can buy direct from the growers.

Fun Fact

Viento is Spanish for "wind," but although the state park with this name sits in one of Oregon's windiest places, it was actually named for the three railroad tycoons who built the first railroad in the area: Villard, Endicott, and Tollman.

Scenic Mt. Hood Railroad (all ages)

110 Railroad Ave.; (800) 872-4661 or (541) 386-3556; www.mthoodrr.com. Morning and afternoon excursions plus brunch and dinner trains. Call for hours, excursion types, and fees.

The 1906 train, which departs from the Mt. Hood Railroad Depot, is a link between the Columbia River Gorge and the foothills of this area's other natural wonder, Mt. Hood, the state's highest peak. Holiday trains in winter are a big draw.

Hood River Water Play (ages 10 and up)

(541) 386-9463 or (800) 963-7873; www.hoodriverwaterplay.com. Open daily; call for hours and fees.

Want to test your might against the famous Columbia Gorge winds? This is one of many surf shops in town, but it offers special kids' programs and rental equipment.

Jackson Park (all ages)

13th and May Streets; (800) 366-3530. Open dawn to dusk. Free.

Families are the center of the fun every Thurs evening in Aug, with the Families in the Park entertainment series. Bring a picnic and enjoy the program.

Saturday Farmer's Market (all ages)

Parking lot between Fifth and Seventh, and Cascade and Columbia; (800) 366-3530; http://hrsaturdaymarket.wordpress.com. Open Sat 9 a.m. to 3 p.m. mid-May through Sept. Free.

Pick up luscious fruit, produce, and other delights from local growers at this open-air market.

Viento State Park (all ages)

Located about 8 miles west of Hood River; (541) 374-8811 or (800) 551-6949; www.oregon stateparks.org. $ day-use fee.

Viento is one of several state parks that sit alongside the Columbia River. A mix of maple, fir, willow, and pine nestle with tent and trailer sites, making this a pretty place to plunk down for a night's rest. There's a ¼-mile nature trail to **Viento Lake,** where the wetlands

Top Hood River **Events**

April
Hood River Blossom Festival. Blossoming pear and apple orchards create an exquisite backdrop for Hood River's springtime festival. (800) 366-3530 or (541) 386-2000.

July
Hood River Cherry Days. Fresh-picked cherries and all kinds of specialty products are part of the Hood River Fruit Loop's annual Cherry Days, which features cherry tasting, cherry picking, farm tours, kids' activities, and a variety of other events located throughout the valley. (541) 386-7697; www.hoodriverfruitloop.com.

August
Gravenstein Apple Days. With—you guessed it—plenty of apples and apple-inspired goodies to sample, this might be just the pick for a lunch stop. (541) 386-7697.

October through November
Hood River Valley Harvest Fest. An annual celebration that expresses appreciation for the bounty of fall harvest with food booths, arts and crafts, and pumpkin carving. (800) 366-3530 or (541) 386-2000.

Rasmussen Farms Pumpkin Funland. Sometimes beginning as early as September, the farm's Pumpkin Funland usually runs through mid-Nov and includes a Halloween hunt, pumpkin bowling, and a corn-husk maze. (541) 386-4622 or (800) 548-2243; www.rasmussenfarms.com.

December
Mt. Hood Railroad Christmas Tree Train. If you're traveling through here during the winter, this magical train ride will make your holiday special with carolers, a country-style holiday meal, and, if you're not far from home, the chance to pick up a Christmas tree. (800) 872-4661; www.mthoodrr.com.

For more information on Hood River events, call (800) 366-3530 or (541) 386-2000 or visit www.hoodriver.org.

Fun Fact

Hood River is the windsurfing capital of the world.

surrounding it provide a good spot for bird-watching. The **Starvation Creek Trail** takes you 1 mile along a section of the Historic Columbia River Highway.

Cascade Locks and Cascade Locks Historical Museum (ages 5 and up)

Located in Cascade Locks Marine Park, west of Hood River; (541) 374-8619; www.cascade locks.net. Open daily noon to 5 p.m. May through Sept. Free, but donations welcome.

"Cascade" refers not to the mountain range to the east but to the cascading waters once in this part of the Columbia's journey to the sea. Located in the park are displays that describe the river's history. An outdoor barn contains a variety of wagons, and a small building houses the first steam locomotive in the Northwest.

Columbia Gorge **Sternwheeler** (ages 6 and up)

Board from Marine Park in Cascade Locks, 20 minutes west of Hood River on I-84 at exit 44; (503) 224-3900 or (800) 224-3901; www.sternwheeler.com; e-mail: sales@sternwheeler .com. Daily cruises May through Oct, $$$$ adults, $$$–$$$$ children depending on cruise. In Dec the sternwheeler departs from the seawall in Gov. Tom McCall Waterfront Park in Portland for special holiday cruises. Call for other specialty cruises and off-season schedules.

When you board the sternwheeler *Columbia Gorge,* you combine a history lesson with a step back in time. Riverboats took Lewis and Clark on the first stage of their journey that eventually brought them to the wild waters of the Columbia River. Considerably tamed since the days of their expedition, the river now reflects the history as well as the natural beauty of the Columbia Gorge. The riverboat captain provides a narrative about the Lewis and Clark expedition, travelers along the Oregon Trail, and the traditions of local Native Americans, who still fish from platforms, as has been done for centuries.

Marine Park (all ages)

355 Wanapa, Cascade Locks; follow Main Street to the park; (541) 374-8619. Open daily dawn to 10 p.m. Free.

The story of Lewis and Clark's trip with Sacajawea and her papoose and how they navigated the treacherous Columbia with its many chutes comes alive here. Now several dams have tamed the once-wild river. Native Americans sometimes fish here in the traditional manner. A marina is also available in the park.

Hood River Fruit Loop (ages 5 and up)

A 35-mile loop drive; (541) 386-7697; www.hoodriverfruitloop.com. Hours vary at farm stands and farms along the route. See printable map and list of vendors on the website or call for brochure. Free.

During harvest season there's no richer place for tasting the fruits of nature than the Hood River valley. Thousands of acres of lush orchards and rich farmland form the foreground, with Mt. Hood in the background—it's definitely an opportunity for photographs! A wide variety of vendors are open along the route for produce and delicious products made from local fruits and berries. The produce changes through the seasons: strawberries and raspberries in June; cherries, apricots, and blueberries in July; peaches in Aug; apples and pears in Aug and Sept. October brings chestnuts for roasting and sunny orange pumpkins.

Mountain View Cycle (all ages)

205 Oak St.; (541) 386-2453; www.mtviewcycles.com. Open daily 9 a.m. to 6 p.m. Mountain bikes, road bikes, kids' bikes, and trailer rentals $$$–$$$$ per 3 hours or day.

Located in historic downtown Hood River, Mountain View Cycle rents mountain, road, and children's bikes as well as trailers for towing toddlers.

History Museum of Hood River County (ages 5 and up)

300 Port Marina Dr.; (541) 386-6772; www.co.hood-river.or.us/museum. Open late spring through fall; call for seasonal hours and prices.

Native American artifacts and pioneer relics, as well as displays on the development of the lumber and fruit-growing industries in the region, make this museum a worthwhile stop.

Western Antique Aeroplane & Automobile Museum

1600 Museum Rd. at Ken Jernstedt Airfield 4S2; (541) 308-1600; www.waaamuseum.org. Open daily 9 a.m. to 5 p.m. $$$ adults, $$ kids 5 to 18, 4 and under free.

If anyone in the family likes cars or planes, this is the place to go. WAAAM has 95,000 square feet holding one of the largest collections of operating antique planes and cars in the country, plus motorcycles, tractors, military vehicles, and more. These aren't creaky old relics—all have been painstakingly restored and still run. A hands-on area for kids includes a submarine interior, and on the second Saturday of the month, special events allow you to watch the planes in flight or even hitch a ride in one of the vintage vehicles.

Mt. Hood

Winter isn't the only season for enjoying this majestic mountain, which at 11,235 feet is Oregon's tallest peak. Summer brings hikers, mountain climbers, anglers, boaters, and bird watchers to the slopes. Multiple campgrounds—many boasting alpine lakes—are packed throughout summer and fall, and runners flock to Timberline Lodge for the annual Hood to Coast Relay and the Mt. Hood Pacific Crest Trail Ultramarathon. The winter

Top Mt. Hood **Events**

July
Oregon Trail Quilt Show. This special rhododendron weekend event sponsored by the Cascade Geographic Society brings together heritage quilts—such as ones hand-sewn by those who made the 2,000-plus-mile Oregon Trail journey westward—with more modern counterparts. Arts and crafts, homemade goodies, storytelling, and music will all entice youngsters while you enjoy the quilts. (503) 622-4798; www.cgsmthood.com.

September
Mt. Hood Huckleberry Festival & Barlow Trail Days. Held at Mt. Hood Village, 65000 E. US 26, and also sponsored by the Cascade Geographic Society, this event focuses on pioneer history and the plentiful huckleberries turning blue all over the mountain. (503) 622-4798; www.cgsmthood.com.

recreation activities usually extend from late fall through early spring, with year-round skiing available at Timberline Lodge. Snowshoeing, cross-country skiing and inner-tubing bring families up. Several ski resorts on the mountain offer everything from beginner hills to steep, mogul-covered slopes. Night skiing, ski and snowboard rentals, and lessons are available at each site. Sno-Park passes are required Nov 1 through Apr 30 and are available at the Hood River or Zigzag ranger stations located on US 30 beyond Mt. Hood Meadows or at the Forest Service's information center at Mt. Hood RV Village, 13 miles east of Sandy on US 26. Check road conditions before driving to the mountain (800-977-6368 or 511 within Oregon; www.tripcheck.com), and be sure to carry chains.

Mt. Hood Meadows (ages 5 and up)
Located on US 35; (503) 659-1256; www.skihood.com. Call for snow levels, prices, and hours.

With 2,150 skiable acres, this is the largest resort on the mountain. The "Meadows" usually opens after mid-Nov, depending on snow levels, of course. It is a full-service facility that offers instruction, child care, restaurants, plus parks and pipes for young skiers and snowboarders.

Cooper Spur Mountain Resort (ages 5 and up)
10755 Cooper Spur Rd.; (541) 352-7803 (snow report); (541) 352-6692 (lodging and dining); www.cooperspur.com. Call for snow levels, hours, and fees.

This ski area specializes in presenting affordable winter fun for the whole family, offering 10 runs for skiing and snowboarding and a tubing center. A day lodge and restaurant provide a place to warm up, and a newly expanded deck allows guests to soak up sunshine while keeping track of the rest of their party, as almost the entire ski area is viewable from the base lodge. The Nordic Center provides just over 4 miles of groomed trails, and separate snowshoe trails are also available. Probably the best deal on the mountain is the $20 lesson, which provides unlimited all-day access to roving skiing and snowboarding instructors.

Mt. Hood Skibowl (ages 5 and up)

87000 E. US 26, Government Camp; (503) 272-3206 or (800) 754-2695; www.skibowl.com. Open daily in winter; call or check the website for summer hours and pricing.

You'll find skiing, extensive night skiing, snowboarding, and tubing in winter. In summer your kids will be thrilled by the Adventure Park's 1,000 acres of rides, including a ½-mile-long mountain-hugging luge that takes you down S-curves in sleds complete with brake levers that even young children can control—you go as fast or as slow as you like. A race course for fancy go-karts, pony rides, bungee jumping, and zip-lining get adrenaline pumping. More mellow interpretive nature trails and a "sky chair" that takes hikers and mountain bikers to the top of the lift so they can walk or ride down make this an unforgettable family fun spot for any taste in any season.

Summit Ski Area (ages 5 and up)

Located at the east end of Government Camp on US 26; (503) 272-0256; www.summitski area.com. Open weekends and holidays 8:30 a.m. to 4 p.m. Call for snow levels. $$$$ all-day lift ticket, $$$ tube rental.

You'll find a great slope for kids and inner tubes for all sizes you can rent. Snowboarding and alpine skiing. The lines can be long on weekends but the rope tow to the top of the slope makes it easier for families to tube all day without getting tuckered out. A café serves snacks and cocoa. Snowboarding and alpine skiing are also available, as well as a popular weekend ski school for kids.

Teacup Lake Nordic Center (ages 6 and up)

Located on US 35 (look for Teacup Lake Sno-Park signs); e-mail: info@teacupnordic.org. $$ day-use donation.

Both groomed and ungroomed cross-country trails take off from a variety of Sno-Parks (plowed parking areas) in the vicinity. Restrooms, plus a warming day lodge (Wed and weekends), are available.

Timberline Lodge and Ski Resort (ages 5 and up)

Off US 26; (503) 272-3158 (lift tickets); (503) 222-2211 (snow report); (800) 547-1406 (reservations); www.timberlinelodge.com; e-mail: information@timberlinelodge.com. Call for snow levels, hours, and prices.

Timberline enjoys the longest ski season in North America, with more than 1,000 acres of skiable terrain. The Magic Carpet lift supports a wide range of children's learning programs. Foot passengers are also allowed on the **Magic Mile Sky Ride** daily, weather and lift lines permitting. Ages 6 and under **free** of charge when accompanied by parents.

Fun Fact

Timberline Lodge posed for the exterior shots of the Overlook Hotel in the 1980 horror movie *The Shining*, based on the Stephen King novel. Timberline requested that director Stanley Kubrick change the sinister Room 217 of the novel to 237 so guests wouldn't avoid the real room 217.

If you're just visiting the mountain for the day, summer or winter, stop by the lodge to appreciate the impressive views and equally impressive 1930s construction of this National Historic Landmark. Built as a WPA project, the lodge has the classic rough-hewn, massive scale of the period. Have your kids try to find the various animals carved into wooden structures throughout the building.

The Dalles

The early French *voyageurs* gave the name Le Dalle, or "the trough," to the falls at a Native American fishery about 6 miles above the current town site because of the frequency with which they were pulled under by the force of the water at the bottom of the falls. The falls have long since been covered with calm waters pooled behind the Dalles Dam.

Columbia Gorge Discovery Center
& Wasco County Historical Museum (ages 5 and up)

5000 Discovery Dr.; (541) 296-8600; www.gorgediscovery.org. Open daily 9 a.m. to 5 p.m. Tours start at 10 a.m. $$ adults, $ ages 6 to 16, 5 and under free.

You'll want to spend the whole day in this 50,000-square-foot facility, exploring two museums, talking with "pioneers" in the Oregon Trail Living History Park, walking the interpretive trail, or having lunch in the Basalt Rock Cafe. This is the official interpretive center for the Columbia River Gorge National Scenic Area, and its exhibits on geology, wildlife, and ancient cultures will add meaning to your travels in the gorge.

Fun Fact

The world's largest rosary collection is exhibited at the Columbia Gorge Interpretive Center just across the Columbia from Hood River, near White Salmon, Washington. A local resident collected the exhibit.

Fort Dalles Museum (ages 5 and up)

15th and Garrison Streets; (541) 296-4547; www.fortdallesmuseum.org. Open daily in summer 11 a.m. to 4 p.m.; call for off-season hours. $, children 6 and under free.

Housed in the last remaining building of Fort Dalles, the museum was built in the wake of the Whitman massacre across the river. Originally the surgeon's quarters, the building now aptly serves to tell the story of the early decades of the community. The grounds contain a wide range of horse-drawn vehicles, and across the street you can visit an old homestead, granary, and barn.

Dalles Dam (all ages)

Tours are offered by appointment from the visitor center at the end of Bret Cladfelter Way off exit 87 of I-84; (541) 296-9778 (information) or (541) 506-7819 (tour appointments). Free.

A tour of the dam provides a lot of history as well as fun. The pool of water behind the dam covers two Native American sites: a sacred burial ground and the ancient fishing grounds of **Celilo Falls.** Photographs in the **Seufert Visitor Center** show the fishing platforms built over basalt rocks so the Yakima Nation Indians could spear salmon as they jumped the falls on their migration upriver. You'll also see petroglyphs that were recovered before the dam was built. The center's collections and interpretive displays provide background on Lewis and Clark and other local history.

Riverfront Park (all ages)

Take I-84 to exit 85; (541) 296-9533; www.nwprd.org. Open dawn to dusk. Free.

Give your teenagers a relatively safe place to try out sailboarding. The offshore islands protect beginners from both the main river current and barge traffic. Equipment rentals and lessons are available through vendors operating at the park in the summer.

Memaloose State Park (all ages)

Eleven miles west of The Dalles; accessible only from the westbound freeway; (541) 478-3008 or (800) 551-6949; (800) 452-5687 for campground reservations; www.oregonstate parks.org. Campground open mid-Mar through Oct; day-use area open year-round. Call for hours and campground fees; day-use area free.

Top Event in The Dalles

April

Northwest Cherry Festival. A parade, live music, health fair, food court, and crafts are all a part of this weeklong celebration of cherry blossoms. (541) 226-2231; www.thedalleschamber.com.

You can see the lower and only remaining of two Memaloose Islands, which were sacred Native American burial grounds. Memaloose is the Chinook Indian word for "island of the dead." The park provides a cool summer oasis in the hottest part of the gorge.

The Dalles Talking Murals (all ages)

Located on a dozen building walls around historic downtown; www.historicthedalles.org. Keys for activating sound are $ (including a keepsake key ring), good for life, and available from the chamber of commerce (404 W. Second), Klindt's Booksellers (315 E. Second), and the Art Box (517 E. Second).

The Dalles has made history by adding talking narration to its already fascinating murals—a first in the nation. With 35 historically accurate murals currently wired for sound and plans for more to be added over the next few years, this is an enchanting way to spend a leisurely afternoon. The underpass linking the downtown area to the river has been renovated recently, so enjoy a stroll to the riverfront after your mural tour.

Deschutes River State Recreation Area (all ages)

Located east of The Dalles on Highway 206; (800) 551-6949 or (541) 739-2322, (800) 452-5687 for campground reservations; www.oregonstateparks.org. Day use free.

This is where the Deschutes River flows into the Columbia. Recreation options include hiking, cycling, camping, horse-riding, boating, and—most popular—fishing. The Deschutes is one of Oregon's finest fishing rivers, popular among local Native Americans who dip-net fish from platforms along the riverbanks. An exhibit provides information about the pioneers who turned south just beyond here to follow the Barlow Trail spur of the Oregon Trail rather than risk disaster on the Columbia River. A mountain-bike trail takes off from the park entrance and follows an old railroad bed for 17 miles alongside the Deschutes. For a shady walk, take the **Atiyeh Deschutes River Trail** through white alder and birch forest. Look for oriole nests that resemble hanging baskets. This is rattlesnake country, so be careful!

Mayer State Park (all ages)

Located off I-84 10 miles west of The Dalles; (800) 551-6949 or (503) 228-9561; www.oregon stateparks.org. $ day-use fee.

Call ahead to arrange for a free naturalist-led tour. A swimming area in a small lake on the west side of the park is perfect for little ones. From the park, take the 9-mile scenic drive

Fun Facts

- The Dalles is one of the oldest inhabited locations in North America, serving as a center of Native American trade for at least 10,000 years.
- The Dalles is one of the oldest incorporated cities in the United States.

to Rowena Crest, a viewpoint high above the river that gives access to the Tom McCall Nature Preserve on the Rowena Plateau.

Tom McCall Nature Preserve

Located on the Rowena Plateau, 8 miles west of The Dalles (Mosier or Rowena exits from I-84); (503) 230-1221; www.nature.org. Open daily. No dogs. Free.

This premier wildflower meadow, preserved by the Nature Conservancy, is best visited between Apr and late May, when the blooms reach their peak. Hiking paths weave across the meadow and along the cliffs, but be aware of ticks, poison oak, and rattlesnakes.

Where to Eat

IN THE DALLES

Cousins' Restaurant. 2116 W. Sixth St.; (541) 298-2771; www.cousinsrestaurant.com. Homestyle breakfast, lunch, and dinner spot well known for its cinnamon rolls, turkey sandwiches, and pot roast. $–$$

IN HOOD RIVER

The Crazy Pepper. 103 Fourth St.; (541) 387-2454; www.thecrazypeppercantina.com. This Mexican restaurant has excellent food, good prices, fast service, and kids' favorites (hamburgers with fries, hot dogs, and grilled cheese). $–$$

Sixth Street Bistro. 509 Cascade Ave.; (541) 386-5737. Hearty and well-prepared American fare and a healthier-than-normal kids' menu. $$

Sophie's Restaurant. 1810 Cascade Ave.; (541) 386-1183; http://sophieshoodriver.com. Imaginative Northwest plates to please a variety of palates—from simple roast chicken to more adventurous choices. An elegant but family friendly place—in fact, it's named after the owners' young daughter. $$–$$$

IN MT. HOOD

El Burro Loco. 67211 E. Highway 26, Welches; (503) 622-6780; www.burroloco .net. From-scratch modern Mexican food with home-smoked meats, a kids' menu, and great cocktails. $–$$

Huckleberry Inn. Government Camp Loop Road; (503) 272-3325. Open 24 hours a day, it's a great breakfast or lunch stop. $–$$$

The Ice Axe Grill and Mt. Hood Brewing Company. Government Camp Loop Road; (503) 272-3172; www.iceaxegrill.com. Families are more than welcome at this mountainside dining establishment. Parents can enjoy the local brew and more adult entrees while kids partake of classic pub hamburgers and pizza. $$–$$$

Timberline Lodge. Timberline Access Road off US 26; (503) 272-3391; www.timberline lodge.com/dining. After a day in the snow, there's no cozier spot than a sofa looking out on the mountain at the **Ram's Head Bar** (kids allowed) $$–$$$. The Blue Ox Bar offers pizzas, salads, and sandwiches. For breakfast, brunch, and lunch, the Cascade Dining Room has lots of delicious options (try the French toast) in a casual setting. Dinner's spendy and more subdued, but try early evening, when kids eat free. Reservations required for dinner. Breakfast, brunch, and lunch $$–$$$; dinner $$$$

IN PORTLAND

Portland has so many incredible and family-friendly restaurants, it's hard to narrow them down to just a handful. But these are great, reasonably priced spots in each of the main areas of town.

DOWNTOWN/THE PEARL DISTRICT

Alexis Restaurant. 215 West Burnside St.; (503) 224-8577; http://alexisfoods.com. Greek cuisine and bellydancers. $$$

Mothers' Bistro. 212 Southwest Stark St.; (503) 464-1122; www.mothersbistro.com. Fantastic comfort food for breakfast and lunch. $$–$$$

Old Town Pizza. 226 Northwest Davis St.; (503) 222-9999; www.oldtownpizza.com. A legendary, and supposedly haunted, pizza place. $$–$$$

SOUTHEAST

Bob's Red Mill. 5000 Southeast International Way, Milwaukie; (503) 607-6455; http://bobsredmill.com. Part restaurant, part store, part mill and museum. $–$$

Hopworks Urban Brewery. 2944 Southeast Powell Blvd.; (503) 232-4677; www.hopworksbeer.com. Pizzeria and family friendly brewery. $$

J&M Cafe. 537 Southeast Ash St.; (503) 230-0463; www.jandmcafepdx.com. A super-friendly place with great food and coffee and an eclectic clientele, all of which makes it a quintessential Portland breakfast and lunch spot. $-$$, cash only.

Por Que No?. 4635 Southeast Hawthorne Blvd.; (503) 954-3138; www.porquenotacos.com. Inexpensive nouveau Mexican; margaritas for grownups. $–$$

Slappy Cakes. 4246 Southeast Belmont St.; (503) 477-4805; www.slappycakes.com. Make your own pancakes—too fun! $$

NORTH/NORTHEAST

Laurelwood Public House. 5115 Northeast Sandy Blvd.; (503) 282-0622; www.laurelwoodbrewpub.com. One of the original family brewpubs. $$

Russell Street Bar-b-que. 325 Northeast Russell Street; (503) 528-8224; www.russellstreetbbq.com. Great southern food. Cool kids' menu. $$–$$$

Tasty and Sons. 3808 North Williams Ave.; (503) 621-1400; www.tastynsons.com. One of Portland's best breakfasts makes the wait worthwhile. $–$$

SOUTHWEST

Marco's Cafe. 7910 SW 35th Ave.; (503) 245-0199; www.marcoscafe.com. Kid-friendly staff and menus for breakfast, lunch and dinner in this Multnomah Village favorite. $$

Old Spaghetti Factory. 0715 Southwest Bancroft; (503) 222-5375; www.osf.com. Kid-pleasing menu with a Willamette River view. $$

The Original Pancake House. 8601 Southwest 24th Ave. at Barbur Blvd.; (503) 246-9007; www.originalpancakehouse.com. Hotcake (and breakfast) heaven. $$

NORTHWEST

Papa Haydn. 701 Northwest 23rd Ave.; (503) 228-7317; www.papahaydn.com. High-end bistro fare plus eye-popping desserts—all with a great view of 23rd Avenue happenings. $$$–$$$$

Swagat Indian Cuisine. 2074 Northwest Lovejoy St.; (503) 227-4300; www.swagat.com. Inexpensive Indian buffet and restaurant. $$

MULTIPLE LOCATIONS

Mio Sushi. www.miosushi.com. Local sushi chain that's reliably good.

Pastini. www.pastini.com. Inexpensive and elegant pasta that's a perennial family favorite.

Rheinlander/Gustav's. www.gustavs.net. Rotisserie meat, fondue, great kids' menu and novelty waiters.

IN SANDY

Calamity Jane's Hamburger Parlor.
42015 US 26; (503) 668-7817; www.calamity-janes.com. You can choose from 50 different burgers, and the milk shakes are made with real ice cream. $$

Where to Stay

IN THE DALLES

Celilo Inn. 3550 E. Second St.; (541) 769-0001; www.celiloinn.com. An upscale remodel turned a basic old motel with a great view of the river into one of the nicest hotels in the area. The patio makes an ideal spot for parents to read and sip wine in summer while kids frolic in the outdoor pool. Family suites available. $$$$

Cousins' Country Inn. 2114 W. Sixth St.; (800) 848-9378 or (541) 298-5161; www.cousinscountryinn.com. Kids love the Old West exterior, and you'll love the outdoor swimming pool and indoor spa; in-room coffeemaker, microwave, refrigerator, and gas fireplaces; and access to the fitness center. Some kitchen units. Restaurant next door. $$$

IN HOOD RIVER

Best Western Hood River Inn. 1108 E. Marina Way; (800) 828-7873 or (541) 386- 8905; www.hoodriverinn.com. Air-conditioned riverfront rooms, a restaurant, and a heated outdoor pool and spa are situated right in the heart of the Columbia River Gorge. Dogs OK. $$$–$$$$

Columbia Gorge Hotel. 4000 Westcliff Dr.; (800) 345-1921 or (541) 386-5566; www.columbiagorgehotel.com; e-mail: cghotel@gorge.net. This historic hotel, with its Spanish-style exterior, is all old-world luxury on the inside. The hotel was built in 1921 by lumber magnate Simon Benson on the site of an old Native American meeting ground. An inviting lobby and fireside coffee room don't seem geared to children, but little ones are welcome at this stately old hotel. They'll enjoy exploring the grounds outside, where an arched stone footbridge crosses a small stream that meanders through the property. Family suites are available. $$$$

Hood River Hotel. Oak Street and First; (800) 386-1859 or (514) 386-1900; www.hoodriverhotel.com; e-mail: hrhotel@gorge.net. Built in 1913 and on the National Historic Register, it has been refurbished as an enjoyable hotel with reasonable rates and many rooms overlooking the river. The hotel also boasts a prime location and an accomplished lobby restaurant. $–$$$$

IN THE MT. HOOD AREA

Huckleberry Inn. Government Camp Loop Road, off US 26; (503) 272-3325; www.huckleberry-inn.com. A restaurant, kitchenettes, and laundry facilities make this small inn an especially handy place to stay during ski season. $$$–$$$$

Timberline Lodge and Ski Resort. Off US 26 about 60 miles east of Portland; (800) 547-1406 or (503) 272-3311; www.timberline lodge.com. The oldest resort on the mountain is a convenient and incredible place to reserve for a winter ski vacation—or summer outdoor fun. Families can spend hours admiring the huge beams, carved stairways, and massive stone fireplace in this National Historic Landmark that was built as a WPA project. Historic photos and memorabilia, plus a game room, multiple restaurants, and an outdoor heated pool provide something for the whole family. $$$$

Trillium Lake Basin Cabins. 32798 Mineral Creek Dr., Government Camp; (503) 819-7952; www.trilliumlake.com; e-mail: info@ trilliumlake.com. E-mail preferred unless calling for lodging within 48 hours. Located at the base of Multorpor (Skibowl East), the cabins are close to the downhill ski centers along a lovely stream. From your cabin door you can walk to the ski area and ski right onto an extensive system of cross-country trails or hike to Trillium Lake, where you can also camp in the summer. E-mail for rates.

IN PORTLAND
Crowne Plaza Hotel Portland Downtown. 1441 NE Second Ave.; (503) 233-2401; www.ichotelsgroup.com.Though not technically downtown, it's right across the river via walking, biking on courtesy bicycles, or riding light rail. Heated indoor pool. $$$–$$$$

DoubleTree Lloyd Center. 1000 NE Multnomah St.; (503) 281-6111 or (800) 996-0510; www.doubletree.com. Glass elevators give you a bird's-eye view of the modern, spacious lobby and the Portland environs. There are two formal restaurants plus a friendly family-style coffee shop. Just across the street is the Lloyd Center mall, with an ice-skating rink, dozens of eateries, and enough shops to provide hours of entertainment for everyone. $$$$

Hotel deLuxe. 729 SW 15th Ave.; (866) 895-2094 or (503) 219-2094; www.hoteldeluxe portland.com. A spacious lobby with ornate wainscoting and an enormous chandelier creates a warm welcome in this family-oriented facility located on the MAX line. A reasonably priced restaurant, laundry service, and 1 p.m. checkout make this place a hidden gem in downtown Portland. Free parking and continental breakfast. Some suites. $$$$

McMenamin's Kennedy School. 5736 NE 33rd Ave.; (503) 249-3983 or (888) 249-3883; www.mcmenamins.com. Let your kids fall asleep in class—at this remodeled old school that's now a sweet hotel, restaurant, pub, and movie theater. The saltwater soaking pool is a delight. $$$$

IN SANDY
Best Western Sandy Inn. 37465 US 26; (800) 359-4827 or (503) 668-7100. A spa, indoor pool, suites, continental breakfast, and exercise room await you in this establishment near Mt. Hood. $$$$

For More Information
Beaverton Area Chamber of Commerce. 12655 SW Center St., Suite 140, Beaverton, OR 97005; (503) 644-0123; www .beaverton.org; e-mail: info@beaverton.org.

Columbia River Gorge Visitors Association. 2149 W. Cascade, #106A, Hood River, OR 97031; (800) 984-6743; www.crgva.org; e-mail: info@crgva.org.

The Dalles Area Chamber of Commerce. 404 W. Second St., The Dalles, OR 97058; (800) 255-3385 or (503) 296-2231; www.thedalleschamber.com; e-mail: info@ thedalleschamber.com.

Hood River Chamber of Commerce. 720 E. Port Marine Dr., Hood River, OR 97031; (541) 386-2000 or (800) 366-3530; www .hoodriver.org; e-mail: info@hoodriver.org.

Molalla Area Chamber of Commerce.
P.O. Box 578, 105 E. Main St., Suite 3, Molalla,
OR 97038; (503) 829-6941; www.molalla
chamber.com; e-mail: info@molalla.net.

**Oregon's Mt. Hood Territory/Clacka-
mas County Tourism & Cultural Affairs.**
88900 E. Highway 26 Business Loop, Government Camp, OR 97028; (503) 655-8490; www
.mthoodterritory.com.

Port of Cascade Locks Visitor Center. P.O.
Box 307, Marine Park Drive, Cascade Locks, OR
97014; (503) 374-8619; www.cascadelocks.net.

Portland/Oregon Visitors Association.
1000 SW Broadway, Suite 2300, Portland, OR
97205; (800) 962-3700 or (503) 275-9750; (877)
678-5263 (hotel reservations); Walk-in Information Center, 701 SW Sixth Ave., Pioneer
Square; (541) 275-8355; www.travelportland
.com; e-mail: info@travelportland.com.

Sandy Area Chamber of Commerce.
38963 Pioneer Blvd., Sandy, OR 97055; (503)
668-4006; www.sandyoregonchamber.org.

**Washington County Visitors Asso-
ciation.** 11000 SW Stratus St., Suite 170,
Beaverton, OR 97008; (800) 537-3149 or
(503) 644-5555; www.visitwashingtoncounty
oregon.com.

**West Columbia Gorge Chamber of
Commerce (Troutdale, Multnomah
Falls, Cascade Locks).** 226 W. Historic
Columbia River Hwy., Troutdale, OR 97060;
(503) 669-7473; www.westcolumbiagorge
chamber.com; e-mail: info@westcolumbia
gorgechamber.com.

**Woodburn Area Chamber of Com-
merce.** P.O. Box 194, 124 W. Lincoln St.,
Woodburn, OR 97071; (503) 982-8221; www
.woodburnchamber.org; e-mail: welcome@
woodburnchamber.org.

The Willamette Valley

T he verdant fields and hills of Oregon's Willamette Valley represented the dream that brought 300,000 people from the middle west of the young nation on a 2,000-mile trek laden with untold hardship. It was the promise of land so rich you could sow corn in the morning and harvest it in the afternoon, of rivers teeming with fish, and of forests running thick with deer and elk. Today the Willamette Valley is still the agricultural heartland of the state. Nursery items, hay, and grass seed are leading products, but it's the wine and produce that are the most fun. The Oregon vineyards produce world-class pinots and other varietals that draw tasters and aficionados in a constant stream from Mar through Oct. In summer you're never far from a roadside fruit and vegetable stand, where you can buy produce that was washed on the vine with the morning's dew. U-pick fields abound, too, starting with strawberries in late May or early June, moving through peaches and cherries in July, then raspberries and blueberries in Aug. In fall, apples, pears, walnuts, and filberts are ready for gathering. For easy entertainment, leave the interstate and the highways behind and travel the valley's web of back roads, picturesque byways that roll through lush meadows topped by popcorn clouds, past sagging barns and rolling hills covered with grapevines or filbert groves, and into sweet towns full of history and interesting eateries.

Newberg & McMinnville

Champoeg State Heritage Area (ages 5 and up)

Located 7 miles east of Newberg off Highway 99W; take exit 278 west from I-5. (800) 551-6949 for information; (800) 452-5687 for reservations; www.oregonstateparks.org. Park open dawn to dusk. $ day-use fee.

Once a small town site and in 1843 the seat of the first provisional government body on the West Coast, Champoeg (sham-poo-ee) is now a quiet riverside retreat not far from the

THE WILLAMETTE VALLEY

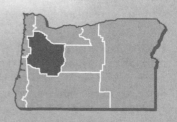

Top Events in Newberg & Mt. Angel

September

Pioneer Farmstead Day. Old-time crafts, entertainment, and lessons in butter churning, spinning, blacksmithing, and other pioneer skills at Champoeg State Heritage Area. (503) 678-1251.

Oktoberfest. Visit this Bavarian celebration in Mt. Angel on a weekday to avoid the crowds. Although the Biergarten is for adults only, much of the entertainment, such as pony rides, miniature carnival rides, puppet shows, and magicians, is geared to families with young children. (503) 845-9440; www.oktoberfest.org.

bustle of the big city. Before it was used by settlers, the site was a Kalapuya Indian village. Much of this area's history is described in the exhibits at the visitor center, near the park entrance. Ten miles of walking and cycling trails are good ways to explore, and a map is available at the visitor center that shows both the paths and the original location of town buildings swept away by an 1860 flood. Tour **Newell House** and the **Pioneer Mothers Log Cabin Museum,** and in summer take a guided walk to tour historic **Manson Farmstead** and old Champoeg town site. Saturdays in July and August are Living History days, where costumed guides demonstrate 19th-century farm skills.

99-W Drive-In Theatre (all ages)

Located in the heart of Newberg on Highway 99W at 3110 Portland Rd.; (503) 538-2738; www.99w.com. Drive-in open Fri through Sun late Apr through Oct; $$ adults, $ kids, minimum car charge $$$, 5 and under free. Call or go online for showings and season dates.

Step back to sock-hop days at one of the last remaining drive-in movie theaters in the area that has been showing first-run movies since 1953, and is still operated by the original family. An old-time concessions stand sells fresh, hot popcorn and treats at what seem like old-fashioned prices, and before the first showing at dusk, families walk around and chat, play at the playground, or check out the car-club vehicles that often gather here. Kids in pajamas and beds in the back of pickups are common sights, and everyone will love the vintage concession movies and short reels, plus the birthday and community announcements, that kick off each evening's showings. Arrive early, as sell-outs are common, especially in summer, and bring cash—no debit cards are accepted.

Flying M Ranch (ages 5 and up)

23029 NW Flying M Rd., Yamhill, 10 miles west of McMinnville; (503) 662-3222; www.flying-m-ranch.com; e-mail: flyingm@bigplanet.com. Open year-round; call for hours. Bunkhouse motel rooms and cabins sleeping 2 to 10 $$$$; rustic camping $$$; hourly horseback ride $$$$; daylong ride $$$$. Call for times and reservations.

Kid-Friendly **Book**

Best Hikes with Kids: Oregon. Bonnie Henderson, 2007; paperback.

Set in the foothills of the Coast Range along the North Yamhill River, the ranch offers a rustic country experience within easy reach of the city. In addition to year-round horseback rides, you can enjoy fishing, swimming, volleyball, and other sports and walking the many trails through forest and meadow. The lodge dining room serves breakfast, lunch, and dinner.

Evergreen Aviation & Space Museum (ages 3 and up)

500 NE Capt. Michael King Smith Way, 1 mile east of McMinnville off Highway 18; (503) 434-4180; www.sprucegoose.org. Open daily 9 a.m. to 5 p.m. $$$$ adults, $$$ students, children 4 and under free.

Get "up close and personal" with historic, world-famous aircraft—the most famous of which is the Hughes Flying Boat, affectionately called the Spruce Goose. At the time the biggest airplane ever built, its history is one of personal sacrifice, determination, and technological development. The museum houses a number of other aircraft plus a new IMAX theater and offers hands-on activities for visitors of all ages.

Aurora

Aurora, a small community northeast of Woodburn, began as a German-American communal society. The followers of religious visionary Wilhelm Keil established the first West Coast religious commune in 1855, and its appearance has changed little since then. In fact, the center of town has been designated a National Historic District. You can reach Aurora by traveling east about 2½ miles from exit 278 on I-5 or by driving north on Highway 99E from Woodburn for about 8 miles.

Top Aurora **Events**

June

Strawberry Festival. Hosted by the Old Aurora Colony, the shortcake and ice cream social helps raise funds for the museum. (503) 939-0312.

August

Aurora Colony Days. Historic town celebration of its pioneer past. Museum entrance is free during this event. (503) 678-2288.

Old Aurora Colony Museum (ages 5 and up)

15018 Second St.; (503) 678-5754; www.auroracolony.org; email: info@auroracolony.org. Open Tues through Sat 11 a.m. to 4 p.m., Sun noon to 4 p.m.; closed Mon and the month of Jan. $.

A guide takes you through the old ox barn and a rough log cabin as well as other original buildings used by commune members. Your kids will appreciate the frontier-life demonstrations that emphasize the amount of work necessary to survive day-to-day. The museum also sells a self-guided walking tour for the town's many historical buildings.

Salem

Just 20 years ago Salem was a sleepy town that housed Oregon's capitol, but in recent years the city has metamorphosed into a bustling center of commerce and culture. Renovated historic buildings, coffeehouses, and department stores all add to the fabric of Salem's spirited city blocks.

State Capitol (ages 8 and up)

900 Court St. NE; (503) 986-1388; www.leg.state.or.us/capinfo. Building open weekdays 7:30 a.m. to 5 p.m. Self-guided tours available throughout the year; on weekdays during summer months building tours available hourly 9 a.m. to 3 p.m., tower tours until 4 p.m. Free.

Salem's most visible and most visited landmark, the capitol building is white marble topped with a 23-foot-high sculpture of the golden Oregon Pioneer. Inside, large murals depict elements of Oregon's history on a grand scale. Give your kids a taste of both history and contemporary state government with a stop at the capitol building.

A. C. Gilbert's Discovery Village (all ages)

116 Marion St. NE, under the Marion Street Bridge that crosses the Willamette; (800) 208-9514 or (503) 371-3631; www.acgilbert.org. Open Mon through Sat 10 a.m. to 5 p.m., Sun noon to 5 p.m. $$ ages 3 to 59, $ toddlers and seniors, 1 and under free.

This place is a must on your Salem itinerary. A. C. Gilbert is the man who gave children of the 1940s and 1950s the original Erector sets, chemistry sets, and other fun and educational toys. The two historic houses plus the outdoor area have become a hands-on exploratorium for children, with innovative exhibits and activities in the sciences, arts, and humanities. Plan to spend several hours here because the kids will want to try everything at least twice.

Willamette Heritage Center
and Mission Mill Museum (ages 5 and up)

1314 Mill St., off 12th Street SE; (503) 585-7012; www.missionmill.org. Open Mon through Sat 10 a.m. to 5 p.m. $$ adults, $ seniors and students, under 6 free.

Take a tour of the mill, church, and three historic houses that date from the 1840s. There's also a charming gift shop with old-fashioned ambience.

Top Salem **Events**

April

Oregon Ag Fest. The last weekend in April, kids (and grownups) can touch, taste, and experience life on a farm and learn how the food they eat is raised or grown. Kids can ride a pony, watch chicks hatch, milk a "cow," and enjoy wagon rides, food, and performances geared for families. A unique way to kick off spring! (503) 535-9353; www.oragfest.com.

July through August

Great Oregon Steam-Up. During this event at the **Western Antique Powerland Museum,** kids have a chance to ride on some of their huge examples of antique farm equipment, and there are demonstrations of old-style threshing, flour milling, and blacksmithing. (503) 393-2424; www.antiquepowerland.com.

August through September

Oregon State Fair. Walk through the animal exhibition areas and laugh at the crowing roosters and odd-looking ducks, guess which bunny should get the blue ribbon, and watch the 4-H kids trying to keep their pigs clean before the show. Dozens of food booths offer everything from hot corn on the cob slathered with butter to Thai noodles. (503) 947-3247; www.fair.state.or.us.

Enchanted Forest (all ages)

8462 Enchanted Way SE, Turner; located between exits 244 and 248 just off I-5 7 miles south of Salem; (503) 371-4242; www.enchantedforest.com. Open Mar 15 through Sept; call for hours and schedule. $$, children 2 and under free. Extra fees for large rides.

Some little ones may not be ready for the Haunted House or the Ice Mountain or Timber Log rides, and it may take a while to convince them that walking into the witch's mouth won't mean they will be eaten, but everything else is appropriate for any age. Bring your own picnic basket, or dine at the cafeteria that serves hot dogs and burgers.

Western Antique Powerland Museum (ages 5 and up)

3995 Brooklake Rd. NE, Brooks; (503) 393-2424; www.antiquepowerland.com. Open Wed through Sun 9 a.m. to 5 p.m. Mar through Oct. Call for special programs. $$, children 12 and under free.

This vast collection of antique farm equipment, from steam engines and kerosene tractors to horse-drawn plows and sowers, is massive enough to grab the attention of kids of all ages.

Bush Pasture Park (all ages)

Located off Mission Street between High and 12th Streets; (503) 363-4714 or (503) 588-6261; www.cityofsalem.net/Residents/Parks. Call for hours. Park and art center free. Bush House Museum open Tues through Sun 2 to 5 p.m. Oct through Apr, noon to 5 p.m. May through Sept. $, children under 6 free.

The beautiful **Bush House Museum** (www.oregonlink.com/bush_house) and its surrounding gardens, plus the 1882 **Conservatory** and **Bush Barn Art Center,** all provide an agreeable setting for an afternoon family outing. In July the 3-day Salem Art Fair draws artists and craftspeople from all over the state who sell their high-quality wares in the park's shady grove.

Silver Falls State Park (all ages)

Located in the Cascade foothills, 26 miles east of Salem by way of Highway 22 and Highway 214; (503) 873-8681, ext. 31 (information); (800) 452-5687 (campground reservations); www.oregonstateparks.org. Call for hours. Camping and $ day-use fees are charged in summer. Campground closes for winter months except for B loop (RV camping). Leashed dogs are allowed in the park, but not along some trails.

The park includes over 25 miles of trails for hiking, biking, and horseback riding and also has 10 waterfalls, half of which cascade more than 100 feet down basalt bluffs. **The Trail of Ten Falls,** a 9-mile hike along gently sloping trails, takes you through stunning forests, alongside beautiful streams that beckon on hot days, and past waterfalls and geologic wonders that will amaze you. Plan at least 5 hours for the whole loop, or take shorter hikes from the north and south parking areas. At the South Falls day-use area, take a gently sloping ½-mile loop that passes behind South Falls and under its dramatic basalt overhang. With an almost immediate payoff, even the littlest legs will manage, and nearby picnic spots, lawns, and a developed swimming area make Silver Falls a great place to while away a summer day. Call for a brochure and maps or download them from the website.

Oregon Garden (all ages)

In Silverton, 15 miles northeast of Salem off I-5; (503) 874-8100 or (877) 674-2733; www.oregongarden.org. Call for special events schedule. Open daily in summer 9 a.m. to 6 p.m.; 10 a.m. to 4 p.m. Oct through Apr. $$ adults, $ ages 8 to 17, 7 and under free. Gordon House admission $ (reservations required for tours).

Determined to become a rival to the famous Butchart Gardens in British Columbia, the Oregon Garden is growing to become a world-class botanical garden of 240 acres. There are a variety of gardens, including a pet-friendly garden and the Children's Garden, plus natural meadows and wetlands, an ancient oak grove, and a lovely loop trail through a variety of plant specimens. A summer concert series and other seasonal events are making this a premier

destination in Oregon. A free tram that runs Apr through Oct allows even the youngest and oldest legs to enjoy the grounds, and a new tree house, dinosaur dig area, and electric train will engage kids of all ages. Be sure to ask for a "Kids' Quest" activity book at the visitor center. The Gordon House, the only house that architect Frank Lloyd Wright ever designed in Oregon, was moved to the garden in 2001 and is open to the public. For an overnight treat, stay at one of the rooms of the **Oregon Garden Resort** (800-966-6490), nestled in small buildings around the park, and enjoy a tableside vista at the Garden View Restaurant. Before you go, check current events and monthly blooming schedules online.

Riverfront Park

200 Water St. in downtown Salem; (503) 588-6261; www.cityofsalem.net/residents/parks. Open 5 a.m. to midnight year-round. Free.

Riverfront Park has 23 acres of walking paths and grassy areas along the Willamette River, plus playgrounds and an amphitheater that hosts Summer Movies in the Park. It's also home to A. C. Gilbert Discovery Village, Salem's Riverfront Carousel (503-540-0374), and the EcoEarth Globe—a huge orb of tile icons that local artists and students made to display the world's diversity.

Willamette Queen **Sternwheeler** (ages 8 and up)

City Dock at Riverfront Park in Salem; (503) 371-1103; www.willamettequeen.com. Call for prices, schedules, and reservations (required).

The graceful sternwheeler was once an important mode of transportation on the Willamette River, taking people and products to their destinations. Now passengers enjoy leisurely lunch, dinner, and excursion cruises and riverbank sites from the deck.

Monmouth

Oregon's only "dry" town is located about 15 miles southwest of Salem. It's also home to Western Oregon University, the state's distinguished 4-year college for students seeking credentials in education, among other academic disciplines.

Paul Jensen Arctic Museum (ages 5 and up)

Located at Western Oregon University, 590 W. Church St.; (503) 838-8468; www.wou.edu /president/advancement/jensen. Open Wed through Sat 10 a.m. to 4 p.m. Admission is free, but donations are appreciated.

Your kids will enjoy seeing the more than 3,000 artifacts gathered by Jensen, who was once president of the college and who traveled to the Arctic on several expeditions. Children shiver at the diorama of wolves snarling at a massive caribou. Special attractions are a sod house and a 27-foot walrus-skin boat, which were given to Dr. Jensen by inhabitants of St. Lawrence Island.

Albany

Historians credit Albany with having the most varied historic buildings in the state. Many, built between 1875 and 1915, are in three districts, all of which are on the National Register of Historic Places. Self-guided walking- or driving-tour maps describe the houses and their history, and are available at the Albany Visitors Center (250 Broadalbin SW, Suite 110, 541-928-0911).

Top Albany Area Events

Summer

River Rhythms Summer Music Series. Located in Albany's beautiful Monteith Park, this Thursday-night program brings in nationally known entertainers. Arrive early to stake out seating with blankets or lawn chairs. Bring your picnic basket or select from a variety of food vendors.

June

Linn County Pioneer Picnic. Held every year since 1887, this is the oldest annual celebration in Oregon. Participate in horseshoe tournaments, watch the kiddie parade, and enjoy the logger's jamboree and a flower show. Held in Brownsville's Pioneer Park. (541) 466-5709.

August

Wah Chang Northwest Art & Air Festival. This 3-day festival combines two Albany events—the Great Balloon Escape and Albany Airport Days—with a juried art show and sale, children's hands-on art, displays of vintage aircraft, airplane and hot-air-balloon rides, food, and live music. More than 40 hot-air-balloons from the western United States launch each morning, weather permitting, from West Albany High School. Many balloons stage a "Night Glow" at Timber Linn Park at dusk on Friday.

December

Christmas Parlour Tour. Step back in time as you view the parlours of several historic homes beautifully decorated for a Victorian holiday. Costumed carolers and vendors add extra festivity, and your ticket price includes hot drinks, entertainment, and rides on trolleys and wagons.

For information on these Albany events, call (800) 526-2256 or (541) 928-0911; http://albanyvisitors.com/albany-events.

Covered **Bridges**

Oregon has more covered bridges than any other state west of the Mississippi, many of them in the northern Willamette Valley. With covers, the giant wooden trusses supporting a bridge could last almost a century; without a cover, they could rot in less than a decade. Many can be seen in and around Linn County. For locations and more information, visit the Covered Bridge Society of Oregon website at www.covered-bridges.org.

Monteith House Museum (ages 5 and up)

518 Second Ave. SW; (800) 526-2256 or (541) 928-0911. Open Wed through Sun noon to 4 p.m. mid-June through Sept, other times by appointment. Free; donations appreciated.

Visit this home for a closer look at one of the most authentic restored buildings in Oregon and the first frame structure constructed in Albany in 1849.

Wavery Lake Park (ages 3 and up)

On Pacific Boulevard and Salem Avenue; (541) 917-7777. Park open daily year-round; paddleboat rentals June through Labor Day, weather permitting. Call for days and hours. Free. Paddleboat rentals $ per half-hour.

Once a log-holding pond, this little lake has become a roadside gem. Feed the resident ducks, have a picnic, walk around the lake, or rent a paddleboat for fun.

Albany Regional Museum (all ages)

136 Lyon St. SW; (541) 967-7122; www.armuseum.com; e-mail: armuseum@peak.org. Open Mon through Fri noon to 4 p.m., Sat 10 a.m. to 2 p.m., other times by appointment. Free.

Old Albany memorabilia, photos, and artifacts fill this fun regional museum. Peer into a turn-of-the-20th-century mercantile and sit in a chair from a shoe-shine stand that was popular in Albany for decades.

Linn County Historical Museum (ages 5 and up)

101 Park Ave., Brownsville, 16 miles south of Albany; (541) 466-3390; www.co.linn.or.us /museum. Open Mon through Sat 11 a.m. to 4 p.m., Sun 1 to 5 p.m. Free; donations appreciated.

Relics of pioneer life are displayed in settings much as they would have appeared during Oregon's early days. Seven old railroad cars have been incorporated into the museum, as well as a covered wagon that arrived in 1865 by way of the Oregon Trail and a collection of miniature sleighs and horse-drawn vehicles. An exhibit on the Calapooia (or Kalapuya) Indians documents some of the history of this culture, which was decimated by smallpox brought by missionaries.

Fun Fact

Albany is home to Oregon's broadest range of historic architectural styles.

Corvallis

Corvallis, home to Oregon's oldest state university, is the quintessential college town. It's also a good central location from which to explore the coast, wildlife refuges, and charming rural communities.

Oregon State University (ages 5 and up)
Campus entrance is at the corner of 14th and Southwest Jefferson Way.

Take a walk along the many campus walkways and enjoy the abundant landscaping, public artwork, and varied architecture while kids run off their energy.

Corvallis Bike Paths (ages 5 and up)
(800) 334-8118 or (541) 757-1544. Always open. Free.

In all, there are more than 25 miles of bike paths and bike lanes in Corvallis. The city is fringed with several sections of paths set off from the roadways to offer safe cycling for families with children. A favorite route is the wide former roadway that connects Oregon State University with the **Benton County Fairgrounds** at 53rd. The mile-long section runs through fields where cows, horses, and llamas graze and past the **Irish Bend Covered Bridge.**

 Another favorite cycling spot is along the Willamette in **Riverfront Park.** From the parking area near the boat ramp at the end of Tyler Avenue and First Street, you can cycle south to a small loop where the Mary's River flows into the Willamette. You can also continue out to **Avery Park,** along the Mary's River, and on to **Bruce Starker Arts Park,** where you can feed ducks on the ponds or let the kids explore the play structure and fountain. In summer, concerts are often held in the grassy amphitheater. Nearby shops and restaurants make this area a pleasant place to while away an afternoon.

Majestic Theatre (all ages)
115 SW Second Ave.; (541) 758-7827; www.majestic.org; e-mail: mail@majestic.org. Call for hours, prices, and schedules.

This completely renovated 1913 vaudeville house features a wide range of concerts, plays, and productions for families year-round. You're likely to find puppet shows, storytellers, dance performances, and at least one kid-oriented play each season

Marys Peak (ages 5 and up)
From Corvallis take Highway 34 west about 18 miles to Marys Peak Road (FR 30); (541) 750-7000. Open dawn to dusk. $ day-use fee.

The most recognizable landmark to the west of Corvallis, Marys Peak offers prime family recreation. In spring and summer wildflowers blaze on the hillsides near the peak of the 4,097-foot mountain, and in wintertime the hillsides ring with children's shrieks as they hurtle down snowy slopes on inner tubes and sleds. Two trails serve both hikers and cross-country skiers, depending on the season, and the 360-degree view from the summit is something you won't want to miss. Camping is available between late May and Oct at six sites near the summit.

Alsea Falls (ages 5 and up)
Farther west on Highway 34, turn south at the small town of Alsea toward Monroe; you can also reach the falls from Highway 99W south of Corvallis, off the Benton County Scenic Loop Drive through Alpine; (800) 334-8118 or (541) 757-1544; (503) 375-5646 for campground information. Call for hours. Free day use.

Just driving to Alsea Falls is a wonderful adventure. From Highway 99W you pass through the quaint little hamlets of Alsea and Alpine that are tucked away in Oregon's forested coastal range. From Highway 34 you'll travel several miles of gravel road winding through dense forest. A small campground, a well-maintained picnic area, and an easy 1⁹⁄₁₀-mile

Family Favorites in the
Willamette Valley

1. Champoeg State Heritage Area, Newberg

2. Bush Pasture Park, Salem

3. Silver Falls State Park, near Salem

4. Marys Peak, near Corvallis

5. Alsea Falls, near Corvallis

6. Oregon Garden, Silverton

7. A. C. Gilbert's Discovery Village, Salem

8. Lane County Historical Museum, Eugene

9. Eugene Saturday Market

10. SPLASH! Lively Park Swim Center, Springfield

An Adventure to Remember

There's nothing more exhilarating than a drive in northwestern forests on a fall afternoon. When you travel south from Corvallis and drive west on winding Highway 34, you will come upon Alsea Falls, one of the most scenic waterfalls west of the Cascade Mountains. The falls, which are an easy walk from the parking lot for people of all ages, slither over monstrous black basalt boulders and continue meandering to a shallow stream. Picnic tables line this fragrant forest and invite you to tarry near the water's gentle sounds.

loop await you at Alsea Falls. Take the easy hiking path at the trail sign and enjoy a walk among second-growth hemlock and Douglas fir.

Sheep Barns, Oregon State University (all ages)
7565 NW Oak Creek Dr.; (541) 737-4854; http://ans.oregonstate.edu/news/lambing.htm. Open 9 a.m. to 2 p.m. daily. Free, but donations welcome.

If you're lucky, you'll witness the birth of a baby lamb or watch a mother tenderly washing her newborn. Lambing time varies annually but is usually in Feb and early Mar. Call for peak viewing times.

Avery Park (ages 5 and up)
Located along the Marys River south of US 20 at the foot of SW 15th Street; (541) 766-6918; www.ci.corvallis.or.us. Open dawn to dusk. Free.

The park delights children with its unusual playground equipment. "Dinosaur bones" and a full-size retired train engine get the kids' vote for the park's favorites. They're located to the left of the park entrance, beyond the small community rose garden. To the right of the entrance, there's another play structure accessible to children of all physical abilities. Trails lead through the woods to the Marys River for wading.

McDonald-Dunn Forest (ages 5 and up) ...
Trail begins at the Forestry Club Cabin in Peavy Arboretum, about 5 miles north of Corvallis off Highway 99W; (541) 737-4452; www.cof.orst.edu. Open dawn to dusk. Free.

Oregon State University owns this research forest, which offers several walking, mountain-biking, and horse trails. A trail map and brochure, which points out 15 stops that demonstrate forest-management practices, are usually available at the trailhead.

Finley Wildlife Refuge (ages 5 and up)
26208 Finley Refuge Rd., off Highway 99W, 10 miles south of Corvallis; (541) 757-7236; www.fws.gov/willamettevalley/finley. Open dawn to dusk. Free.

Hundreds of thousands of migrating waterfowl winter along the Willamette Valley and find a safe haven at this 5,325-acre refuge, where you and your children can enjoy walks throughout the year. Even very young children can manage the **Woodpecker Loop Trail,** which winds over 1¼ miles of gentle terrain through forest, meadow, and wetland environments. Have your kids approach the pond slowly and watch and listen for the squeaks of the frogs as they leap into the water. A brochure, usually available at the trailhead (at a small parking lot about 3½ miles west of Highway 99W on Refuge Road) identifies the woodpeckers you might see as well as plant and other animal species along the trail.

Benton County Historical Museum (ages 5 and up)

1101 Main St., located in Philomath, 7 miles west of Corvallis; (541) 929-6230; www.benton countymuseum.org. Open Tues through Sat 10 a.m. to 4:30 p.m. Free.

The museum is housed in what was the first college in the territory. Its interpretive exhibits provide insights into the region's pioneer and early industrial life. A rotating art exhibit and a portion of the Horner Collection—consisting of natural-history and archaeological artifacts—are other interesting dimensions of the museum.

Osborn Aquatic Center (all ages)

1940 NW Highland Dr.; (541) 766-7946. Call for hours and swim times. $.

The recent addition of Otter Beach—an outdoor area with water cannons, floor geysers, a play structure, pools and falls, and a 22-foot slide—makes this a place for year-round water fun for everyone in the family.

Top Corvallis **Events**

July
Da Vinci Days. Named for that famous Renaissance artist, scientist, and inventor Leonardo da Vinci, this event attracts thousands for 3 days of art, science, and fun. The Children's Village provides youngsters with activities that change annually, such as fish printing—taking a scaly flounder or rockfish, dipping it in ink, and rolling it on paper to create an indelible impression—or a long, 4-foot-high wooden easel that snakes about 40 feet through the park with buckets of chalk provided. Music on 3 stages sets the background sound. (541) 757-6363; www.davinci-days.org.

September
Fall Festival. Arts and crafts booths, food booths, live music, and entertainment focus on creativity. Kids get a chance for some hands-on creativity of their own. (541) 752-9655; www.corvallisfallfestival.org.

Eugene

Eugene, Oregon's second-largest city, is located at the confluence of the Willamette and McKenzie Rivers in the midst of farmland and forests that stretch to the foothills of the Cascade Mountains to the east and the Oregon Coast Range to the west. The University of Oregon is housed here on a beautiful campus crisscrossed with walking paths. Several lush Eugene parks invite outdoor enthusiasts to jog, cycle, and walk.

Rhododendron Garden at Hendricks Park (all ages)

Located at the foot of Summit Avenue, off Agate Street; (541) 682-4800; www.eugene-or .gov/portal/server.pt. Always open. Free.

A blur of glorious color peaks in the springtime with more than 6,000 rhododendrons— both native and hybrid. May is the best month for a visit to this 12-acre garden, but at any time of year you can enjoy a walk through this lush, wooded park. Free guided tours are offered each spring.

Science Factory (all ages)

2300 Leo Harris Pkwy., off Centennial; (541) 682-7888; www.sciencefactory.org; e-mail: info@sciencefactory.org. Open Wed through Sun 10 a.m. to 4 p.m., closed major holidays and UO football home game days. Call for planetarium hours. $ exhibit or planetarium, $$ for both, children 2 and under free.

Science Factory is a hands-on, user-friendly environment in which kids can explore natural wonders, all the while learning about physics and science concepts. They can shout into an echo tube, experiment with the force of pendulums, or watch what happens when they electrify a bubble. The planetarium is one of the largest facilities of its kind between San Francisco, California, and Vancouver, British Columbia. It offers year-round programs on touring the solar system, exploring the night sky across the seasons, or learning about cosmic phenomena.

University of Oregon Museum of Natural History (ages 5 and up)

1680 E. 15th Ave.; (541) 346-3024; http://natural-history.uoregon.edu. Open Wed through Sun 11 a.m. to 5 p.m. $, children 2 and under free.

Kids get a strong sense of Oregon's very early history through the museum's displays of Native American artifacts, including a pair of 9,000-year-old sagebrush sandals. Changing exhibits explore other cultures throughout the world.

Lane County Historical Museum (ages 5 and up)

740 W. 13th Ave.; (541) 682-4242 or (541) 682-4239; www.lanecountyhistoricalsociety.org. Open Tues through Sat 10 a.m. to 4 p.m. $, children under 5 free.

With collections dating from the 1840s, your kids will imagine themselves along the Oregon Trail, getting dressed up for a flapper's party in the 1920s or riding an early child's

Top Eugene **Events**

June through July

Oregon Bach Festival. The critically acclaimed festival features a series of children's performances as well as free noon concerts. Most performances are located at the Hult Center for the **Performing Arts.** (800) 457-1486 or (541) 682-5000; www.oregonbachfestival.com.

July

Oregon Country Fair. Every summer it's as if the clock had stopped somewhere in the late '60s. The Oregon Country Fair draws an amazing crowd of old hippies and new yuppies and their families for what one coordinator called "a walking Whole Earth catalog." The event offers an amazing variety of food booths to satisfy carnivores, vegetarians, and vegans alike. Entertainment ranges from vaudeville and mime to folk and rock 'n' roll. The Energy Park demonstrates alternative energy sources, and the Community Village offers exhibits on political, social, cultural, spiritual, and environmental concerns. The Kid's Loop and Youth Stage are designed to engage the youngest fairgoers. (Note: Though it is mostly discouraged, some fairgoers may dispense with clothing.) (541) 343-4298; www.oregoncountryfair.org.

Obon and Taiko Festival. Enjoy a summer evening of Japanese folk dances (audience participation encouraged), Taiko drumming, children's activities, Asian food, and craft booths. (800) 547-5445; www.eugenetaiko.com.

September

Eugene Celebration. The annual downtown Eugene Celebration held in mid-September has a Kid Zone with standards such as face painting and puppet shows along with more adventurous activities like trampolines, tightropes, and tumbling. You can even make your own snow cone with pedal power! Dozens of food booths and continuous live entertainment make this the largest 3-day street party in the state. (541) 681-4108; www .eugenecelebration.com.

Fiesta Latina. Annual Latin-American cultural celebration featuring food, local art, music, and dancing at Island Park in Springfield. (541) 357-9052; www.fiestalatinaoregon.com.

Rafting the McKenzie River

Explore the river with a variety of whitewater guide services (ages 10 and up):

- **Oregon Whitewater Adventures.** 39620 Deerhorn Rd., Springfield; (800) 820-7238 or (541) 746-5422; www.oregonwhitewater.com; e-mail: info@ oregonwhitewater.com. Guided raft trips $$$$.

- **Oregon River Sports.** 4000 Franklin Blvd.; (541) 334-0696 or (888) 790-7235, www.oregonriversports.com; e-mail: ors@oregonriversports.com. Raft rentals and guided trips $$$$. Also canoe and kayak rentals for use on the canal in Alton Baker Park daily in summer. $$ per hour.

bicycle with odd-sized wheels. Inquire about historical craft demonstrations and request a guided tour from one of the museum's docents.

Oregon Air and Space Museum (ages 5 and up)

90377 Boeing Dr., off Airport Road; (541) 461-1101; www.oasm.info. Open Wed through Sun noon to 4 p.m., closed Sun Nov through Mar. Call about special events. $$ adults, $ ages 6 to 17, children 5 and under **free.**

The growing museum now includes an F-4 Phantom jet, a 40-year-old Cessna L-19 that flew in the Korean War, and the oddly shaped Bullet, a home-built plane that never made it off the ground as a commercial venture. Exhibits trace the development of the space industry, and a gift shop sells model planes, T-shirts, and books.

Paul's Bicycle Way of Life (all ages)

152 W. Fifth Ave.. Open 10 a.m. to 6 p.m., weekends 10 a.m. to 5 p.m. Rentals $$$ per day.

Eugene is a town that reveres cycling. You can tell because of the extensive bike paths and lanes throughout the town and the investment in sophisticated cycling bridges that cross the Willamette and McKenzie Rivers. Paul's rents bikes and trailers and provides trail maps and advice (including how to keep your bike from being stolen).

Fifth Street Public Market (all ages)

Located at 296 E. Fifth St.; (541) 484-0383; www.5stmarket.com. Open 10 a.m. to 7 p.m. Mon through Sat, 11 a.m. to 5 p.m. Sun.

Two floors of shops, restaurants and ethnic-flavored eateries capture Eugene's eclectic essence. French and Middle Eastern cafes nestle with fresh coffee purveyors and fabulous bakeries. Artisan booths with wood-framed photographs stand near boutiques with hand-blown glass objects and earthen pottery.

Eugene Saturday Market (all ages)

At Eighth and Oak Streets downtown; (541) 686-8885; www.eugenesaturdaymarket.org. Open rain or shine Sat 10 a.m. to 5 p.m. Apr through mid-Nov; Holiday Market held in Lane County Fairgrounds Exhibit Hall, 13th and Jefferson; call for dates and hours.

Here's another venue that's uniquely Eugene but with even more unusual entrepreneurial enterprises—from farmers selling fresh-cut flowers and garden-grown fruits and vegetables to artisans with quilts, tie-dyed kids' clothing, jewelry, and wonderful wooden hand-crafted toys. It's billed as Oregon's oldest weekly open-air crafts festival. The international food court lets you experience tastes of the world.

SPLASH! Lively Park Swim Center (all ages)

6100 Thurston Rd., Springfield; (541) 747-9283 or (541) 736-4244; www.willamalane.org. Call for swim times. $ single, $$$ family. Discounts for local residents.

The first indoor wave pool on the West Coast opened its doors in Springfield in 1989 and has been drawing hordes of families ever since. The huge pool contains not only the wave pool but a larger-than-usual children's wading pool (complete with floating rubber duckies), a Jacuzzi, a lap pool, and a 136-foot waterslide. You can bring your cooler and eat at one of the many tables. Family changing rooms are equipped with private showers, potties, and sinks, so your little ones don't have to go into the larger dressing room alone. The noise level seems overwhelming sometimes, but that helps contribute to the "lively" atmosphere.

Willamalane Park (ages 8 and up)

1276 G St.; Swim Center at the corner of 14th and G; (541) 736-4104; www.willamalane.org. Park open daily 6 a.m. to 10 p.m. Free. Call Swim Center for hours and special play swim times; $.

This 14-acre park includes a swim center, basketball court, football/soccer field, horseshoe pit, playground, softball field, tennis court, and a very popular skate park. More like an enhanced street scene than the more typical collection of sloping bowls and half-pipes, the skate park features chunky, abrupt shapes with definite corners and a "picnic table" in the middle, a set of "stairs," and a very real fire hydrant.

Springfield Museum (ages 5 and up)

590 Main St.; (541) 726-2300; www.springfieldmuseum.com. Open Tues through Fri 10 a.m. to 4 p.m., Sat noon to 4 p.m. $, children 18 and under free.

A variety of changing exhibits and a permanent collection of objects ranging from pioneer toys to men's ties invites even locals to visit more than once.

Dorris Ranch Living History Filbert Farm (ages 5 and up)

At the intersection of S. Second and Dorris Streets; (541) 736-4544; www.willamalane.org. Open daily 6 a.m. to 10 p.m. Free.

Experience Oregon's history with a visit to Dorris Ranch. Now a living-history farm, it welcomes families to walk among the 75 acres of lush orchards, 75 acres of riverfront forest,

Fun Fact

Dorris Ranch in Springfield was the first commercial filbert orchard in the United States, beginning in 1892.

and 40 acres of pasture and wetlands. A 1½-hour self-guided walking tour takes you through each of these environments and to the Historic Village featuring a homestead, Native American plank house, and fur trapper's cabin.

Mt. Pisgah (ages 6 and up)

34901 Frank Parrish Rd.; to reach the trailhead, take I-5 south of Eugene to the 30th Avenue exit, then follow signs to Mt. Pisgah Arboretum. Cross the bridge over the Coast Fork of the Willamette River, then turn right and take the trailhead from the parking lot at the end of the road; (541) 747-3817; http://mountpisgaharboretum.org. $ day-use fee.

It's fairly steep in places, but the views from the top make the climb worth it. The sighting pedestal on the mountaintop will tantalize your kids. Local outdoors author Bonnie Henderson suggests bringing lots of paper and crayons so kids can create rubbings of the bas-relief fish, birds, leaves, and shells that decorate the 40-inch-tall bronze pedestal. The relief map on top identifies visible landmarks. Watch for poison oak along the trail and "cow pies" underfoot. Most of the 7 miles of hiking paths crisscrossing the 208-acre park are now all-weather trails. The arboretum has created several self-guiding brochures for children to learn from on walks through the area.

Fern Ridge Lake (ages 5 and up)

Located 12 miles from downtown Eugene by way of Clear Lake Road off Highway 99W; (541) 688-8147; http://corpslakes.usace.army.mil/visitors. Open dawn to dusk. Minimal parking and day-use fee.

Here's another spot that's popular with the locals for camping, picnicking, swimming, waterskiing, sailing, and sailboarding. Perkins Peninsula Park offers a swim area, playing field, boardwalk, and interpretive nature trail.

Fall Creek State Recreation Area (ages 5 and up)

Located off Highway 58 about 15 miles southeast of Eugene; (541) 937-1173 or (800) 551-6949, (800) 452-5687 for campground reservations; www.oregonstateparks.org. Always open. $ day-use fee.

When the summer heat starts to get to you, take the family to one of the many nearby swimming holes. Fall Creek has a number of campgrounds, and a picnic area borders the stream that flows into the reservoir. A few swimming holes beyond the Puma Creek Campground offer a little more privacy.

Fall Creek National Recreation Trail (ages 5 and up)

Located about 15 miles west of Eugene on Highway 58; take the turnoff at Jasper-Lowell through the town of Lowell, turn right at North Shore Road, and continue for about 11 miles. The 14-mile trail begins opposite the Dolly Varden Campground on the creek's south bank. For maps and information, visit the Willamette National Forest office at 211 E. Seventh Ave. in Eugene; (541) 465-6521; www.stateparks.com/fall_creek_lane.html.

An old-growth forest and paths lush with maiden and sword ferns give hikers a true sense of getting away from it all without a long or tedious drive.

Aufderheide section of
the West Cascades Scenic Byway (all ages)

Located east of Eugene; follow Highway 58 to Highway 126 and turn at FR 19. The Aufderheide drive follows the South Fork of the McKenzie River and the North Fork of the Middle Fork of the Willamette River from Oakridge (30 miles southeast of Eugene) to the small community of McKenzie Bridge. The West Cascades Scenic Byway continues north to Estacada, near Portland. (541) 225-6300. Open dawn to dusk. $ day-use fee at some parking areas (National Forest Day Pass).

This is a beautiful drive, along which there are many places to stop so the kids can run and explore in old-growth forests of red cedar and Douglas fir and woodland streams and waterfalls. Of particular interest to children is the Delta Nature Trail, a ½-mile loop through towering old-growth trees, some of which are up to 500 years old. Stop by the Middle Fork Ranger Station in Oakridge or the Westfir Lodge Bed & Breakfast to obtain a free audio cassette that describes what you'll see along the way.

Salt Creek Falls (ages 5 and up)

Located an hour southwest of Eugene; turnoff located off Highway 58; look for Salt Creek Falls sign. (541) 465-6521; www.waterfallsnorthwest.com. Open May through Oct. $ day-use fee (National Forest Day Pass).

Oregon's second-highest waterfall, which tumbles over tall basalt cliffs, presents a blend of history and natural beauty as well as outdoor recreation. Interpretive panels tell of the ladies and gentlemen who rode the train to this spot for a day's picnic outing in the 1920s and of the 7,000-year-old evidence of Molalla and Kalapuya Indian activity in these canyons. Walking trails lead to shaded picnic spots and an observation platform that gives you a bird's-eye view of the 286-foot falls. A 2½-mile loop hike to Diamond Creek Falls takes about 2 hours.

Waldo Lake (ages 5 and up)

Located in the high Oregon Cascades southeast of Eugene; (541) 937-2129; www.fs.fed.us /r6/centraloregon. $ day-use fee (National Forest Day Pass).

Waldo Lake is one of the purest, clearest lakes in the world, according to water specialists. At an elevation of 5,414 feet, the lake's summer recreation period is fairly short. Three Forest Service campgrounds provide a few amenities (like flush toilets) that make camping less rustic. Hiking trails connect to other lakes, such as tiny Betty Lake, which is shallow enough to warm for swimming in the summer. Mountain bikers frequently use the 22-mile Waldo Lake Trail, which circles the lake. Trail information is available from the Oakridge Ranger Station on Highway 58 near Oakridge.

Odell Lake and Crescent Lake (all ages)

Located on West Odell Road off Highway 58, approximately 70 miles east of Eugene; (541) 433-3200; www.fs.fed.us/r6/centraloregon. Always open. $ day-use fee.

Boat rentals, swimming beaches, hiking trails, picnic areas, and campgrounds make these lakes easy to enjoy with the family. In winter the lodges are open for cross-country skiers or for downhill enthusiasts skiing at nearby Willamette Pass. Three resorts offer cabins and lodge rooms, boat rentals, and restaurants. Odell Lake Lodge offers cross-country ski rentals, and Crescent Lake Resort rents snowmobiles. All are open year-round; call for hours and rates.

- **Odell Lake Lodge.** East end of Odell Lake; (800) 434-2540 or (541) 433-2540; www .odelllakeresort.com.
- **Shelter Cove Resort.** On west end of Odell Lake; (800) 647-2729; www .sheltercoveresort.com.
- **Crescent Lake Resort.** (541) 433-2505; www.crescentlakeresort.com.

Willamette Pass (ages 5 and up)

Southwest of Eugene on Highway 58; (541) 345-7669; www.willamettepass.com. Call for lift ticket hours and rates, and for summer gondola hours and rates.

You'll find daytime and night skiing on many groomed runs and one of the best ski instruction programs for children anywhere. Skiing begins when the snow covers the slopes, usually in Dec. There are also several miles of groomed cross-country trails. The Cascade Summit Lodge has a restaurant for skiers who need to warm up with a cup of steaming cocoa and a bite to eat. In summer, the Skyway Gondola provides access to alpine hiking trails and incredible views.

Where to Eat

IN ALBANY

Novak's Hungarian Restaurant. 2306 Heritage Way SE; (541) 967-9488. A legend in Albany, Novak's warm and inviting ambience is obvious right when you walk in the door. Delicious homemade breads and noodle dishes will appeal to the kids while Mom and Dad experiment with some of the more exotic cuisine. $$–$$$

Wine Depot & Deli. Two Rivers Market, 300 Second Ave.; (541) 967-9499. This is a good spot to pick up sandwiches for a picnic lunch or salads and desserts for a quick family dinner. $

IN CORVALLIS

Broken Yolk Café. 119 SW Third St.; (541) 738-9655. Fresh and often organic breakfast and lunch, organic coffee, and a kids' play area. $$

Local Boyz Hawaiian Café. 1425 NW Monroe Ave.; (541) 754-5338. Authentic Polynesian and Hawaiian fare, including lots of kid-pleasing meat-and-rice dishes. $$

Nearly Normal's. 109 NW 15th St.; (541) 753-0791. A casual eatery in an old house near Oregon State campus, it offers a nice variety of vegetarian and international cuisine. Ingredients are as fresh as can be. Kid-friendly. $–$$

New Morning Bakery. 219 SW Second; (541) 754-0181. Open for desserts, breakfast, lunch, and dinner. Incredibly decadent pastries are available. Affordable monster-size cookies and delicious salads and soups give everybody something to savor. A children's play area is equipped with toys, books, and kid-size tables and chairs. $

IN EUGENE

Glenwood Restaurant. 2588 Willamette (541-687-8201) and 1340 Alder (541-687-0355). Casual food and atmosphere; voted best family dining by *Eugene Weekly* many times. Arrive early on weekends to avoid crowds of hung-over college students. $–$$

Newman's Fish Company. 1545 Willamette St.; (541) 344-2371. It's an easy location to miss, but don't pass up the opportunity to have truly fresh and delicious fish and chips. Outdoor counter service and seating. $–$$

Oregon Electric Station. Fifth and Willamette; (541) 485-4444. This is the splurge restaurant—meals are good but pricey. Kids will adore eating in an old train boxcar or the 1912 train depot. $$$$

Taco Loco. 900 W. Seventh Ave.; (541) 683-9171. A lively and visually stimulating eating establishment that serves Mexican and Salvadorean food, it was voted People's Choice Best Mexican for several years in local restaurant surveys. $–$$

IN SALEM

Macleay Country Inn. 8362 Macleay Rd. SE; (503) 362-4225. Along with steaks and seafood, Spud-fish is the restaurant's signature dish—fish and chips with a batter made from potatoes. $–$$

Thai Orchid. 285 Liberty St. NE; (503) 391-2930. A small Willamette Valley chain that offers consistent, fresh Thai. $$

Willamette Burger Company. 1405 Broadway; (503) 399-9992; http://willamette burgerco.blogspot.com. Voted Best Restaurant in 2010 by the local paper, this isn't your standard burger joint. Locally sourced, handmade ingredients—even homemade tater tots and fries, mayo, and buns. The kids will love coloring on the butcher-paper tablecloth while you wait for your meal. $–$$

Where to Stay

IN ALBANY

Econolodge. 1212 Price Rd. SE; (541) 926-0170 or (888) 321-3352. Cable TV. Pets welcome. Seasonal pool. $$

Quality Inn. 1100 Price Rd. SE; (541) 928-5050; www.qualityinn.com/hotel-albany-oregon-OR165. Indoor heated pool, free breakfast, and clean rooms. Near the Expo Center. $$–$$$

IN CORVALLIS

Best Western Grand Manor. 925 NW Garfield; (541) 758-8571; www.bestwestern.com. Large, comfortable rooms with refrigerators and microwaves; fireplace rooms available. Outdoor heated pool and complimentary hot breakfast. $$$$

Corvallis Budget Inn. 1480 SW Third St.; (541) 752-8756. A clean and comfortable hotel at a great price. $

Holiday Inn Express Corvallis. 781 NW Second St.; (877) 859-5095; www.hiexpress .com. A central location, clean rooms, and river views are pluses here, and the heated indoor pool, PB&J bar, cookies in the evening, and yummy morning cinnamon rolls make this popular for families. $$$$

IN EUGENE

Best Western New Oregon Motel. 1655 Franklin Blvd.; (541) 683-3669. Reasonably priced rooms have refrigerators, and there's a complimentary continental breakfast. Families will also appreciate the indoor pool, whirlpool tub, sauna, and exercise room after a day of traveling. $$–$$$

Broadway Inn. 476 E. Broadway; (541) 344-5233; www.eugenebroadwayinn.com. Recently upgraded, this centrally located, modest hotel is a good value, with an outdoor heated pool, microwaves, and refrigerators in comfortable rooms. $–$$

Campus Inn. 390 E. Broadway; (877) 313-4137 or (541) 343-3376; www.campus-inn .com; e-mail: eugene@campus-inn.com. Centrally located. In-room refrigerators, coffee, Internet access. Free breakfast, parking, newspaper. $$

Phoenix Inn Suites. 850 Franklin Blvd.; (800) 344-0131 or (541) 344-0001; www .phoenixinn.com. At this centrally located hotel, you'll receive a complimentary breakfast and have access to a pool, Jacuzzi, and fitness center. $$–$$$

IN SALEM

Best Western Mill Creek Inn. 3125 Ryan Dr. SE; (800) 346-9659 or (503) 585-3332. Fitness room, pool; free breakfast at the Denny's next door beats the typical continental offerings. In-room fridge, microwave, and all-new beds in 2010. Free shuttle to Salem Airport. $$$–$$$$

Econolodge. 3195 Portland Rd. NE; (503) 585-2900. Free in-room coffee; outdoor heated pool. Refrigerators and microwaves. $$–$$$

The Grand Hotel. 201 Liberty St. SE; (503) 540-7830 or (877) 540-7800; www.grand hotelsalem.com. The first hotel in the city to earn its EarthWISE green certification, the Grand is large, comfortable, and centrally located. $$$$

IN WOODBURN & SILVERTON

Champoeg State Heritage Area. (800) 452-5687 for reservations; www.oregonstate parks.org. The campground and park are northwest of Woodburn, due west of Wilsonville; take exit 278 from I-5 and follow signs to the park. $

For More Information

Albany Visitors Association. 250 Broadalbin St. SW, Suite 110, Albany, OR 97321; (800) 526-2256 or (541) 928-0911; www.albany visitors.com.

Aurora Chamber of Commerce. 21558 Highway 99E, Aurora, OR 97002; (503) 939-0312; www.auroracolony.com

Corvallis Tourism. 553 NW Harrison Blvd., Corvallis, OR 97330; (800) 334- 8118 or (541) 757-1544; www.visitcorvallis.com; e-mail: info@visitcorvallis.com.

Eugene Area Chamber of Commerce. 1401 Willamette St., Eugene, OR 97401; (541) 484-1314; www.eugenechamber.com; e-mail: info@eugenechamber.com.

McKenzie River Chamber of Commerce. P.O. Box 505, Walterville, OR 97413; (541) 822-3350; www.mckenziechamber.com; e-mail: mcrvco@aol.com.

Monmouth-Independence Chamber of Commerce. 309 Pacific Ave. N, Independence, OR 97361; (503) 838-4268; www.micc-or.org; e-mail: micc@ micc-or.org.

Newberg Chamber of Commerce. 415 E. Sheridan, Newberg, OR 97132; (503) 538-2014; www.chehalemvalley.org.

Salem Convention & Visitors Association. 18 High St. SE, Salem, OR 97301; (800) 874-7012; www.travelsalem.com.

Travel Lane County. 754 Olive St., Eugene, OR 97401; (800) 547-5445 or (541) 484-5307; www.travellanecounty.org.

Willamette Valley Visitor's Association. 250 Broadalbin St., Suite 110, Albany OR 97321; (866) 548.5018; www.oregonwine country.org.

Woodburn Area Chamber of Commerce. 124 W. Lincoln St., P.O. Box 194, Woodburn, OR 97071; (503) 982-8221; www .woodburnchamber.org.

Central Oregon & the Cascades

I n many ways central Oregon is the state's playground. It's here that we can find virtu-ally any kind of outdoor recreation that teases our ambitions—mountain climbing, rock climbing, whitewater rafting, canoeing, kayaking, windsurfing, skiing, swimming, hiking, bicycling, fishing, and horseback riding. The area's climate is ideal for the outdoor-bound. In summer less rain falls here than in many other areas of the state. Winter brings snow to the mountains, but a well-equipped highway department keeps roads passable.

Posh family resorts at Sunriver, Black Butte, Seventh Mountain, and Eagle Crest, among others, draw visitors every season of the year. The forests, rivers, and lakes of the region create a lush backdrop for camping and outdoor recreation. And there is a wealth of educational opportunities for outings to lava fields, museums, and historic sites. You'll want to take your time here and then return to see what new experiences each season has to offer.

Bend

Drake Park and Mirror Pond (all ages)
Take Bond Street and turn on Franklin Street heading west to NW Riverside Boulevard; (541) 389-7275; www.bendparksandrec.org. Always open. Free.

A wide variety of waterfowl plays a predominant role in this aptly named section of the Deschutes River, which flows through the town of Bend. There is even a pair of swans from Queen Elizabeth's royal swannery here. Picnic on the broad green parkland that hugs the shore and frolic at the children's playground (with restrooms!) that's just across the bridge at Harmon Park.

CENTRAL OREGON & THE CASCADES

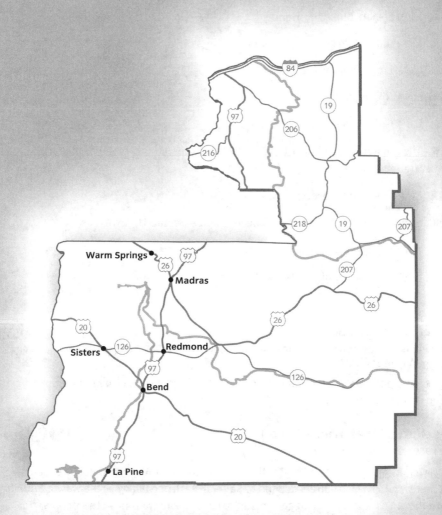

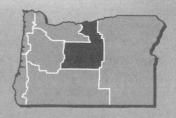

Family Favorites in Central Oregon

1. High Desert Museum, Bend

2. Museum at Warm Springs, Warm Springs

3. Lava Lands Visitor Center, Bend

4. Lava River Cave, Bend

5. Lava Cast Forest, Bend

6. Mt. Bachelor Ski Resort (winter and summer), Cascade Lakes Scenic Highway

7. Pine Mountain Observatory, Bend

8. Osprey Observation Point, Cascade Lakes Scenic Highway

9. Three Creek Lake, south of Sisters

10. Reindeer Ranch at Operation Santa Claus, Redmond

Robert Sawyer Park (all ages)

Located just ½ mile northwest of the Bend River Mall; (541) 389-7275; www.bendparksand rec.org. Day use. Free.

This 66-acre park has both developed and natural settings, with picnic tables, drinking water, and toilets.

Deschutes River Trail (all ages)

(541) 389-7275. Day use. Free.

Equally enticing for fishing and hiking, the 3-mile **Deschutes River Trail** follows the Deschutes from NW First Street in Bend to **Sawyer Park** and nearly all the way to **Tumalo State Park.** You'll see lots of joggers, mountain bikers, and walkers on this popular trail. Off Century Drive (Cascade Lakes Scenic Highway), FR 41 leads to several trailheads within the Deschutes National Forest, with 9 miles of trail through lava flows and pine forests. The paths range from easy to moderate. A National Forest Day Pass is required for parking at the trailheads. For more information, visit the website at www.fs.fed.us/r6/central oregon and search for Deschutes River Trail.

Pilot Butte State Scenic Viewpoint (all ages)

Take NE Greenwood, which winds to the top of the butte; (800) 551-6949; www.oregonstate parks.org. Always open. Free.

To get a great view of the Cascades and the surrounding area without going far from town, take a short trek to this volcanic cinder cone within the city's limits. It provides a perfect 360-degree view of the various peaks—Mt. Hood, Jefferson, Washington, Three-Fingered Jack, Broken Top, Bachelor, Newberry Crater, and the Three Sisters—as well as the Deschutes River as it wends its way north. Bring your own thirst quencher, as there is no water in the park.

Des Chutes County Historical Museum (all ages)
129 NW Idaho; (541) 389-1813; www.deschuteshistory.org. Open Tues through Sat 10 a.m. to 4:30 p.m. $, children under 12 free with a paid adult admission.

Artifacts from the county's colorful history give insight into the lives of Native Americans, fur trappers, and pioneers.Exhibits bring the history of the timber and railroad industries to life. Visit the website to download a 20-minute audio tour of seven downtown Bend historic sites.

High Desert Museum (all ages)
59800 S. Highway 97, located just off US 97, 3.5 miles south of Bend; (541) 382-4754; www .highdesertmuseum.org. Open daily May through Oct 9 a.m. to 5 p.m.; Nov through Apr 9 a.m. to 4 p.m.; closed Thanksgiving, Christmas, and New Year's Day. Adult admission $$–$$$, depending on season; youth $$, and children under 4 free. Ten percent discount for guests of specified local lodging.

Besides the spectacular array of exquisite dioramas, there's a Desertarium with live animals scurrying about in their natural habitats, a homestead exhibiting the details of harsh pioneer life in the central desert, and a forestry exhibit with a working sawmill. The museum also sponsors special programs and live animal presentations at regular intervals throughout the day.

Lava Lands Visitor Center (ages 5 and up)
Located 11 miles south of Bend on US 97; (541) 593-2421; www.fs.fed.us/r6/centraloregon. Visitor center is open daily May to mid-Oct 9 a.m. to 5 p.m. $ car entrance fee (National Forest Day Pass).

You'll feel as though you're in another world entirely, as if you've somehow landed on the moon on this volcanic cinder cone, where the 360-degree view is stunning. Imagine, as you look at the remains of a 9-mile-long, 7,000-year-old lava flow, what it must have looked like as a molten river. Two self-guided interpretive trails take you over the lava fields and through an adjoining pine forest. Another trail rims Lava Butte, which rises 500 feet above the visitor center. Regular programs include guided walks, demonstrations, and talks on the human and volcanic history of the region.

Lava River Cave (ages 10 and up)
Located about 12 miles south of Bend off US 97 (1 mile south of the Lava Lands Visitor Center); (541) 383-5300 or (541) 593-2421; www.fs.fed.us/r6/centraloregon. Open Wed through Sun from early May through mid-Oct (daily July through Labor Day) 9 a.m. to 5 p.m.

An Adventure to Remember

You'll have a deeper knowledge of the hardships early pioneers faced after visiting central Oregon's High Desert Museum, a veritable treasure chest of natural-history, anthropology, and wildlife displays. A rustic cabin, tiny as today's fabricated toolshed, reflects the pioneer settlers' keen ability to make use of every nook and cranny. Costumed docents answer any questions. The spare multipurpose room holds cast-iron pots and pans, a wooden washboard, a pine-framed bed, and an open pantry, demonstrating among other things how dramatically complex our society has become since the turn of the 20th century. During the live raptor program, kids can view injured or orphaned birds of prey. Afterward wildlife educators give kids a chance to feel a hawk's wing and examine a kestrel's skull. Also on the museum grounds are a tiny stream and pond where large rainbow trout swim and rocky beds where otters frolic and porcupines lounge. An old sawmill, a Basque sheepherder's wagon, and exhibits on Native American and pioneer history all reflect the museum's painstaking attention to detail. If you go nowhere else during your stay in central Oregon, be sure to visit this extraordinary museum.

Requires National Forest Day Pass $. Allow 1.5 hours to explore the cave; lantern rentals stop at 4 p.m.

How would you like to take your kids out for a bit of spelunking? One of the more fascinating discoveries around central Oregon happened when a trapper stumbled across a huge cave while hunting in 1889. In 1923 geologists studying the cavern realized that it continued underground far deeper than any cave previously discovered. This cave is the longest uncollapsed lava tube in Oregon, extending nearly 5,200 feet from end to end, and is part of the Newberry National Volcanic Monument. Bring flashlights and extra batteries or rent propane lanterns at the entrance. Wear sweaters and long pants because the cave is always about 42 degrees. Get ready for an experience that will have your kids shivering, not from the cold, but because it's a bit spooky to be underground in a long cavern lighted only by your flashlights. Their imaginations will run riot. Stairs take you down into the cave, where ice stalactites and stalagmites form in winter. Children love the echo chamber, where you can hear voices from farther ahead return as strange sounds.

Lava Cast Forest (ages 5 and up)

Located 14.8 miles south of Bend; take US 97 south, then turn east directly across from the Sunriver turnoff for 9 miles to the trailhead; (541) 383-5300 or (541) 593-2421; www.fs.fed .us/r6/centraloregon. Open daily May through Oct dawn to dusk. $ vehicle permit (National Forest Day Pass).

Somewhat deceptively named, this isn't really a forest of trees embedded in a lava flow 7,000 years ago. Rather, you'll find the hollow impressions left by trees caught in the path of a flow, casting molds in the hardening lava as they burned away. Explore the area on a paved, self-guided mile-long nature trail.

Mt. Bachelor (ages 3 and up)
Located 22 miles west of Bend on Cascade Lakes Highway; (800) 829-2442 or (541) 382-2442; www.mtbachelor.com; (541) 382-7888 for ski report. Open daily; call for hours. $$$$, children 5 and under free**. Surcharge on holidays. Child care available.**

Families can find both summer and winter recreation at Mt. Bachelor, Oregon's highest and now largest ski area, with 3,686 acres of skiing on 71 runs, a season that runs from Nov to May, and an average of 395 inches of fresh snow per year. Ski rentals are available, including a complete selection of children's alpine and Nordic skis. Tubing is also popular. Afterward, warm up with a cup of hot chocolate or a piping-hot lunch in one of six day lodges. The cafe remains open in the summer, too, and the rental shop switches from skis to mountain bikes. The summer excursion chair takes you on a scenic trip to Pine Marten Lodge at the 7,200-foot level, where you can enjoy lunch or dinner with incredible views. Several designated hiking trails at the top allow you to explore the full panorama of central Oregon.

Central Oregon Lava **Trivia**

- The volume of rock in the Lava Butte Lava Flow is 380 million cubic yards. Assuming a paved road 24 feet wide and 6 inches thick, there is enough rock in the flow to pave 160,000 miles of road—enough to circle the world six and a half times.

- The lava flow from Lava Butte is 30 to 100 feet thick and covers over 9 square miles.

- The 22½-acre Lava River Cave was donated to the State of Oregon for use as a park in 1926 by the Shevlin-Hixon Lumber Company.

- The cave is about 6,200 feet long and as wide as 50 feet in places, and the ceiling is as high as 60 feet in some areas.

- The Lava River Cave area has three ecosystems: warm and dry climate surrounding the entrance; warm and moist microclimate at the entrance; and the cool, moist, and dark environment of the cave itself.

- At the point where the cave crosses beneath US 97, its roof is 50 feet thick.

Trail of Dreams Sled Dog Rides (ages 3 and up)

Located at Mt. Bachelor, operating hours vary during winter season; (800) 829-2422 or (541) 382-2442; www.mtbachelor.com. $–$$$$. Advance reservations recommended.

A variety of sled-dog rides are offered, including a 1-mile Children's Mini-Thriller Expedition that lasts about 10 minutes for kids 11 and under. Kids can also go on standard trips that last about an hour.

Rafting (ages 8 and up)

A number of outfitters in the area offer whitewater rafting trips on the Deschutes, one of Oregon's most challenging whitewater rivers. Most trips average about $$$$ per person, more for multi-day trips. Some rent rafts, river kayaks, or float tubes. In addition to those operating from area resorts, other outfitters include:

- **All Star Rafting.** (800) 909-7238; www.asrk.com.
- **River Drifters.** (800) 972-0430; www.riverdrifters.com.
- **High Desert River Outfitters.** (800) 461-5823; www.highdesertriver.com.
- **Sun Country Tours.** (800) 770-2161 or (541) 382-6277; www.suncountrytours.com.
- **Imperial River Co.** (541) 395-2404 or (800) 395-3903; www.deschutesriver.com.

Pine Mountain Observatory (ages 6 and up)

Located 30 miles southeast of Bend. Take US 20 to Millican, then turn 9 miles south from the marked road; (541) 382-8331 (after 3 p.m.); http://pmo-sun.uoregon.edu. Open to the public late May through Sept Fri and Sat evening or by special appointment, weather permitting. Call first. Suggested donation $.

The University of Oregon's astronomical research facility features 15-, 24-, and 32-inch telescopes, plus multiple portable telescopes. Guides lead scoped and naked-eye viewing tours. Scientific discoveries made here have been published worldwide. This is the only major observatory in the northwestern United States. There's a primitive campground (no water) across the road. Bring a small flashlight and warm clothing when you visit; at 6,500-foot elevation, the evenings are brisk even in summer.

Sunriver Resort (all ages)

Located about 15 miles southwest of Bend via US 97; (800) 801-8765 or (541) 593-1000; www.sunriver-resort.com; e-mail: info@sunriver-resort.com. Resort always open.

Sunriver, one of the first resorts to combine a lodge with private home development, is a premier family resort. From horseback riding to ice-skating, mountain biking to whitewater rafting, the resort offers an array of recreational opportunities with something to please everyone. Kids' day camps in summer?

- **Bike Barn.** (541) 593-3721. Rent a bike here to explore 35 miles of paved paths, or mountain-bike on Bend/Sunriver-area trails.
- **Fort Funnigan.** (541) 593-4609. Daily programs and certified child care for kids ages 3 to 10.

- **Marina.** (541) 593-3492. Rent a canoe, kayak, raft, or stand-up paddle-board, plus shuttle pickup/delivery.
- **Paintball Paradise.** (541) 388-0129. Paintball exploits for the 12 and over set.
- **Sunriver Stables.** (541) 593-6995. Trail rides for ages 7 and up; pony rides for the toddler set.
- **Wanderlust Tours.** (800) 962-2862 or (541) 389-8359; www.wanderlust.tours.com. Guided canoe, hiking, snowshoe, and volcano tours.
- **North and South swimming pools.** (800) 801-8765. Three outdoor pools, one with a 50-foot water slide. Or get fit at the 3-lane lap pool at **Sage Spring Club and Spa,** (541) 593-7890.

All these activities cost extra, of course, but the advantage is a well-planned "one-stop-shopping" approach located in the heart of Oregon's lovely high desert region. **Goody's** (541-593-2155), with the aroma of fragrant homemade waffle cones wafting through the air, is the refreshment stop of choice for families.

Sunriver Nature Center & Observatory (ages 2 and up)

Located 18 miles south of Bend in Sunriver Resort at 57245 River Rd.; turn right on Abbott Drive, follow signs to Circle 3, then take River Road; if you reach the marina and stables, you've gone too far; (541) 593-4394; www.sunrivernaturecenter.org. Open daily 9 a.m. to 5 p.m. in summer; Tues through Sat 10 a.m. to 4 p.m. rest of year. $ includes daytime viewing in the observatory. The observatory is open 10 a.m. to 2 p.m. and 9 to 11 p.m. daily (except Mon night) in summer, call for hours rest of year. Evening admission $–$$ adults depending on season, $ children 12 and under.

Families can learn more about astronomy at the observatory and about wildlife and natural and cultural history through living-history programs, nature trails, a botanical garden, and hands-on activities and interpretive exhibits. Call for classes and special events.

Sun Mountain Fun Center (ages 3 and up)

300 NE Bend River Mall; (541) 382-6161; www.sunmountainfun.com. Open Sun through Thurs 10 a.m. to 11 p.m., Fri and Sat 10 a.m. to 1 a.m. $–$$, cafe $–$$.

This 5½-acre indoor and outdoor facility offers a variety of activities for kids of various ages, including go-karts, mini-golf, water wars, batting cages, bowling, billiards, video arcade, cafe, and rooms for parties.

Shevlin Park (all ages)

Located 3 miles west of Bend on Shevlin Park Road; (541) 389-7275; www.bendparksandrec .org. Open all year dawn to dusk. Free.

Over 600 acres of forested land offers several trails that wander up Tumalo Creek, where kids enjoy exploring in the water in summer. Several new facilities offer pleasant picnic spots. This is also a popular site for cross-country skiing in winter.

Top Bend **Events**

June

Balloons Over Bend. Watch more than 20 hot-air balloons soar simultaneously from the ground. At dusk join the Night Glow, where families can get up close to illuminated balloons as they're inflated. Food, live music, face painting and bounceable inflatables top it off.

July

July 4th Festival & Pet Parade. This historic small-town parade with a twist brings out the family pets—be they dogs, llamas, horses, or even stuffed animals. Anyone can take part. Afteward, join 3-legged races, watermelon eating, and other festivities in Drake Park. (541) 389-7275; http://bendparks andrec.org.

Cascade Cycling Classic. Racers from around the globe compete in challenging cycling events. Spectators especially favor the evening criterium races. Kids' race. (541) 388-0002; www.mbsef.org/CascadeCyclingClassic.

August

Sunriver Music Festival. Classical and pops music plus a children's concert are a sure bet for your resort stay. (541) 593-1084; www.sunrivermusic.org.

Cascade Lakes Scenic Highway (all ages)

To reach the highway from Bend, take Franklin Avenue west past Drake Park, then follow the signs; (541) 383-5300; www.byways.org. The road beyond Mt. Bachelor is closed in winter and often doesn't open until June. **Free.**

Also called Century Drive because it's almost 100 miles of beautiful scenery, this road circles a chain of impressive mountain lakes. Take a week or two to explore the area, if you can, stopping at a different lake every night or getting to know one or two very well. The highway runs through the heart of what was once a "ring of fire" chain of volcanic mountains. You'll see a wide range of geologically significant volcanic features, from stratovolcanoes and lava domes to cinder cones, ashflow tuffs, shield volcanoes, and large deposits of pumice and ash. **North and South Twin Lakes** are considered perfect examples of maars: round, deep volcanic crater lakes with no inlet or outlet. **Devil's Garden** is a small spring-fed meadow at the edge of a barren lava flow where astronauts once trained for the Apollo moon missions.

Todd Lake (ages 3 and up)

Located about 25 miles west of Bend off the Cascade Lakes Scenic Highway; (541) 383-4000; www.fs.fed.us/r6/centraloregon/recreation. Call for hours and annual winter closures that often extend from Nov into May. $ day-use fee (Northwest Forest Pass).

You'll have to carry your camping gear in from the parking area about 200 yards, but the reward is a beautiful wedge of clear mountain water in an alpine meadow, with a view of **Broken Top** in the background. A path circles the lake and provides a perfect opportunity for exploring. In August the lakeshore comes alive with frogs, which guarantee the kids extra fun. Tables on the west shore provide shady spots for having lunch, but you can also take your picnic basket and blanket and dine in a sunny meadow on the north shore.

Boating (ages 3 and up)

You can rent canoes, kayaks, and other watercraft at **Tumalo Creek Kayak & Canoe,** 805 SW Industrial Way; (541) 317-9407; www.tumalocreek.com. Guided trips, lessons, and classes also available; life jackets for kids and infants available.

Elk Lake (ages 5 and up)

Located 33 miles southwest of Bend on Cascade Lakes Highway (not accessible by car in winter); (541) 383-4000; www.fs.fed.us/r6/centraloregon; resort: (541) 480-7378; www.elk lakeresort.net. $ day pass, $ camping, lodge cabins $$-$$$$

Three Forest Service campgrounds and two picnic areas provide a base of operation if you're camping, or the resort is the place to stay if you want a bit more comfort. This 390-acre lake is popular for small sailboats and sailboards as well. In summer the lodge offers canoe/kayak, pedalboat, rowboat, pontoon boat, and paddleboard rentals. A summer music festival draws locals and travelers alike. In winter the lodge will bring you in from the Mt. Bachelor Sno-Park by Sno-Cat for cross-country ski holidays. The **Pacific Crest Trail** runs adjacent to the resort, and there are numerous mountain-bike trails to explore.

Osprey Observation Point (all ages)

Located on the west shore of Crane Prairie Reservoir, 45 miles southwest of Bend; (541) 383-5300; www.fs.fed.us/r6/centraloregon/wildlife. $ day-use fee (National Forest Day Pass).

Watch ospreys circling over the lake and listen to their piercing cries calling to one another as they seek their dinner from the lake below. The osprey was once an endangered species, but with the ban on DDT and with protected habitats such as this one, they are now a more common sight on Oregon lakes and rivers. This area remains one of a handful of designated osprey nesting sites in the United States. Take the ¼-mile nature trail from

Fun Fact

Part of the film *How the West Was Won* was shot on location at Dutchman Flat, an unusual pumice desert just west of Mt. Bachelor.

the parking lot and help your kids spot the huge nests atop tall poles. It's quite a sight to observe an osprey make a successful dive, then return to the nest with a wriggling trout clutched in its talons.

La Pine

The **Cascade Lakes Scenic Highway** turns east again on Highway 42, toward La Pine. On the way, take Highway 43 to **Pringle Falls** along the Deschutes River.

Newberry National Volcanic Monument (all ages)
Located 24 miles south of Bend on US 97; (541) 383-5300; www.fs.fed.us/r6/centraloregon. Call for hours and winter closures. $ car entrance fee (National Forest Day Pass).

Newberry was designated a national monument in 1990 for its unique geologic, scenic, recreational, and scientific value. The giant caldera within Newberry Crater holds two crystal-clear alpine lakes, Paulina and East, as well as the Big Obsidian Flow. Native Americans used the sharp black obsidian to make tools and spear- and arrowheads. If you come across a historical or cultural artifact along the trail, such as an Indian arrowhead, feel free to pick it up and hold a piece of history in your hands for a moment, but then replace it so those who follow you might also appreciate its significance. To remove any such artifact is against federal law.

Walk with your kids along the 1-mile interpretive trail through the center of the flow, but caution them about the cutting edges of this dense volcanic glass. In August this area is alive with frogs migrating up the flow from Lost Lake—your kids will go wild!

Throughout the summer, park naturalists at Newberry National Volcanic Monument offer free educational and interpretive programs, usually at a small outdoor amphitheater near the Big Obsidian Flow.

Fun Fact

The Big Obsidian Flow at the Newberry Volcano was created 1,300 years ago and now covers 700 acres.

Sisters

When first driving into this small western town, you could be forgiven for thinking the calendar has dropped about 100 years. If it weren't for the cars, the town's clapboard falsefront buildings and wooden boardwalks would make you believe you were back in the Old West. Many of the shops are geared for tourists, but your kids will appreciate the ice cream parlor on Main Street.

Metolius River Recreation Area (all ages)
Just 8 miles west of Sisters; (541) 595-6711 (Camp Sherman Store); www.metoliusriver.com. Free.

The headwaters of the Metolius River rush full force out of the ground, a sight that will amaze your kids and rekindle your own appreciation of the wonders of nature. This is one of the premier fly-fishing rivers in the state, completely set aside for catch-and-release angling. Good places to get a look at some lunkers are on the small viewing platform near the bridge where the river flows in front of the Camp Sherman Store, about 5 miles north of US 20, and at the state hatchery about 5 miles beyond. The store is a full-service deli and grocery, so you can stock up for your river picnic, and also has one of the best selections of hand-tied flies I've come across.

Hoodoo Ski Area (ages 3 and up)
Located 22 miles northwest of Sisters; (541) 822-3799; (541) 822-3337 (snow report); www .hoodoo.com. Call for hours. Day care available for ages 18 months to 4 years. Skiing $$$$, $$$ on Tightwad Tuesdays and for Fri and Sat night skiing, children under 5 free. Tubing $$$ for 10 runs or $$$$ for an all-day pass, $ bunny hill, tube rental $5.

Hoodoo, which offers excellent downhill skiing with a variety of slopes, is the second-oldest ski area in Oregon. The groomed cross-country trails at the resort can be enjoyed for a fee, but equally fun trails take off from the Sno-Park below the mountain. The Autobahn Tube Hill is a kid's paradise, with multiple 800-foot tubing runs and a bunny hill for tamer tubers or sledders. A new lodge has delighted skiers with dining options for a variety of tastes.

Black Butte Ranch (all ages)
Off US 20, 13 miles east of Sisters; (866) 901-2961 or (541) 595-6211; www.blackbutteranch .com. Open daily year-round: $–$$ recreation, $$$–$$$$ lodging.

The ranch offers a variety of recreational activities: 4 swimming pools, 23 tennis courts, 16 miles of bicycle paths, an equestrian center, an arcade, a climbing wall, basketball courts, boating, and fly-fishing (catch-and-release only), as well as playgrounds and recreation programs. In winter, cross-country skis and snowshoes can be rented at the Sports Shop for use at nearby Sno-Parks or on the ranch, as long as there's at least 6 inches of snow.

Many hiking trails are available on and off the ranch, including some with spectacular views leading to the top of Black Butte. Area trails range in difficulty from easy walks to distinctly challenging. The recreation center has a guidebook that outlines the options. A chain of spring-fed lakes provides a waterway for boating, and you can rent canoes, kayaks, or paddleboats at the lodge pool for use on Phalarope Lake. If you want to take canoes or kayaks to nearby Suttle or Clear Lakes, you can rent them from the recreation center. Life jackets are provided with the rental.

Guided trail rides take off daily in summer from the **Black Butte Stables** (541-595-2061). Wear long pants and sturdy shoes or boots with heels. Riders must be at least 7 years old and meet size, strength, and balance requirements. Riding lessons are available by appointment only. Call about special options such as wilderness rides, wagon rides, chuckwagon dinners, and cattle drives.

Suttle Lake (all ages)

Located 14 miles west of Sisters on US 20; (541) 595-2628; www.hoodoo.com for information; (877) 444-6777 or www.recreation.gov for reservations. Day use $.

Remnants found in the ashy soil around Suttle Lake indicate that Native Americans camped and fished here as many as 10,000 years ago. In the 1920s Europeans built a lodge at Suttle Lake and established it as an ideal alpine spot to while away a summer vacation. Today visitors can fish, water-ski, windsurf on choppy days, or drift quietly when the water is still as glass. A sandy beach is ideal for swimmers, though the water can be chilly until late in the summer. For slightly warmer water, head to nearby Scout Lake, the swimming spot of choice for Sisters locals. Stay at one of three campgrounds at Suttle (or one at Scout), reserve a yurt or rustic cabin, or enjoy the modern but natural rooms at **The Lodge at Suttle Lake** (541-595-2628; www.thelodgeatsuttlelake.com), where each room is named for a Native American symbol reflecting the room's style. The lodge opened in 2005 after three prior lodges, built in the '20s, '30s, and '40s, respectively, each burned down.

Three Creek Lake (all ages)

Located about 17 miles south of Sisters on FR 16; (541) 549-7700 (Sisters Ranger Station); www.fs.fed.us/r6/deschutes. Call for hours and snow closures. $ day-use fee (National Forest Day Pass). Campsites are first-come, first-served.

You'll find this alpine lake is a beautiful spot to spend a weekend, a week, or just an afternoon. The shore has a shallow, gradual shelf that is perfect for wading, and the small marina rents rowboats by the day or the hour. The water in this lake is so clear that you can see to the bottom at its deepest point, some 30 feet below the surface. Two primitive

Fun Fact

Sisters is Oregon's llama capital and is literally surrounded by llama ranches.

Top Events in Sisters

June

Sisters Rodeo. A parade, pancake breakfast, and four rodeo performances draw people from all over the state. (541) 549-0121 or (800) 827-7522; www .sistersrodeo.com.

Wizard Falls Kids Day. Usually held the second Saturday in June, this event lets kids 10 and under fish in the big pond for lunker trout. (541) 579-7700 or (541) 595-6611.

July

Sisters Outdoor Quilt Show. All the buildings in town are festooned with hundreds of quilts on the second Saturday in July. (541) 549-6061; www.sisters outdoorquiltshow.org.

campgrounds offer about 20 spots along the shore. At 6,550 feet, the lake water is brisk all summer; if you're camping, bring pants and sweatshirts for chilly nights and mornings (bug spray comes in handy, too). A small stream runs into the lake from **Little Three Creek Lake** above. Stroll a short path around the lake, or walk along the stream in search of brook trout or other critters. The lush green meadow surrounding Little Three Creek comes alive during August when tiny frogs make their way from the lake to the forest. In winter several Sno-Parks offer cross-country skiers and snow-shoers access to the backcountry.

Wizard Falls (ages 5 and up)

Located about 5 miles north of Camp Sherman on US 20; just east of Black Butte, turn north at sign for Metolius River and drive to FR 1419; (541) 549-7700 (Sisters Ranger Station). Open as weather permits. Free.

The Metolius River passes through a narrow channel of deep rock and forms these grand falls. The spot is as hazardous as it is beautiful, so keep your kids on the bridge when you stop to admire it. Take a walk up the **Canyon Creek Trail** along the Metolius for some gorgeous scenery.

Wizard Falls Fish Hatchery (all ages)

Located just across the bridge at Wizard Falls, 5 miles downstream from Camp Sherman; (541) 595-6611 (hatchery) or (541) 549-7700 (Sisters Ranger Station). Open 8 a.m. to 7 p.m. year-round as weather permits. Free.

The kids can feed the enormous brook trout, including some unusual specimens like albino trout, with food available from a coin-operated dispenser. Interpretive displays describe the life of a trout and how the hatchery helps enhance the native populations of brown and rainbow trout and kokanee salmon in the river.

Redmond
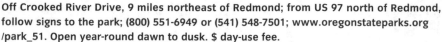

Smith Rock State Park (all ages)

Off Crooked River Drive, 9 miles northeast of Redmond; from US 97 north of Redmond, follow signs to the park; (800) 551-6949 or (541) 548-7501; www.oregonstateparks.org /park_51. Open year-round dawn to dusk. $ day-use fee.

This is a mecca for rock climbers and photographers. Your kids are probably too young to climb, but you can watch climbers scale the rock faces in the park, then rappel down on brightly colored ropes. The 641-acre park is filled with dramatic rock spires rising above the Crooked River Canyon. Walk along 2 miles of developed trails to the river or ridge (keep to the trail to reduce erosion) and watch for wildlife such as mule deer and nesting geese, hawks, falcons, golden eagles, and ospreys (keep an eye open for rattlesnakes).

Ogden State Scenic Viewpoint (all ages)

Located off US 97 9 miles north of Redmond; (800) 551-6949. Open year-round dawn to dusk. **Free.**

Even the most fearless in the family will be awed by the steep plunge into Hells Canyon you can see from the walkway along the river. Unless you have a fear of heights, walk the old US 97 bridge across the canyon and read about the railroading and pioneer history of the area. Picnic grounds and big lawns make this a great rest stop, but note that dogs aren't allowed out of cars here for their own safety—some have jumped over the wall and fallen into the canyon.

Petersen Rock Garden and Museum (all ages)

Located off US 97 at 7930 SW 77th; (541) 382-5574. Open 9 a.m. daily, museum closes at 5 p.m., grounds close at dark. $, children under 6 **free.**

The late Rasmus Petersen spent 17 years gathering rocks from around his Redmond home and crafting them into this 4-acre park of miniature bridges, monuments, lily ponds, towers, and gardens.

Operation Santa Claus (all ages)

4355 W. Highway 126; located 2 miles west of Redmond; (541) 548-8910. Open daily dawn to dusk. **Free.**

Christmas in July? Make that Christmas all year at Operation Santa Claus reindeer ranch. More than 100 reindeer live at this ranch, where the owners believe in keeping the spirit of the holiday going all year. Take a self-guided tour and come see the newborns in May and June.

Halligan Ranch (ages 5 and up)

Located at 9020 S. Highway 97; (541) 420-1334; www.halliganranch.com. Call for information on operating hours, reservations, and rates.

Top Redmond **Events**

July

Fourth of July Parade. If you're here during Fourth of July weekend, help this friendly community celebrate Independence Day by cheering participants in an old-fashioned parade. (541) 923-5191.

July and August

Deschutes County Fair and Rodeo. Four rodeos, a carnival, country music concerts, and a parade in downtown Redmond are highlights of this almost century-old event. (541) 548-2711; www.expo.deschutes.org. $$ (free for kids 5 and under).

Chamber Music on the Green. Concerts offered outdoors July through August. (541) 923-5191; www.redmondcofc.com.

The Halligan Ranch offers day hikes and overnight trips with llamas for families. The ranch has more than 50 llamas, and visitors of all ages can experience hands-on grooming, petting, feeding, and leading. The walks take place on a portion of the 230-acre ranch, with guides providing information on local history, rock fences, ranch structures, and, of course, llamas.

Cascade Swim Center (ages 5 and up)

465 SW Rimrock Dr.; (541) 548-6066; www.raprd.org. $.

The swim center features a 25-meter pool, basketball and sand volleyball courts, a pre-school park, horseshoe pits, and picnic areas.

Borden Beck Wildlife Preserve (ages 4 and up)

Located 5 miles west of Terrebonne on Lower Bridge Road; (541) 548-7275; www.raprd.org. Free.

The newest addition to Redmond's recreational facilities is the Borden Beck Wildlife Preserve. Through the annual donations of the Beck family, the preserve is maintained in its natural state for local residents and visitors to enjoy. It features nature and hiking trails, picnic areas, fishing and swimming in the Deschutes River, and wildlife viewing.

Madras

Lake Billy Chinook (all ages)

Two miles southwest of Madras; take US 26 to Culver Highway, then follow signs to the lake; (800) 551-6959; www.oregonstateparks.org. Call for hours and winter closures. $ vehicle permit.

Three rivers feed into the waters of Lake Billy Chinook, named for an Indian guide who helped Captain John Frémont in his mapping expeditions to Oregon. The lake is now a haven for summer water fun in the midst of Oregon's high desert country.

Cove Palisades State Park (all ages)

On Lake Billy Chinook at 7300 SW Jordan Rd.; (800) 551-6949 or (541) 546-3412 for information or www.oregonstateparks.org; (800) 452-5687 or www.reserveamerica.com for reservations. Open daily. $ day-use fee.

The park straddles the Deschutes and Crooked Rivers arms of the lake and is the center of much recreational activity. Boat ramps, swimming beaches, campgrounds, and picnic tables are provided. The two campgrounds, one on the Deschutes River and another overlooking the Crooked River from the cliffs above, are closed in winter. There are three public day-use areas and a private restaurant that's open May through Sept. Rustic lakeshore cabins are available for rent, and there are 10 miles of hiking trails to explore.

Cove Palisades Resort & Marina (541-546-9999), on the Crooked River arm of the lake, rents fishing and waterskiing boats, patio boats, and Jet Skis. In summer, park rangers offer interpretive programs. Just up from the Deschutes Campground to the northeast, you'll find a large boulder of basalt with Indian petroglyphs. You can walk to the beach along a trail across from the entrance station at the campground, but keep your eyes and ears open for rattlesnakes.

Round Butte Overlook Park (all ages)

Located 15 miles southwest of Madras off Belmont Lane; (503) 464-8515; www.portland general.com. Open daily May 25 through Sept 30 8 a.m. to dusk. Free.

The park on the rim of the Deschutes River Canyon includes a picnic area and interpretive center overlooking Round Butte Dam and Lake Billy Chinook. The annual weekend long Eagle Watch in late Feb draws hundreds to witness one of Oregon's largest gatherings of winter migratory bald eagles. Early risers can join Sunday's 5:30 a.m. Sunrise Eagle Tour each year.

Top Madras **Event**

May

Collage of Culture. Country music, hot-air balloons, Latin salsa, traditional Native American dances, and ethnic food—what more could you want in this event that celebrates cultural diversity? (541) 475-2350 or (800) 967-3564; www.madras chamber.com.

Richardson's Recreation Ranch (all ages)

Located 11 miles north of Madras (off US 97) near milepost 81; (541) 475-2680; www.rich ardsonrockranch.com. Open daily 7 a.m. to 5 p.m. Mar to Oct; 9 a.m. to 4 p.m. Nov to Apr, weather permitting; arrive by 3 p.m. if you want to dig. $.

Kids of all ages can enjoy an afternoon of rockhounding here, digging for thunder eggs— those drab, round rocks that, when split in two, reveal formations like miniature worlds in crystal, opal, agate, or cinnabar.

The thunder egg is the Oregon state rock, and its name comes from an Indian legend about a battle between the thunder spirits residing in Mt. Jefferson and Mt. Hood. When they became angry at each other, the spirits hurled the agate-filled balls at one another, sounding their thunder with each toss. The result of their ire is resting in rock beds, about 4,000 acres of which are within the Richardson family ranch. Digging is available daily, weather permitting, and rock picks are provided. Thunder-egg splitting services are also available at the shop, and finished rock products are sold. Rocks are priced by the piece or the pound for what you take out.

Warm Springs Indian Reservation

Kah-Nee-Ta Resort (all ages)

To get to Warm Springs and the resort, take US 26 for 25 miles northwest from Madras or 119 miles southeast from Portland; (800) 554-4786 or (541) 553-1112; www.kahneeta.com. $–$$ (recreation), $$$–$$$$ (lodging).

Everyone will enjoy the traditional aspects of a stay at this tribal-owned and -operated resort that retains the rugged natural beauty of its surroundings. Kids love swimming in the pools, one fed by hot springs and the other with a fountain depicting bears holding salmon spouting water. Activities include salmon bakes and fry bread, dancing and drumming, and storytelling and singing. You can rent cabins, lodge rooms, tepees, or campsites for RVs. Recreation also includes fishing and kayaking on the Deschutes, hiking along trails, horseback and pony riding, working out at the fitness center, and playing tennis, miniature golf, and golf.

Museum at Warm Springs (ages 3 and up)

2189 US 26; (541) 553-3331; www.museumatwarmsprings.org. Open daily Apr through Oct 9 a.m. to 5 p.m.; call for hours Nov through Mar. $$ adults, $ ages 5 to 12, 4 and under free.

The homeland for roughly 5,000 members of the Warm Springs, Wasco, and Northern Paiute tribes, Warm Springs Reservation has developed a thriving tourist industry as well as a center that seeks to enlighten visitors about the rich traditions of Northwest Native American culture. The stunningly beautiful museum is one place you won't want to miss. Completed in 1993, the 25,000-square-foot facility was created to provide a legacy to the generations that follow and houses the largest collection of Native American artifacts

Fun Fact

Kah-Nee-Ta Village was named for an Indian woman, Xnitla, which means "root digger." She was a scout and a spiritual leader who used the natural hot springs and indigenous plants and roots for medicinal purposes and religious ceremonies.

under one roof in the United States. The history of the Confederated Tribes unfolds in a state-of-the-art permanent exhibit of audiovisual presentations and displays, which include prized heirlooms from tribal families, historic photographs, and murals. Traditional dwellings—a tule mat lodge, wickiup, and plankhouse—show how people lived in ancient villages. Beadwork, basketry, clothing, and other artifacts are also displayed. A multimedia exhibit draws you into the traditional singing, drumming, and dancing of the tribes, which is a marvelous experience to appreciate with your family. Walking trails along Shitike Creek lead to picnic areas and an amphitheater where performances and demonstrations are staged in the summer.

Olallie Lake National Scenic Area (ages 5 and up)

Located 32 miles south of US 26 off FR 42; (541) 822-3381; www.fs.fed.us/r6/mthood or www.olallielakeresort.com. Call for hours and seasonal closures. $ vehicle fee (National Forest Day Pass); lodging $–$$$$.

Top Warm Springs **Events**

February

Lincoln's Pow-Wow. Celebrated in Simnasho on the weekend of Lincoln's birthday, the event features authentic Native American arts and crafts, food, stick games, traditional dancing, and singing.

June

Pi-Ume-Sha Pow-Wow. This annual celebration of the treaty that established the Warm Springs Reservation is held on the weekend closest to June 25 and includes Native American dancing, singing, an endurance horse race, food, crafts, a parade, a rodeo, and a golf tournament.

For both events, contact the Confederated Tribes of Warm Springs at (541) 553-3243; www.warmsprings.com; e-mail: info@warmsprings.com.

This area covers nearly 11,000 acres in both the **Mt. Hood National Forest** and the **Warm Springs Reservation.** The many lakes that dot the region of pine and fir forests reflect the grandeur of Mt. Hood to the north and Mt. Jefferson to the west. New owners are restoring the Olallie Lake Resort, which offers small cabins and yurts for rent, as well as a store with fishing and camping supplies and row boat rentals, and are adding flush toilets and showers. No motors or swimming are allowed on the lake because it provides drinking water for local residents. You can swim in **Head Lake** and **First Lake,** both just off the road to the north of Olallie Lake. Three-mile **Olallie Trail** circles Olallie Lake, and spur trails lead to several other lakes. You can pick up a map of area trails from the ranger station near the entrance to the scenic area or at the resort store on Olallie Lake. Access to Olallie Lake is not suitable for trailers and requires a car in good condition.

Where to Eat

IN BEND

Caffe Yumm. 325 SW Powerhouse Dr.; (541) 318-9866. This Oregon franchise focuses on healthy, whole (and often organic) foods for a variety of tastes, from Asian-inspired bowls to wild salmon burgers. Lots of vegetarian, vegan, and gluten-free options, too. $$

Dandy's Drive-In. 1334 NE Third St.; (541) 382-6141. This Bend institution opened in 1968; the current owner met his wife while working there as a teenager in high school in the 1970s. Kids will love watching roller-skating carhops deliver your food to one of 18 car stalls. Try the Grand bacon cheeseburger or a milk shake made from local Eberhards ice cream. $

Deschutes Brewery. 1044 NW Bond St.; (541) 382-9242. Though this brewery and pub caters to the beer-loving set, the friendly vibe, fresh menu, and plenty of kid-pleasing items make it a favorite for lunch and dinner among families, too. Gluten-free menu available. Arrive early to avoid a long wait. $$

Flatbread Community Oven. 375 SW Powerhouse Dr.; (541) 728-0600. Kids can choose their own pizza ingredients, arrange them on the pizza, and then watch it bake in the open-hearth oven. And since this is one of only a couple dozen pizzerias in the United States to earn certification by Naples' Vera Pizza Napoletana Association, adults will surely love it, too. $$–$$$

Tumalo Feed Company. 64619 W. US 20; (541) 382-2202; www.tumalofeedcompany .com. Listed as one of *Sunset Magazine*'s "11 Great Steakhouses of the West." Kids receive crayons and paper, and they can choose a prize out of the saddlebags if they clean their plates (or do their best). Children under 5 eat free, and up to age 12 eat for $6.95.

Westside Bakery and Cafe. 1005 NW Galveston; (541) 382-3426; http://westside bakeryandcafe.com. On the way out of town, heading toward the Cascade Lakes Scenic Highway, you'll come across this dining establishment with unusual and eclectic decor that includes a red-nosed moose head, old movie posters, and Native American paraphernalia. The menu offers a wide variety of options for both parents and children. You can even grab goodies to go from the bakery. $$

IN SISTERS

Bronco Billy's Ranch & Grill. 190 E. Cascade St.; (541) 549-7427; www.broncobillys ranchgrill.com. At this favorite watering hole, you can also find lunch and dinner with a western flair. Barbecued ribs, links, and chicken are renowned rib-sticking entrees. $–$$$

Kokanee Cafe. 13173 SW FR 1419; located 15 miles west of Sisters in Camp Sherman;

(541) 595-6420; www.kokaneecafe.com. Many would agree that this hidden gem offers the best of Northwest cuisine. Fresh local ingredients are always featured in the small but carefully chosen list of featured dinner entrees. Closed Nov through Apr; call first for hours. $$$–$$$$

Papandrea's Pizza. 442 E. Hood; (541) 549-6081; www.papandreaspizza.com. This cozy pizza parlor has a very local, friendly feel. $$–$$$

IN MADRAS

The café and bakery at Great Earth Natural Foods. 46 SW D St.; (541) 475-1500. A great stop for breakfast, lunch, or early dinner (open until 7:30 p.m. weekdays and 4 p.m. Sat), or to stock up on organic foods for your picnic. $–$$

Where to Stay

IN BEND

Bend Riverside Motel. 1565 NW Wall St.; (800) 284-2363 or (541) 388-4000; www.bendriversidemotel.com. The large property sits on the Deschutes River next to Pioneer Park. Less-expensive rooms are cramped, but for slightly more you get room to stretch out and views of the river. An indoor pool, sauna, and a tennis court are available. $$–$$$

Black Butte Ranch. 12930 Hawks Beard, Black Butte Ranch; (800) 452-7455 or (541) 595-6211; www.blackbutteranch.com; e-mail: info@blackbutteranch.com. The year-round resort offers lodge rooms and condominiums, as well as private homes rented by the day or week. Cycling on miles of paved trails, plus tennis, swimming, and golf, rounds out many a family vacation. $$$–$$$$

Entrada Lodge. 19221 Century Dr.; (888) 505-6343; www.entradalodge.com. Situated a few miles west of Bend among tall pine trees, this peaceful place is close to Mt. Bachelor and a ¾-mile walk or bike ride to

the Deschutes River. It doesn't offer all the fanfare that other establishments do, but it includes a free continental breakfast, an outdoor pool, and a whirlpool. $$–$$$

McMenamins Old St. Francis School. 700 NW Bond St.; (877) 661-4228 or (541) 382-5174; www.mcmenamins.com; e-mail: info.osf@mcmenamins.com. Sleeping in school? It's possible—and fun—at this reconfigured old Catholic school in downtown Bend. With an in-house brewery, large tiled soaking pool, and movie theater filled with couches where you can eat pizza while you watch a free flick (with lodging), this is like no school you've ever attended! Dining $$–$$$, recreation $–$$, lodging $$$$.

Sunriver Lodge and Resort. 1 Center Dr.; (800) 801-8765; www.sunriver-resort.com; e-mail: info@sunriver-resort.com. Lodge rooms, private homes, and condos are available on a nightly and weekly basis. Horseback riding, mountain biking, and whitewater rafting in summer, plus ice-skating, sledding, and nearby skiing in winter, make this a perfect "one-stop" resort site. $$$–$$$$

IN LA PINE

Best Western Newberry Station. 16515 Reed Rd. and US 97; (800) 210-8616 or (541) 536-5130. Continental breakfast, an indoor swimming pool, and a spa give families a pleasant respite. $$–$$$

Paulina Lake Resort. E. Paulina Lake Road; (541) 536-2240; www.paulinalakelodge com. The resort is open May through Sept and mid-Dec through mid-Mar. Camping is available along the lakes and Paulina Creek. Paulina Lake Resort and **East Lake Resort** (541-536-2230; www.eastlakeresort.com) both offer cabins. They also provide boat rentals and restaurants serving breakfast (East Lake only), lunch, and dinner (Paulina only). Paulina is also open for winter recreation. $$–$$$$

IN MADRAS

Best Western Madras Inn. 12 SW Fourth St.; (541) 475-6141; www.bwmadrasinn.com. Continental breakfast, a pool and sauna, and an exercise room are offered here. $$–$$$

Sonny's Motel. 1539 SW US 97; (800) 624-6137 or (541) 475-7217. Kitchenettes and laundry facilities are available. Pets allowed. $$–$$$$

IN REDMOND

Eagle Crest Resort. 1522 Cline Falls Rd.; (800) 682-4786; www.eagle-crest.com. Three golf courses, a spa and health club, multiple indoor and outdoor pools, kitchenettes, and a restaurant give families plenty of options. $$$–$$$$

Historic New Redmond Hotel. 521 SW Sixth St.; (541) 923-7378; e-mail: nrdh@bhghotels.com. Although the hotel was built in 1927, the rooms are modern and comfortable. Exercise room, spa, free continental breakfast, and free parking. $–$$$

IN SISTERS

Best Western Ponderosa Lodge. 500 US 20W; (541) 549-1234 or (800) 549-1234; www.bestwesternsisters.com. Continental breakfast, a swimming pool, and spa pool are offered to guests, who will also appreciate the proximity to downhill skiing, golf, and fishing. $$–$$$

Comfort Inn at Sisters. 540 US 20W; (541) 549-7829 or (800) 228-5150. Continental breakfast is available here, and pets are allowed with prior approval. You'll also find an indoor swimming pool and laundry facilities. RV spaces are available at the adjacent Mountain Shadow RV Village. $$–$$$$

The Lodge at Suttle Lake. 13300 US 20; (541) 595-2628; www.thelodgeatsuttlelake .com. Choose from historic, rustic, or water-front cabins or lodge suites with a great view of the lake. $$$$

Sisters Historic Motor Lodge. 511 W. Cascade; (541) 549-2551; e-mail: sisml@uci .net. Full breakfast is provided, and you'll be close to golf, skiing, tennis, and fishing. Kitchenettes are also available. Pet-friendly. Nonsmoking. $$–$$$$

IN WARM SPRINGS

Kah-Nee-Ta High Desert Resort and Casino. 6823 Highway 8; (800) 554-4786 or (541) 553-1112; www.kahneeta.com. Choose from lodge rooms, village rooms, cabins, tepees, and RV sites. Kayaking and whitewater rafting opportunities are available on the Deschutes, along with hiking, horseback riding, soaking in the hot-springs pools, working out at the fitness center, and playing tennis or golf. Two restaurants serve American and Northwest cuisine. The casino is lively and the resort museum is outstanding. $$–$$$$

For More Information

Bend Chamber of Commerce. 777 NW Wall St., Bend, OR 97701; (541) 382-3221; www.bendchamber.org.

Bend Visitor & Convention Bureau. 917 NW Harriman, Bend, OR 97701; (877) 245-8484; www.visitbend.com.

Central Oregon Visitors Association. 661 SW Powerhouse Dr., Suite 1301, Bend, OR 97702; (800) 800-8334 or (541) 389-8799; www.visitcentraloregon.com or www .covisitors.com.

Confederated Tribes of Warm Springs. 1233 Veterans St., Warm Springs, OR 97761; (541) 553-3333; www.warmsprings.com; e-mail: info@warmsprings.com.

La Pine Chamber of Commerce. On US 97 at the south end of town; 51425 Highway 97, Suite A, La Pine, OR 97739; (541) 536-9771; www.lapine.org; e-mail: info@lapine.org.

Madras Chamber of Commerce. P.O. Box 770, 274 SW Fourth St., Madras, OR 97741; (541) 475-2350 or (800) 967- 3564; www .madraschamber.com.

Prineville–Crook County Chamber of Commerce. 390 NE Fairview, Prineville, OR 97754; (541) 447-6304; www.visitprineville.com.

Redmond Chamber of Commerce. 446 SW Seventh St., Redmond, OR 97756; (541) 923-5191; www.visitredmondoregon.com.

Sisters Area Chamber of Commerce. P.O. Box 430, 291 E. Main Ave., Sisters, OR 97759; (866) 549-0252 or (541) 549-0251; www.sisterscountry.com; e-mail: info@sisters country.com.

Sunriver Area Chamber of Commerce. P.O. Box 3246, Sunriver, OR 97707; (541) 593-8149; www.sunriverchamber.com; e-mail: info@sunriverchamber.com.

Southern Oregon

T he southern region of Oregon encompasses the diversity of the whole state: coast, mountains, valleys, high desert. Your choices for family fun are equally diverse—from bird watching on Oregon's largest lake to exploring its only national park, from riding a wild river to watching Shakespeare performed in one of the world's pre-eminent Shakespearean theaters. In winter southern Oregon is transformed into a frosty playground. In summer the warm, dry weather provides an open invitation to outdoor recreation.

Ashland

Ashland's population of more than 20,000 swells to triple that when the renowned Shakespearean festival season is at its peak. While we wouldn't recommend introducing your children to Shakespeare with a play like *King Lear,* the theater inevitably offers three of the Bard's 12 comedies on its playbill each year. Experiencing a play in the open-air Elizabethan Theatre is wonderful, but spend a little extra to rent a cushion and lap robe—it will make all the difference if the night becomes chilly. Main Street and Lithia Park provide ample daytime entertainment nearby; another popular pastime in Ashland is dining, and for a town this size, there are a number of remarkably good restaurants.

Oregon Shakespeare Festival (ages 6 and up)

15 S. Pioneer St.; (541) 482-2111 (for brochure and information); (503) 482-4331 (tickets); www.osfashland.org. Plays run Feb through Oct. Call for prices and schedules.

Three theaters, the **Elizabethan Theatre,** the **Angus Bowmer Theatre,** and the **New Theatre,** all offer top-notch productions. The Bowmer offers both Shakespeare and contemporary plays, while the Elizabethan is primarily dedicated to the Bard.

SOUTHERN OREGON

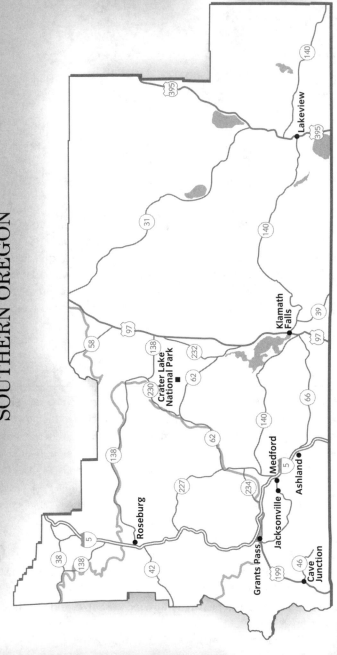

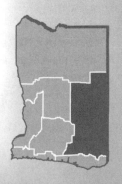

Oregon Shakespeare Festival Backstage Tours (ages 6 and up)

15 S. Pioneer St.; (541) 482-4331; www.osfashland.org. Reservations required. Open Tues through Sun late Feb to late Oct, 10 a.m. Prices range from $$ to $$$, depending on the season.

With an actor as a guide, you get a behind-the-scenes look at how a theatrical production is put together. Your kids will especially enjoy the costumes and props, which they're allowed to touch.

Oregon Shakespeare Festival Green Shows (all ages)

15 S. Pioneer St.; (541) 482-4331; www.osfashland.org. Shows Tues through Sun during the OSF season at 6:45 or 7:15 p.m. depending on time of year. Free.

Billed as "the show before the show," there's something for every taste in these half-hour performances—from hip-hop to ballet, strings to singers and puppets and pyrotechnics—on "the Bricks" outside the Elizabethan and Bowmer Theatres. Call for schedule.

Oregon Cabaret Theatre (ages 8 and up)

First and Hargadine Streets; (541) 488-2902; www.oregoncabaret.com. Plays run Feb through Dec. Call for prices and schedule.

This theater presents entertaining musicals, revues, and comedies in a nightclub setting in a historic church. Preshow gourmet brunches and dinners are available by reservation, and you can buy preshow snacks, or beverages and desserts at intermission.

Emigrant Lake (all ages)

Located 6 miles southeast of Ashland, on Highway 66; (541) 774-8183. Open dawn to dusk. $ vehicle pass.

Emigrant Lake has long been a popular spot for waterskiing, fishing, and swimming. This reservoir has a 280-foot twin-flume waterslide (open June to Sept, $$) that will keep your kids squealing and happy for hours. Lakeside camping is also available.

Farm Tours at Willow-Witt Ranch (all ages)

658 Shale City Rd.; (541) 890-1998; www.willowwittranch.com. Tours Sat at 1 p.m. by advance reservation. $$ adults, kids free.

Fun Fact

A treaty between the United States and Spain established the current southern border between Oregon and California. The treaty was signed in 1819.

Get a glimpse of life on a working ranch in the mountains outside of Ashland, where you'll learn about sustainable agriculture by interacting with pack goats, milk goats, horses, pigs, ducks, and other pastured poultry. Or stay the night ($$$$ for a 2-queen studio) and experience farm life hands-on.

Hyatt Lake (all ages)

Located about 20 miles east of Ashland on Highway 66; (541) 482-2031. Open dawn to dusk. $ day-use fee; camping $$.

You'll find more water recreation as well as winter fun at Hyatt Lake, a high Cascade lake that will reward you with a view of Mt. McLoughlin. There are two private resorts on the lake as well, run by the same company (www.hyattlakeresorts.com; 541-482-3331):

- **Hyatt Lake Resort.** 7979 Hyatt Prairie Rd. Pizza parlor and convenience store plus cabins, RV sites, tent sites, and boat, canoe, and paddleboat rentals.
- **Camper's Cove Resort.** 7900 Hyatt Prairie Rd. Newly remodeled restaurant and lounge, plus cabins ($$$–$$$$) and RV spaces.

Mt. Ashland (ages 5 and up)

1745 Highway 66, located 18 miles from the city center heading south; (541) 482-2897; www.mtashland.com. Usually opens Thanksgiving weekend; call for hours. Lift tickets $$$–$$$$.

With 4 chairlifts and more than 20 ski runs on a 1,150-foot vertical slope, Mt. Ashland should be on the to-do list for any family that enjoys downhill skiing. A ski school and rental shop cater to those interested in trying the slopes for the first time, and the day lodge offers meals and great views. Summer hiking is terrific here, too. The Pacific Crest Trail crosses Mt. Ashland Inn's parking area, and several spur trails lead to scenic viewpoints and picturesque streams.

Wild and Scenic Rogue River Rafting (ages 5 and up)

Many local outdoor operators run trips out of Ashland, including:

- **Noah's River Adventures.** 53 N. Main St.; (800) 858-2811 or (541) 488-2811; www .noahsrafting.com. Call for schedule. Half- or full-day Rogue River scenic float trips ($$$$) are mellow enough for young kids and seniors; whitewater and multi-day trips also available ($$$$). Family discount plans available.
- **Adventure Center.** 40 N. Main St.; (800) 444-2819 or (541) 488-2819; www.rafting tours.com. Call for schedule; runs early spring to early fall. Half-day or all-day trip $$$$. Discounts available for families. This company runs 8 different rivers, including the Rogue and wild Upper Klamath, and supplies transportation, gear, and food. It also offers a simple float trip for families with preschool-age children.
- **Raft the Rogue.** 21171 Highway 62, Shady Cove; (800) 797-7238; www.rafttherogue .com. Call for schedule; runs early spring to early fall. Rentals $$$–$$$$ per person. This company rents the rafts and delivers you to the river—you do the rest!

Top Ashland **Events**

June
Feast of Will. This celebration dinner in Lithia Park, complete with period music and dancing, marks the opening of the Elizabethan Theatre each season. (541) 482-4331.

July
4th of July Celebration. For more than 100 years, Ashlandians have been gathering for one of Oregon's most charming and unique small-town parades and a festival in nearby Lithia Park, followed by a dramatic fireworks show. (541) 482-3486.

October
Children's Halloween Parade. Kids, families, and others parade through downtown Ashland in an amazing and wacky, but family friendly, display of costumes. (541) 482-3486.

December
Holiday Festival of Lights. Be sure to attend the community's yuletide festival if you're in the area during the holidays. It lasts the whole month. (541) 482-3486.

Year-round
Southern Oregon University Theatre Arts. The university presents a variety of classics, musicals, and contemporary plays each academic year. (541) 552-6348; www.sou.edu/THTR/season.html.

Lithia Park (all ages)
Located just off Siskiyou Boulevard; (541) 488-5340; www.ashland.or.us. Open dawn to dusk. Free.

A green and lovely place, Lithia Park is at the heart of this romantically small town. Designed by John McLaren, the architect who gave San Francisco Golden Gate Park, Lithia Park is now a recognized National Historic Site. Near the entrance to the park is a small fountain, bubbling forth mineral water from Lithia Springs, which has been said to have curative powers. Kids will love the romping in the playground, exploring the large meadow, and wading in Lithia Creek.

ScienceWorks Hands-On Museum (all ages)

1500 E. Main St.; (541) 482-6767; www.scienceworksmuseum.org. Open Wed through Sat 10 a.m. to 4 p.m., Sun noon to 4 p.m., open until 5 p.m. in summer, $ kids 2 to 12; $$ teens and adults.

This is a state-of-the-art museum for explorers of all ages. It offers interactive exhibits, science shows, and an outdoor garden.

Ashland Rogue Valley Growers' and Crafters' Market (all ages)

At the National Guard Armory at the corner of E. Main Street and Mountain Avenue. Open 9 a.m. to 1:30 p.m. every Tues, Mar to Oct.

Ashland is known for its organic food and handmade arts culture, and this market shows it off well.

Medford

Medford's prosperity turned from gold in the 1800s to agricultural activity—it's still a world center for pears—and it is a major business and medical center in southern Oregon.

Butte Creek Mill (ages 5 and up)

402 Royal Ave. N, Eagle Point; (541) 826-3531; www.buttecreekmill.com; e-mail: info@buttecreekmill.com. Open Mon through Sat 9 a.m. to 5 p.m., Sun 11 a.m. to 5 p.m. Free.

Oregon's only original water-powered gristmill has been operating continuously since 1872, when two 1,400-pound French buhr millstones were brought around Cape Horn by ship, then transported over the mountains by wagon. The building itself, open for self-guided tours, is a living museum. Your kids will be intrigued by the way the waterwheel turns the stones to grind the grains into flour. To continue the old-fashioned family entertainment, bring a picnic to enjoy in the park across the stream, and walk across the Antelope Creek Covered Bridge, also nearby. You can buy Butte Creek Mill products online and at the Country Store located on the property.

Harry and David (ages 5 and up)

1314 Center Dr.; (877) 322-1200, (541) 864-2278, or (541) 776-2277; www.harryanddavid.com. Tours are offered 4 times a day on weekdays, 9:15 a.m. to 1:45 p.m. by reservation. $, children 12 and under free.

If your kids love fruit, take them on a tour of one of the largest mail-order companies in the world. The tour takes you through the plant that packages gift baskets of delectable fruits, from Oregon-grown ruby silk pears to ruby cream bananas; to the candy kitchen where an assortment of chocolate truffles are created before your eyes; and on to the bakery where baklava, loaf cakes, and fruit pastry confections will get your mouths watering—just in time to return to the retail store. You can also visit the store on your own.

Top Medford **Events**

April

Pear Blossom Festival. Among the activities are the 10-mile Pear Blossom Run, bicycle races, arts and crafts, and a parade. (541) 734-7327.

May

Art in Bloom. Artistic renditions of smudge pots. Stuff for kids. http://art-in-bloom.com.

Summer

Bear Creek Park Concerts. Concerts are held in the park on Sunday evenings. (541) 774-2400.

Movies in Bear Creek Park. Free family movies select Saturday nights at 7 p.m. (541) 774-2400.

September

Multicultural Fair. A 1-day event highlighting the region's many cultures through food, music, dance, and arts and crafts. The Storytelling Teepee and muraling activities are especially popular with kids. (541) 618-1910.

November

GingerBread Jubilee. Chefs, caterers, and other locals use all-edible ingredients to create architectural masterpieces. The "houses" are auctioned off for charity but are available for community viewing. A great way to get inspired for the holidays. (541) 779-6972.

December

Winter Light Festival. Tree lighting, kids' crafts, music, food and a visit from Santa are sure to get the whole family in the holiday spirit. (541) 774-2400; www.ci.medford.or.us.

The Farm (ages 3 and up)

51 S. Stage Rd.; (541) 535-1316; www.visitthefarm.org. Open Fri through Sun 10 a.m. to 4 p.m. weather permitting. $.

This is a staple of any Medford visit for our family, because there's no better way for kids to learn about animals than by hanging out with them. Kids can ride ponies and feed and pet pygmy goats, lambs, bunnies, chickens, and even a couple of wallabies. Take time to explore the Adventure Areas, where you can watch sheep shearing, try your hand at (fake) steer roping, or see what's new in the baby exhibit. Bring a picnic lunch to enjoy at covered tables outside, and buy homemade goods and educational books at the gift store.

Fun Fact

When Medford sprang up in the wake of the Oregon and California Railroad, nearby Jacksonville, unhappy with the competition, referred to it as Chaparral City, perhaps as a means of depressing the pretensions of the upstart rival community.

Kid Time! Discovery Experience (ages 1½ to 8)
226 N. Ross Lane; 541-772-9922. Open Mon through Sat 10 a.m. to 5 p.m., Sun 11 a.m. to 4 p.m. $ adults, $$ children 2 and up. Under 2 free.

Educational programs and hands-on activities like the Brainforest, Construction Zone, Toddler Time, Art Alley, and Water Works will keep younger kids engaged.

Medford Railroad Park (ages 3 and up)
Located near the Rogue Valley Mall on Berrydale Avenue off Table Rock Road; (541) 774-2400; www.soc-nrhs.org/medfordrrpark.htm. Open second and fourth Sun, Apr through Oct, 11 a.m. to 3 p.m. Free; donations appreciated.

Train buffs have put together miniature steam, diesel, and electric trains that run along a mile of track. Parents and kids are welcome to take rides. Bring lunch to eat in the picnic pavilion.

Joseph H. Stewart State Recreation Area (all ages)
Located 35 miles northeast of Medford on Highway 62; (800) 551-6949 or (541) 560-3334, (800) 452-5687 (camping reservations). Always open. Free.

The park has a marina with a cafe and store and a swimming beach for cooling off during the summer. It also features 5½ miles of hiking trails and a 6-mile bike trail. Campsites are available, too ($).

Crater Rock Museum (ages 5 and up)
2002 Scenic Ave., Central Point; located 6 miles north of Medford off Highway 99; (541) 664-6081; www.craterrock.com. Open Tues through Sat 10 a.m. to 4 p.m. $ adults and kids over 5; 5 and under free.

The museum offers amazing displays of rocks, minerals, and gems, plus fossils and Native American artifacts. The gift shop displays works from local artists.

Fish Lake Resort (all ages)
Located 30 miles west of Medford and 39 miles east of Klamath Falls off Highway 140; (541) 949-8500; www.fishlakeresort.net. Open year-round. $–$$$$.

You'll find this resort by a Cascade lake near the foot of Mt. McLoughlin. It includes cabins, RV and tent sites, a cafe, store, game room, and boat rentals. The lake offers fishing and swimming, but no speedboats or waterskiing. The site is located near hiking, mountain-biking, and cross-country ski trails.

Jacksonville

Located just west of Medford, Jacksonville, at the entrance to Applegate Gate Valley Wine Country, was at the heart of southern Oregon's gold rush that began in 1852, and the entire town has since been put on the National Register of Historic Places. If you'd like to explore Jacksonville and learn more about its history, take a narrated trolley ride through town.

Self-Guided Audio Tours (all ages)
Rent tours at the Jacksonville Visitors Center, 185 N. Oregon St., or at businesses throughout town, or download them at www.jacksonvilleoregon.org.

Nineteenth-century Jacksonville comes to life in four narrated, self-guided audio tours enlivened with sounds of the era and voices of pioneers who settled southern Oregon. Choose from the tour of Jacksonville's Historic Commercial Core, the Historic Home Tour, the dramatic tales of the Pioneer Cemetery Tour, and the natural history of the Woodlands Trails Tour.

Beekman Bank (ages 6 and up)
Corner of California and Third Streets. Open 1 to 5 p.m. in summer. Free.

The Beekman Bank was Oregon's first bank, opened during the Jacksonville gold rush in 1863 by Wells Fargo agent C. C. Beekman. It's one of several historical buildings now run by the fledgling Jacksonville Heritage Society—including the old jail, the Rectory, and the Beekman House—so hours for all may expand or change as the organization grows.

Children's Museum (all ages)
206 N. Fifth St.; (541) 773-6536. Hours vary. $

This child-oriented attraction is located in the adjoining County Jail. Kids appreciate the pioneer exhibit area, where the usual museum refrain "Look but don't touch" doesn't apply. The collection of antique toys is also a favorite.

Gin Lin Mining Trail (ages 3 and up)
Located 15 miles south of Jacksonville in the Rogue River National Forest; (541) 618-2200 or (541) 899-1812; www.fs.fed.us/r6/rogue-siskiyou. Always open. Free.

The easy ¾-mile trail tells the story of a Chinese miner whose claim on this stretch of the Siskiyous yielded more than $1 million in gold dust. An interpretive brochure, available at the trailhead, describes numbered stops along the way. A guide is also available online.

Top Jacksonville **Events**

February

Chinese New Year Celebration. A parade with lion and dragon teams, plus music, dancers, rickshaw martial arts, and kids' activities, makes for midwinter color and excitement. (541) 899-8118; www.socca.us.

June through Labor Day

Britt Festivals. Renowned musicians converge here to wow audiences in a peaceful outdoor setting. (800) 882-7488; www.brittfest.org.

July

Children's Festival. Held on the Britt grounds, this event is especially fun for children ages 2 to 12. The whole family can enjoy arts and crafts, food, and live entertainment. (541) 774-8678.

December

Victorian Christmas. Strolling carolers and horse-drawn carriage rides add a festive holiday atmosphere in this famous gold-rush town. (541) 899-8118.

Applegate Lake (all ages)

Located in the Rogue River National Forest, 23 miles southwest of Medford; (541) 899-1812 or (541) 899-9220 (store, summer); www.applegatelake.com. Always open, though store and some campgrounds close in winter and water levels may restrict recreational activity. Some free sites; others require a $ fee.

This is a great place to spend the day swimming, boating, fishing, or hiking on one of several trails around the lake. Hartish Park, on the west shore, is a charming spot for picnicking and there are several campsites around the lake.

Grants Pass

The Rogue River is one of the most popular destinations in Oregon, and it runs through Grants Pass. Immortalized by writer Zane Grey, this mighty 215-mile river is famous worldwide for its stunning beauty, from the headwaters in Crater Lake National Park to the Pacific Ocean. The wild and scenic section of the river brings thousands to challenge its whitewater canyons in rafts and kayaks.

Hellgate Jetboat Excursions (ages 8 and up)

966 SE Sixth St.; (800) 648-4874 or (541) 476-2628; www.hellgate.com; e-mail: info@hellgate .com. Operates May through Sept; call for schedules. Hellgate Quick and Scenic Trip (2 hours, 36 miles): $$$$, children 3 and under free.

The original jet boat tour company on this part of the river, Hellgate trips leave from the Riverside Motel, off Seventh Street, to either Hellgate Canyon (made famous by John Wayne's Rooster Cogburn) or Grave Creek. The brunch and dinner trips include a meal at the OK Corral.

Wildlife Images Rehabilitation Center (all ages)

11845 Lower River Rd., 13 miles west of Grants Pass; (541) 476-0222; www.wildlifeimages .org. Tours offered daily by reservation; tour times change per season. Call at least a day ahead for reservations, as tours fill quickly, especially in summer. $$ adults, $ kids 4 to 17, under 4 by donation.

Grants Pass–**Area Parks**

Take both your picnic and a Frisbee to any of the four parks in and near town where your family can play Disc Golf. You toss your whirling disc at the "holes," which are actually wire baskets mounted atop poles.

- **Riverside Park** (all ages). Located downtown on the Rogue River; (541) 471-6435. Open dawn to dusk. Riverside Park has a 9-hole course that is perfect for beginners.

- **Tom Pearce Park** (all ages). Located off Foothill Boulevard about 5 miles from Grants Pass's town center; (541) 474-5285. Open dawn to dusk. This park has a "pro" 18-hole course that's used in competitions.

- **Indian Mary Park** (all ages). Located on Merlin-Galice Road about 10 miles from exit 61 off I-5; (541) 474-5285. Open dawn to dusk. There's a 9-hole course as well as camping and picnicking facilities along the Rogue.

- **Lake Selmac** (all ages). Located 25 miles southwest of Grants Pass off Lake Shore Drive; (541) 474-5285; www.co .josephine.or.us/parks. Open daily year-round. Free for day use; camping $. This 160-acre lake has the only lakeside park in the county system. It's a beautiful spot for fishing, sailing, swimming, hiking, and camping, and there are picnic shelters, ball fields, a playground, and boat ramps.

Top Grants Pass **Events**

May

Boatnik Festival. Adventurous whitewater buffs compete over a 50-mile course on the Rogue River. A parade, art shows, and carnival are also a part of this lively weekend event. Boatnik is one of many events throughout Amazing May, the kickoff of the summer events season. (800) 547-5927 or (541) 476-7717; www.boatnik.com.

July

Back to the Fifties. Downtown Grants Pass steps into the past. Locals dress in retro costume and the streets close for outdoor sock hops, Elvis impersonators, and classic-car cruises. (541) 476-5573.

July & August

Concerts in the Park. Make your way to Riverside Park downtown on Tuesday evenings, 6:30 to 8:30 p.m., for a variety of entertainers. (541) 476-7717.

August

Josephine County Fair. This old-fashioned event with carnival rides and pig races is certain to entertain your brood. A favorite event is the 4-wheel-drive log pull. (541) 476-3215; www.jocofair.com.

August through September

Jedediah Smith Mountain Man Rendezvous. Authentic clothing and muzzle-loaders turn Sportsman's Park into a pioneer settlement filled with brawny mountain adventurers and pioneer women who forged a new life in this vast, wild land. It includes demonstrations of the firearms, lifestyle, clothing, and crafts of that period.

Visitors to this wildlife rescue program get a close-up look at how the center aids and nurtures injured and orphaned animals, including bears, cougars, raccoons, and birds of prey. From May through Oct, weather permitting, catch a vintage open-air trolley at Sixth and G Streets (departs 3 times daily) for a 3-hour trip to the center and back, including the tour ($$$ adult, $$ child including tour).

Grants Pass Historical Walking Tour (ages 5 and up)
(800) 547-5927, (541) 476-7717, or (541) 476-5510; www.visitgrantspass.org. Always open. **Free.**

Take a self-guided walking tour of the town's historical neighborhoods, where you will see some of the most impressive early-20th-century architectural styles in southern Oregon.

Downtown Grants Pass is now a National Historic District, and many of these buildings also house irresistible antiques shops and restaurants. On Sat from mid-Mar through Thanksgiving weekend, stop by the Grower's Market, 9 a.m. to 1 p.m., for fresh produce and local crafts. During summer the market operates on Wed as well.

Valley of the Rogue State Park (all ages)

Located about 10 miles east of Grants Pass, just off I-5 near the town of Rogue River; (800) 452-5687 for reservations; (800) 551-6949 or (541) 582-1118 for information; www.oregon stateparks.org. Open year-round for camping, dawn to dusk for day use. Free day use; $ for camping, depending on season and type of accommodation.

Perhaps one of the most popular campgrounds in the state due to its proximity to I-5, Valley of the Rogue also offers a picnic area along the river, which lets you watch boaters launch rafts and kayaks into this placid body of water. Across the river is the site of a fort, and the land around the park itself was once used briefly as a reservation for Takilma Indians.

House of Mystery at the Oregon Vortex (all ages)

4303 Sardine Creek Rd., Gold Hill; past Valley of the Rogue State Park about 3 miles on I-5; (541) 855-1543; www.oregonvortex.com. Open daily Mar through Oct 9 a.m. to 4 p.m. (last tour at 3:15 p.m.), except summer, 9 a.m. to 5 p.m. (last tour at 4:15 p.m.). $$, 5 and under free.

This is the spot of the Oregon Vortex, which proprietors claim is the area of unusual phenomena that Native Americans called the Forbidden Ground. Kids love the strange sensations produced by trying to stand up straight when the walls and floors around all seem slanted. The visual phenomena are fun to experience, and, who knows, maybe it's not just an optical illusion.

Cave Junction

Cave Junction, Oregon's third-oldest town, sits in what is called the Illinois Valley, where the east and west forks of the Illinois River join on the journey down the Siskiyou mountainsides toward the Rogue River and the sea. More than a dozen creeks find their way into the Illinois in Cave Junction, making rushing waters a common sound just about anywhere in town. **Illinois River Forks State Park** lies less than a mile south of Cave Junction along the West Fork Illinois River. On hot days your kids will appreciate the cooling water and will enjoy splashing among the rocks. There are picnic tables for a leisurely riverside lunch.

Great Cats World Park (all ages)

Located 1.2 miles south of Cave Junction at 27919 Redwood Hwy.; (541) 592-2957; www .greatcatsworldpark.com. Open year-round (by appointment only in Dec and Jan). Call for hours. Adults $$$, kids $$, under 3 free.

The whole family will be mesmerized by the close-up sights of this awesome group of big cats, from lynxes to leopards to lions. Educational programs, animal demonstrations, and guided tours are available.

Oregon Caves National Monument (ages 6 and up)

19000 Caves Hwy., 19 miles from Cave Junction on Highway 46; (541) 592-2100; www.nps .gov/orca. Cave tours closed winter; trails open year-round. Call for tour times, which vary seasonally. $$, under 6 free.

Your children will be awestruck in this underground wonderland. The cavernous spaces, the strange formations, and the sound of water echoing off the marble cave walls all combine to produce an eerie, yet wondrous, experience. Have your kids look for the "ghosts," spectral shapes that hang from the cave ceilings. Cave temperature is a constant 41 degrees, so wear a sweater and slacks and also sturdy shoes. Camera tripods and walking aids such as canes are not allowed in the cave, nor are strollers. Children under 6 are permitted only if they are at least 42 inches tall and can handle the sometimes steep stairways on their own. There's a special free 20-minute tour for those under 42 inches in height.

While you wait for the tour to start, explore aboveground, where a nature trail leads you on a cliff-top loop about 1/10 mile long. Trailside signs identify the plant life, and you're likely to encounter a little wildlife along the way as well. **No Name Trail,** about 1 1/10 miles round-trip, takes you past gurgling mountain streams and mossy cliff sides, through dense forest with wildflowers in the undergrowth. Another trail follows Cave Creek 1 1/5 miles to Cave Creek Campground. Allow several hours for your visit.

Oregon Caves Chateau (all ages)

20000 Caves Hwy.; (541) 592-3400, (877) 245-9022; www.oregoncaveschateau.com. Call for hours. Closed late Oct through mid-Apr. Free for day visitors; $$$–$$$$.

This 1934 chateau is a treasure trove of the past and a designated National Historic Landmark. The 6-story lodge is nestled among waterfalls in the rugged Siskiyou Mountains. Most of the furnishings have been making people comfortable for more than 60 years. Park rangers hold slide talks here, and you can treat your kids to an ice cream cone at the beautiful old wooden soda fountain. Lodging is available from early May through late Oct and fills quickly; make reservations by phone or online.

Fun Fact

The Illinois River got its name from three 1847 pioneers from Peoria, Illinois, who discovered gold on the river. Samuel, John, and Phillip Althouse were among the early placer miners to find gold in southern Oregon.

Out 'N' About Treesort (ages 5 and up)

300 Page Creek Rd., about 10 miles from Cave Junction; (541) 592-2208; www.treehouses .com; e-mail: treesort@treehouses.com. Tours, rentals, horseback riding per hour, tree climbing/rappelling. Call for rates and reservations, which fill far in advance.

One of the most unusual places to stay is a bed-and-breakfast that rents a standard ground-level cabin (very cozy, sleeps 5), and 13 lofty perches in white oak trees. The Family Tree House has two cabins linked by a swinging bridge. Kids think this is the next thing to heaven—or Disneyland. The freshwater swimming pool is fed by river water and the zip-line, Giant Tarzan Swing, and climbing tree offer thrills. Horseback riding is available, with guided trail rides (for ages 8 and older). Tours are offered daily in summer and off-season weekends noon to 5 p.m. You can tour unoccupied tree houses and experience the Mountain View Treeway—a high-rise walkway that includes 90-foot and 45-foot suspension bridges.

Roseburg

Douglas County Museum
of Natural & Cultural History (ages 6 and up)

123 Museum Dr., next to the County Fairgrounds; follow signs from I-5 at exit 123; (541) 957-7007; www.co.douglas.or/museum. Open daily 10 a.m. to 5 p.m., closed Sun Oct through Mar. $ adults, kids 17 and under free.

This is a surprisingly large museum with a nationally acclaimed collection in four separate wings. Exhibits range from the prized million-year-old saber-toothed tiger to an 1890 steam donkey used in local logging camps. Native American artifacts that predate Crater Lake, a "mud wagon" that traveled the roads of 19th-century southern Oregon, and a large collection of historic photographs (the largest in the state) will have your kids enthralled. They'll love the hands-on Discovery Room and Junior Rangers program, too.

Wildlife Safari (all ages)

1790 Safari Rd., Winston; take exit 119 from I-5 at Winston and follow signs on Highway 42 for about 5 miles; (541) 679-6761; www.wildlifesafari.net. Open daily except Christmas 9 a.m. to 5 p.m., 10 a.m. to 4 p.m. in winter. $$$, children 3 and under free. Discounts for Oregon Zoo members.

You'll find an open zoo where emus peck at your car windows and baby pygmy goats in the petting area beg for food in ice cream-cone cups. African elephants provide entertainment twice daily, and for an extra charge they'll "wash" your car. Trains run, weather permitting, within the central Safari Village, and you can grab a bite to eat in the White Rhino restaurant. Check out the petting zoo and botanical gardens, too. Animals may lay low when summer days get really hot, so time your visit for as early in the day as possible.

An Adventure to Remember

Snuggled tightly in the rolling hills of western Douglas County, Wildlife Safari has come a long way since its beginnings in the 1970s as a for-profit open-zoo enterprise. Today the 600-acre savanna successfully provides a natural habitat that closely resembles the native homes of elephants, bears, gazelles, rhinos, zebras, and ostriches, among others. And it's now a member of the Safari Game Search Foundation, a nonprofit organization dedicated to animal conservation, education, research, and rehabilitation. The grounds provide a marvelous opportunity for you and your family to observe animal interaction in an unrestrained, bucolic setting. If you're near Roseburg, include this destination in your travels.

Diamond Lake (all ages)

Located 76 miles east of Roseburg off N. Umpqua Highway. Umpqua National Forest Diamond Lake Ranger District: (541) 498-2531 (weekdays) or (541) 793-3310 (weekends); www .fs.fed.us/r6/umpqua. Three campgrounds with more than 400 campsites; some campsites can be reserved by calling (877) 444-6777 or online at www.reserveusa.com; campsites usually open late May through Sept. Diamond Lake RV Park: 3 miles from Diamond Lake Lodge on the south end of the lake; (541) 793-3318. Diamond Lake Resort: 350 Resort Dr.; (800) 733-7593 or (541) 793-3333; www.diamondlake.net; e-mail: info@diamondlake.net.

Diamond Lake has long been a favorite destination for Oregon families, often discovered while in the area to see the more famous Crater Lake. It's a fabulous year-round destination—swimming, boating, fishing, and hiking in summer; cross-country skiing, snowshoeing, and snowmobiling in winter. The USDA Forest Service maintains several hundred campsites and numerous hiking trails, plus there's an RV park on the south side of the lake. But the true family fun center is **Diamond Lake Resort,** which has it all. It offers lodge rooms, guest cabins, and studios with kitchens, along with a coin-op laundry, grocery store, cafe, dining room, pizza parlor, and service station. The resort's marina, corrals, and bicycling are described below. Call for specific prices.

- **Diamond Lake Marina.** In addition to a full-service bait-and-tackle shop, the marina rents motorboats, patio boats, and paddleboats, bumper boats, and single or double kayaks.

- **Diamond Lake Bicycling.** Also at the marina, Diamond Back mountain bikes are available to rent for riding the 12-mile Forest Service paved bike path around the lake. You'll also find backcountry dirt roads and trails; ask marina staff for directions to the best sites for your family's interests and skill levels. Helmets provided.

- **Diamond Lake Corrals.** Guided horseback rides are available from mid-June until the snow arrives in the fall. One-hour rides leave on the hour 9 a.m. to 4 p.m. (except at noon and 1 p.m.). Three-hour rides depart at 9 a.m. and 2 p.m. An all-day ride takes you to the top of Tipsoo Peak. Suppers from the Chuck Wagon and group wagon and buggy rides are also available. The corrals are closed Sun, except for holiday weekends.

- **Winter Recreation.** In winter the resort offers guided snowmobile tours. There are 8 miles of groomed cross-country ski trails, plus more than 50 miles of marked backcountry trails for all ski abilities. The 12-mile path circling the lake also makes a great ski trail. The North Store offers skis, boots, and poles for rent. Call for prices.

Rafting and Bicycling   (ages 8 and up)

A number of outfitters offer guided fishing and whitewater trips on the North Umpqua River. Two local outdoor specialists are:

- **North Umpqua Outfitters.** 222 Oakview Dr.; (888) 454-9696; www.nuorafting.com; e-mail: info@umpquarivers.com. Call or e-mail for schedules and prices.
- **Oregon Ridge and River Excursions.** P.O. Box 495, Glide, OR 97443; (541) 496-3333 or (888) 454-9696; www.umpquarivers.com. Call for schedules and prices. Oregon Ridge is a reference to mountain-bike excursions, which they also offer.

Top Roseburg **Events**

June through August

Music on the Half Shell. Located in lovely Stewart Park, this free summer series features a variety of music programs ranging from zydeco and Cajun to country and African. Pack a picnic dinner and relax! (800) 444-9584, ext. 10, or (541) 672-2648; www.halfshell.org.

July

Graffiti Week. A regional event that attracts locals and 1950s car owners for car shows, a fun run, concerts, and '50s-style fun. (800) 444-9584.

August

Douglas County Fair. This classic fair attracts surprisingly big-name music acts and offers traditional fair treats. (541) 957-7010.

September

Umpqua Wine, Art, and Food Festival. Umpqua Community College's recently opened School of Viticulture hosts this annual festival for wine lovers and families alike. Kids' favorites are the Wildlife Safari petting zoo, Wizard's Castle, and miniature horses. (541) 459-1385; www.uvwineartand music.com.

Stewart Park (all ages)

Located on Stewart Parkway on the west side of town, off Garden Valley Road; (541) 672-7701. Open dawn to dusk. **Free.**

Kids love climbing on the old steam locomotive in the large playground and exploring the butterfly garden. The 230-acre park also has horseshoe pits and tennis courts, wide green fields, and a nature trail leading from the wildlife pond through an old orchard and along the North Umpqua River. On Tues evenings in summer take your kids to an outdoor concert at the band shell.

Stewart Park also has an excellent skate park at NW Goetz Street. For more information, you can check in with the Umpqua Skaters Association (541-673-1414) or visit the website at www.skateoregon.com/Roseburg/Roseburg.html.

Susan Creek Falls Trail (ages 5 and up)

Starts in the day-use area of the Susan Creek Campground, off Highway 138 about 28 miles east of Roseburg; (541) 440-4930; www.blm.gov/or/resources/recreation. Always open. $; day use **free.**

This trail leads to a group of fascinating Indian mounds. You'll walk through a young forest of mixed conifers and madrones with a thick undergrowth of salal, fern, and huckleberry. At ¾ mile the falls cascade nearly 70 feet down a cliff side into a boulder-bordered pool. Beyond the falls, follow the footbridge up a fairly steep hill for another ½ mile to the mounds—ceremonial rock piles prepared by young men in spiritual quest. These are cultural treasures that should not be disturbed. The campground also houses 31 campsites that are open May through Oct.

Crater Lake National Park

Crater Lake National Park (all ages)

P.O. Box 7, Crater Lake, OR 97604; (541) 594-3000, www.nps.gov/crla for park information; (888) 774-2728, www.craterlakelodges.com for lodging and boat-tour information. Park is open year-round, $$ for 7-day vehicle pass. Camping available when snow clears in early summer, $; the historic Crater Lake Lodge is open late May through mid-Oct, $$$$; and the Cabins at Mazama Village (7 miles from the rim) are open year-round, $$$$. North entrance is located off Highway 138, from Roseburg; 2 visitor centers—Steel Information Center, at the junction of the south entrance road and Rim Drive, and the Rim Village Visitor Center, near the east end of the parking area—provide a wealth of information. The south gate park entrance is off Highway 62, which runs between Medford and Klamath Falls. In winter, this is the only access to the park. Rim Drive is closed in winter, but intrepid Nordic skiers can take the 33-mile unplowed road circling the rim of the lake on skis. Watch for ice, and check with park rangers for avalanche warnings first.

It's difficult not to describe Crater Lake in superlatives: The bluest water, the most dramatic contrasts, and the clearest air all leave visitors invigorated for days. Away from the lake itself, the forests are rich with surprises—deep river canyons, sparkling waterfalls,

Free Things to Do at Crater Lake

- **Mazama Campground Amphitheater.** Your family will enjoy the public programs offered in the amphitheater in summer, including guided nature walks and evening talks.

- **Steel Information Center**. The center shows the movie *Crater Lake* every half hour in summer. (541) 594-3100.

- **Sinnott Memorial Overlook Museum.** This museum has exhibits and displays on the origin and history of the lake. There are also scheduled ranger talks.

bright and delicate wildflowers. You'll want to take your time exploring here. The geology and history of the area are equally fascinating. In the past 750,000 years, explosive eruptions created a series of volcanic peaks along what we now call the Cascade Range. Mt. Mazama, which holds Crater Lake in its peak, was one of these, and for 500,000 years it erupted regularly. About 7,700 years ago the most violent eruption of all took place in a series of massive explosions 42 times more powerful than Mt. St. Helens's 1980 blast. The winds scattered as much as 6 inches of ash over 5,000 square miles, covering 8 states and 3 Canadian provinces. In the **Pumice Desert,** north of the rim, the ash is 50 feet deep. The eruptions emptied the mountain of magma, removing the support for the mountain peak. The peak collapsed, forming the bowl-shaped caldera that, at first, was too hot to hold water. As volcanic activity slowed, the caldera filled with water. The volcano has been silent for 4,000 years.

Many children prefer the Klamath Indian version of events that created the mountain lake. A battle began between the god of the world above, Skell, who lived on Mt. Shasta to the south, and the evil god of the world below, Llao. Skell won the battle, beheading the mountain of Llao and forever ridding the world of his evil influence, leaving in his place a beautiful mirrored lake that reflects the sky. Look for **Llao Rock,** which dominates the northwest portion of the lake and faces **Skell Head,** across the lake on the east side. From the parking lot at the rim, walk the paved path down to the **Sinnott Memorial Overlook,** where a rock shelter hewn from the side of the caldera provides a breathtaking view. A topographical relief map of Mt. Mazama shows the lake, **Wizard Island,** and the surrounding area. Along the park's south entrance road on Highway 62, stop at one of several pullouts or picnic areas to view a breathtaking canyon through which Annie Creek runs more than 250 feet below.

To explore the environs of Crater Lake more deeply, take the **Annie Creek Trail,** which leaves between Loops D and E in the Mazama Campground and follows a 1 7/10-mile loop descending 200 feet to the valley floor and along the stream before ascending the rim to complete the circuit. Other trails to explore are the **Castle Crest Wildflower Trail,** a 2/5-mile loop that begins across from the Steel Information Center just beyond the

Fun Fact

Crater Lake is the deepest lake in North America, the second-deepest in the Western Hemisphere, and the seventh-deepest in the world.

junction of East and West Rim Drives, and the **Godfrey Glen Nature Trail,** about 1 mile beyond Mazama Village on the road to the rim. Rangers sometimes lead walks, or you can purchase inexpensive leaflets at the trailhead. The only safe—and legal—access to the lake is the 1-mile **Cleetwood Cove Trail,** on West Rim Drive about 13 miles from Rim Village. You must be in good physical condition to attempt this steep hike down the walls of the caldera. Once there, you can dip your feet in the water or try your hand at catching some of the kokanee salmon or rainbow trout that remain in the lake, which was stocked with these species between 1888 and the 1940s, when park rangers decided to allow the lake to return to its natural state. During the summer, boat tours of the lake offer up-close views with trips leaving from the Cleetwood Cove dock. The Volcanic Cruise Boat Tour is the only company allowed to have boats on the lake. The trips provide views from inside the caldera. You can also stop and spend some time hiking roughly 1 mile to the top of Wizard Island, returning on a later tour. The 2-hour narrated tour takes you past the **Phantom Ship,** remnants of an older volcano and dike that were exposed after the great eruption. The boat tours operate daily late June through mid-Sept, weather permitting. The Annie Creek Restaurant & Gift Shop near the south entrance is open from early June through Oct. Construction has been ongoing at Rim Village, so contact the park for updated information on concession facilities available.

Klamath Falls

Klamath Falls sits on the southern tip of Upper Klamath Lake, the largest lake in the state at 58,992 acres, with Mt. McLoughlin casting its reflection in the waters. In the summer you can hop aboard a restored 1906 trolley for a ride through the downtown area to get a sense of the area and its history.

Baldwin Hotel Museum (ages 5 and up)
31 Main St.; located in the old Baldwin Hotel; (541) 883-4207. Open June through Sept Wed through Sat 10 a.m. to 4 p.m. Two-hour, 4-floor tour $$, 1-hour, 2-floor tour $; children 4 and under free. Family rates available. Last half-hour tour at 2:30 p.m.

Guided tours take you back to the early 1900s, with the original furnishings and many photographs by the builder's talented daughter.

Children's Museum of Klamath Falls (all ages)

711 E. Main St.; (541) 885-2995; www.cmkf.org. Open Wed through Sat 10 a.m. to 2 p.m. $$.

Kids can experiment with scopes of all kinds, make music in the multimedia area, climb into a real cockpit, or follow the model train through a small-scale countryside.

Favell Museum of Western Art and Indian Artifacts (ages 5 and up)

125 W. Main St.; (541) 882-9996; www.favellmuseum.org. Open Tues through Sat 10 a.m. to 5 p.m. $$ adults, $ ages 6 to 16, children under 6 free.

Arrowheads, ceremonial knives, stone- and beadwork, basketry, and pottery captivate the kids. See the silver treasure from an abandoned wagon train and tour the walk-in vault display of miniature working firearms, including a Gatling gun.

Klamath County Museum (ages 5 and up)

1451 Main St.; (541) 883-4208. Open Tues through Sat 9 a.m. to 5 p.m. $, children 4 and under free.

Natural history, Indian and pioneer history, and agricultural development are all on display in the museum. Your kids will see up close some of the birds and animals they might encounter in the natural areas around Klamath Falls, and they'll learn about the geothermal energy resources that have been used in the area for centuries.

Lake of the Woods (all ages)

Located 42 miles east of Medford and 32 miles west of Klamath Falls off Highway 140; (866) 201-4194; www.lakeofthewoodsresort.com or www.fs.fed.us/r6/frewin. Hours vary by season; call ahead. Lodging: $$$–$$$$; restaurants: $–$$$.

This is a high-mountain lake in the Cascades with Forest Service campgrounds, summer camps, private cabins, picnic area, resort with cabins, restaurant, pizza parlor, store, and boat rentals. Swimming, waterskiing, fishing, and canoeing are available. In summer watch lakeside vintage movies Fri nights; on Sat nights join the dancing at the family barbecue and bonfire.

Volcanic Legacy Scenic Byway

As the name implies, this roadway has been designated a scenic byway for the beauty created by millennia of volcanic activity. In 1999 the federal government awarded All American Road status to this spectacular byway, which includes Crater Lake National Park, the most dramatic feature of the drive. Along the way you'll see a pumice desert, ancient natural chimneys (called fumaroles) along Annie Creek, canyons, and the lush wildlife refuge of Upper Klamath Lake. (800) 445-6728; www.travelklamath.com or www.sova.org /volcanic.

Upper Klamath Canoe Trail (all ages)

Begins at Malone Springs launch 4 miles from the junction of Highway 140 and W. Side Road (take Rocky Point turnoff), northwest of Klamath Falls; (530) 667-2331; www.fws.gov /klamathbasinrefuges/ukcanoe.html. Open dawn to dusk. **Free.**

The canoe trails meander through marshland on the edge of Upper Klamath Lake. You can rent canoes ($$$ per hour) at Rocky Point Resort on Rocky Point Road (541-356-2287; www.rockypointoregon.com).

Klamath & Western Railroad Inc. (all ages)

Located 27 miles north of Klamath Falls at 36851 S. Chiloquin Rd. in Chiloquin; (541) 783-7763; www.hobby-tronics.com/KNW. Open Sun Memorial Day through Labor Day. Call for hours and prices.

The club operates a ⅛-scale train park that is open to the public during summer months. Bring a picnic to enjoy at tables set up for guests. The trains, a mixture of diesel and live steam engines, pull cars with comfortable seats, roomy enough for adults, along thousands of feet of track.

Collier Memorial State Park
and Logging Museum (all ages)

Located 30 miles north of Klamath Falls; (800) 551-6949 or (541) 783-2471; www.oregon stateparks.org. Open dawn to dusk; call for museum hours. **Free.**

The museum side of the park is open year-round and houses rotating exhibits; camping is closed in winter. Straddling the highway, the park has a beautiful picnic area in a shaded ponderosa pine forest alongside the Williamson River and an open-air logging museum across the highway that some claim has the largest collection of logging equipment in the nation. Children appreciate the sense of scale and the absence of "do not touch" signs. There's also an authentic pioneer village with buildings relocated from their original sites.

Fort Klamath Museum (all ages)

Located on Highway 62, 2 miles south of Crater Lake; (541) 381-2230. Open Thurs through Mon 10 a.m. to 6 p.m. June through Sept. **Free;** donations appreciated.

The museum is housed in a military post that was established in 1863. The displays depict the Modoc Indian War of 1872–73. In the park are the graves of the fearless Modoc chief

Fun Facts

- The area boasts the largest wintering population of American bald eagles in the 48 contiguous states.
- Upper Klamath Lake, at 58,992 acres, is the largest lake in Oregon.

Top Klamath **Events**

August

Klamath County Fair & Carnival, and the **Jefferson Stampede Rodeo.** You'll receive a three-for-one series of events that fill your entire weekend. (541) 883-3796; www.kcfairgrounds.org; e-mail: KCFAIR@kcfairgrounds.org.

October

Scarecrow Row & Fall Festival. Join scarecrows in a parade, carve pumpkins, and take wagon rides through town, where food, crafts, and music await. (541) 205-4936.

December

Snowflake Festival. A holiday bazaar, parade, toy show, holiday play, and tree lighting help usher in the season. (800) 445-6728.

Captain Jack and three braves who fought against the US Army in the most extensive Indian war in the West.

Lakeview

First settled in the 1870s by sheep and cattle ranchers, Lakeview calls itself the "tallest town in Oregon" because it has the highest elevation above sea level of any incorporated town in the state.

Schminck Memorial Museum (ages 5 and up)
128 S. E St.; (541) 947-3134. Open Tues through Sat 10 a.m. to 4 p.m.; closed Dec and Jan. $, children under 13 free.

Kids love the doll and toy collection in the basement, and the old vacuum cleaners behind the kitchen area will bring on a few giggles. Baseball fans will covet the silk baseball cards of such early players as Ty Cobb and Rebel Oakes.

Warner Canyon Ski Area (ages 8 and up)
Located 11 miles northeast of Lakeview off Highway 140 in the Fremont National Forest; (541) 947-6040; www.lakecountychamber.org/skihill.html. Call for hours and lift prices.

With more than 20 downhill runs and several miles of Nordic trails, as well as great sledding opportunities, this county-run ski area is a great place for families with a hankering for some outdoor winter fun.

Top Lakeview **Events**

June

Junior Rodeo. For a chance to see young people compete on horseback, come to this event held early in the summer. (541) 947-6040.

September

Lake County Round-Up. The event is held during the Lake County Fair. A wild-cow milking contest is guaranteed to have your kids roaring with laughter. (541) 947-6040.

Fort Rock State Natural Area (all ages)

Located north of Silver Lake, 7 miles off Highway 31; (800) 551-6949; www.oregonstate parks.org. Always open. Free.

This area rises nearly 400 feet from the desert shelf. Archaeologists discovered 9,200-year-old woven sandals here, and one is now housed in the Lake County Museum.

Fort Rock Cave (all ages)

Located 2 miles northwest of the rock, within the Fort Rock State Natural Area; (800) 551-6949; www.oregonstateparks.org. Open daily, year-round. Free.

A ½-mile trail takes you inside an ancient volcanic maar that rose within a 40-mile-wide lake, which Native Americans lived by more than 10,000 years ago.

Lake County Museum (ages 5 and up)

118 S. G St.; (541) 947-2220. Open Mar through Dec; call for hours and days. $, children free.

Historical displays with artifacts portray the Native American culture indigenous to the area. One room features the region's Irish traditions.

Fremont-Winema National Forests

Located 8 miles west of Lakeview on Highway 140; (541) 947-2151; www.fs.fed.us/r6/frewin. Always open. Free.

The Fremont-Winema National Forests cover 2.3 million acres and have an abundance of lakes and streams for you to explore with your kids. **Drews Reservoir** is a popular spot for waterskiing as well as fishing and swimming. **Cottonwood Meadow Lake,** north of Highway 140, is surrounded by aspen and pine forests, with a trail that circles the lake and connects two camping areas. South of the highway, **Lofton Reservoir, Heart Lake, and Holbrook Reservoir** are accessible from various Forest Service roads, and all are well maintained even though some are gravel.

Hart Mountain National Antelope Refuge (all ages)

Located 65 miles northeast of Lakeview and 25 miles west of Plush; the road surface becomes gravel just before climbing the escarpment; (541) 947-3315; www.fws.gov/sheldon hartmtn. Open daily, year-round. Free.

Hart Mountain is accessible on mostly paved roads from the southern Oregon town of Lakeview. The refuge was established in 1936 to protect then dwindling herds of prong-horn antelope. It now also protects mule deer, sage grouse, California bighorn sheep, golden eagles, prairie falcons, and more than 250 other species of game and birds. It's common to see herds of pronghorns and other wildlife as you drive through this incredible area. Morning and evening are when animals are most active. Other features include undeveloped camping, fishing, hiking, historic cabins, and hot-springs bathing.

Warner Wetlands (all ages)

Located 39 miles northeast of Lakeview and 5 miles from Plush; (541) 947-2177; www.blm .gov/or/resources/recreation. Open daily, year-round. Free.

The wetlands are a series of pothole lakes along the western base of Hart Mountain and were established to protect the Warner Valley's unique features and restore critical wildlife habitat. The lakes and ponds go through a natural cycle of drying and filling that increases productivity by recycling nutrients and invigorating plant communities. At Hart Lake walking footpaths provide a nice trip along dikes to bird-viewing blinds. Bring binoculars and a bird identification book. Commonly seen birds include Canada geese, great blue

Family Favorites in Southern Oregon

1. Oregon Shakespeare Festival, Ashland

2. Rogue River, Grants Pass

3. Oregon Caves National Monument, near Cave Junction

4. Crater Lake National Park

5. The House of Mystery, near Grants Pass

6. Favell Museum of Western Art and Indian Artifacts, Klamath Falls

7. Fremont National Forest, near Lakeview

8. Out 'N' About Treesort, near Cave Junction

9. Wildlife Safari, Winston

10. Douglas County Museum of History and Natural History, Roseburg

Christmas Valley **Back Country Byway**

This drive takes you through vastly different scenery than most "scenic" drives, and it covers some of the most geologically interesting country in the state. The area is riddled with caves, a 325-foot rock towering over the desert, a "lost" forest of pines in the middle of the desert, the largest inland sand dune in the state, a giant crater, and a fissure in the earth approximately 2 miles long and up to 70 feet deep. The signed route departs from Highway 31 at the Fort Rock turnoff and follows a variety of roads (paved, gravel, and ghastly) before returning to Highway 31 just south of Silver Lake. A number of alternate routes are marked to help you avoid the ghastly roads if your vehicle doesn't have high clearance.

About 5 miles north of the Fort Rock cutoff and 1 mile off the highway, you'll come across a scene reminiscent of a science-fiction film—**Hole-in-the-Ground.** This massive crater, some 500 feet deep and covering a quarter acre, was formed by an explosion caused when molten lava hit water. In 1966 a group of astronauts used this spot to experience something close to what they expected the moon's surface to be like.

Some 5 miles farther down Highway 31, follow signs to **Fort Rock State Natural Area,** formed more than 5 million years ago when a volcanic explosion of molten rock erupted through a lake. It was in **Fort Rock Cave** near here that the oldest shoes in the world were found in 1938—75 sagebrush sandals made by people who inhabited the valley more than 9,000 years ago. The cave is a National Heritage Site and is open only by a state-park guided tour; call (541) 536-2428 at least 3 days in advance to arrange a tour. In the town of Fort Rock, stop by the **Homestead Village Museum,** open Wed through Sun from Memorial Day weekend through Sept (541-576-2251; www.fortrock oregon.com).

Derrick Cave, located off Derrick Caves Road northeast of Fort Rock, is a 30-foot-high lava tube nearly ¼ mile long with "rooms" nearly 40 feet wide and

herons, cinnamon teals, cormorants, white egrets, white pelicans, sandhill cranes, and yellow-headed blackbirds. Boating in the area depends on fluctuating water levels.

Where to Eat

IN ASHLAND

Alex's Plaza Restaurant. 35 N. Main St.; (541) 482-8818. Sitting alongside Ashland Creek, Alex's has a diverse menu sure to please everyone. $–$$$

60 feet high. It served as a fallout shelter during the Cuban missile crisis, with provisions for 1,000 people in case of nuclear war.

About 2 miles east of Christmas Valley is an area that was a huge lake 10,000 years ago. Now referred to as **Fossil Lake,** it covered the entire basin. This is one of the most significant sites in North America for ice age (Pleistocene) fossils. Note, however, that it is illegal to remove fossils from the area, but you can wander the dusty grounds and imagine the mammoths, camels, and miniature horses that once drank from the lakeshore here.

An alternate route from the byway takes you about 6 miles north of Christmas Valley along a graded gravel road to a fascinating place: **Crack-in-the-Ground.** Nearly 2 miles long and 12 feet wide, the 1,000-year-old fissure reaches a depth of 70 feet in some places. From the parking area, a ¼-mile trail takes you to the opening of the crack, from there descending about 400 yards into the earth. You can walk along an unofficial path at the top if you prefer.

Some 20 miles northeast of Christmas Valley, the **Lost Forest** seems misplaced more than lost—a 9,000-acre pine and juniper forest in the middle of a giant desert. Still, the forest is several thousand years old despite the minimal annual rainfall. The forest borders the largest sand dune in the state that's not next to the ocean. Composed of ash and pumice blown into the valley after Mt. Mazama erupted 7 millennia ago, the dunes cover 16,000 acres and sometimes reach as high as 60 feet.

For more information about the Christmas Valley Back Country Byway, call the Bureau of Land Management at (541) 947-2177 or Oregon State Parks at (800) 551-6949; additional information is online at www.blm.gov/or /resources/recreation.

Creekside Pizza. 92½ N. Main St.; (541) 482-4131. Also nestled along the creek with a full bar, this family friendly pizza place has appeal for grownups, too. $$

Morning Glory. 1149 Siskyou Blvd.; (541) 488-8636; www.morninggloryrestaurant.com. Fresh, good breakfast and lunch at reasonable prices. $–$$

Pangea Grill & Wraps. 272 E. Main St.; (541) 552-1630. A small, friendly place for lunch or dinner with healthy wraps, outstanding fresh soups, and other homemade delights. $–$$

Pasta Piatti. 358 E. Main St.; (541) 488-5493; www.pastapiatti.com. Light yet satisfying "new world" Italian fare in the heart of

Ashland. The outdoor patio is a delightful spot for a summer preshow dinner. $$–$$$

Señor Sam's. 1634 Ashland St.; (541) 488-1262. The specialty is healthy Mexican food. The restaurant received the "Best Burritos" in Ashland vote. $

Zoey's Café. 199 E. Main St.; (541) 482-4794. From delicious ice creams—try the Rogue Valley Pear and Oregon Trail—to calzones, wraps, and sandwiches, this is a family friendly place for freshly prepared foods. $–$$

IN CRATER LAKE NATIONAL PARK

Annie Creek Restaurant. In Mazama Village near the park's south entrance; (541) 594-2255; www.craterlakelodges.com; open June through mid-Sept. If you're not inclined toward the fancier setting of the Crater Lake Lodge restaurant, come here for pizza, pasta, salads, soups, and self-serve ice cream. $$–$$$

IN GRANTS PASS

Grants Pass Pharmacy and Soda Fountain. 414 SE Sixth St.; (541) 476-4262. Wow your kids with a trip to this old-fashioned soda counter for malts, ice cream, and sandwiches. The staff are as friendly as you'll find anywhere. $

The Laughing Clam. 121 SW G St.; (541) 479-1110. The menu at this casual family alehouse and eatery is varied enough to make everyone happy. $–$$

Wild River Brewing & Pizza Co. 595 NE E St.; (541) 471-7487. Here's a pizza place that serves its specialty with a flair. Parents appreciate the local microbrews. $–$$

IN JACKSONVILLE

Bella Union Restaurant. 170 W. California; (541) 899-1770; www.bellau.com. It may be housed in the building where the Bella Union Saloon was one of seven local bars in

1868, but you won't find typical saloon fare in this upscale spot. Instead your choices will include pasta, pizza, steak, and seafood. $$

Pony Espresso. 545 N. Fifth St.; (541) 899-3757. Soups, salads, coffee drinks. Old-time big coffee shop. Porch, drive-thru.

IN KLAMATH FALLS

The Klamath Grill. 715 Main St.; (541) 882-1427. The place where locals meet for hearty breakfasts, including "home-grown pancakes," and lunches. $–$$

Mia and Pia's Pizzeria and Brewhouse. 3545 Summers Lane; (541) 884-4880. A family pizza parlor that features an outdoor patio, kids' games, and glimpses of local history in the decor. It was Klamath County's first microbrewery. $$

IN LAKEVIEW

Happy Horse Deli & Antiques & Collectibles. 728 N. Fourth St.; (541) 947-4996. Along with freshly made soups, salads, and sandwiches, this lunchtime gathering place features rooms filled with precious and not-so-precious antiques, including many regional items. $–$$

Pizza Villa. 44 S. G St.; (541) 947-2531. This family-operated pizza parlor also offers hot sandwiches and features a kids' game area. $–$$

IN MEDFORD

Kaleidoscope Pizza. 3084 Crater Lake Hwy.; (541) 779-7787; www.kaleidoscope pizza.com. This lively and eclectic pizza place has repeatedly won the local paper's Best Pizza award, and it's big enough that your noisy kids won't be noticed. Hearty salads and calzones round out the menu. $$–$$$

Noho's Hawaiian Café. 703 E. Main St.; (541) 245-6919. Hawaiian food like grilled beef, chicken, and pork with yummy sauces and rice that's a sure palate-pleaser for the whole family. $$–$$$

Tin Tin Buffet. 2366 Poplar Dr.; (541) 776-8833. A surprisingly delightful and very clean strip-mall restaurant at the north end of town, close to the freeway. Fill your plate from 4 stations of all sorts of fresh Chinese food—including crab legs and other seafood delights, fresh sushi, lots of fruit, and all the kid-pleasing Chinese standards. Be sure to get a booth overlooking the koi pond! $$

IN ROSEBURG

Alexander's Greek Cuisine. 643 SW Jackson St.; (541) 672-6442; www.alexanders greekcuisine.com. Delicious and authentic Greek food at moderate prices. Facebook friends get discounts. $–$$

Brix. 527 SE Jackson St.; (541) 440-4901. Breakfast and lunch are reliable and delicious, and the staff are cheerful and family friendly. $–$$

Brutke's Wagon Wheel. 227 NW Garden Valley Blvd.; (541) 672-7555. This pasta and prime-rib eatery is a local family favorite. $$$–$$$$

Where to Stay

IN ASHLAND

Ashland Springs Hotel. 212 E. Main St.; (888) 795-4545; www.ashlandspringshotel .com. Ashland's most famous historic hotel treats you to reasonable luxury in the heart of town. Prepare for your day in the lovely lobby, or relax before dinner on the patio, where the kids can look at the fountain and English garden. $$$$

Bed-and-breakfast referrals are available through two different agencies in Ashland: **Ashland B&B Clearinghouse,** (800) 588-0338 or (541) 488-0338; www.bbclearing house.com; **Ashland's B&B Network,** (800) 944-0329; www.abbnet.com.

Hyatt Lake Resort. 7979 Hyatt Prairie Rd.; (541) 482-3331. RV and tent sites are available plus all kinds of activities to enjoy with your kids, including horseback riding, boating, mountain biking, and fishing in summer and cross-country skiing and general snow play in winter. $

Mt. Ashland Inn. 550 Mt. Ashland Ski Rd.; (800) 830-8707 or (541) 482-8707; www .mtashlandinn.com. Located in a large log chalet; all 5 rooms have private baths. The inn's owners will shuttle guests to the ski lodge, only 3 miles up the road. $$–$$$

The Palm Motel. 1065 Siskiyou Blvd.; (800) 691-2360; www.palmcottages.com. A retro hotel with modern amenities and great style, plus a fabulous courtyard garden near the outdoor pool and plenty of space to run around. Rooms have full kitchens and amenities like organic coffee. $$–$$$$

Plaza Inn & Suites at Ashland Creek. 98 Central Ave.; (888) 488-0358; www.plazainn ashland.com. A central location that's off the main drag, with large modern rooms equipped with microwaves and refrigerators, and a lovely view. $$$–$$$$

Stratford Inn. 555 Siskiyou; (800) 547-4741 or (541) 488-2151; www.stratfordinnashland .com. Just 5 blocks from the Shakespeare festival, this inn provides continental breakfast and has laundry facilities, a pool, and a spa. $$$

IN CAVE JUNCTION

Oregon Caves Lodge. 20000 Caves Hwy.; (541) 592-3400; call for open season. This rustic 6-story lodge was built in 1934. Nestled deep in the Siskiyou National Forest, there are plenty of opportunities for outdoor activities, including nearby hiking and cave exploration. $$$–$$$$

IN CRATER LAKE NATIONAL PARK

Crater Lake Lodge. Reservations from Xanterra Parks & Resort, 1211 Avenue C, White City; (541) 830-8700; www.craterlakelodges.com. The historic lodge is located in Rim Village and overlooks the lake. It is open May through Oct. The restaurant offers breakfast, lunch, and dinner. $$$$

Mazama Campground and Lost Creek Campground (tents only). First-come, first-served. Campground spaces cannot be reserved and usually fill up by early afternoon in summer. Open mid-June through Sept. Note that weather may affect campground opening and closing dates. Call (541) 594-3100 for more information. $

Mazama Village Motor Inn. (541) 830-8700; www.craterlakelodges.com. The inn is located in the Mazama Village complex. Open June through Sept. $$$–$$$$

IN GRANTS PASS

Riverside Inn Resort & Conference Center. 971 SE Sixth St.; (800) 334-4567 or (541) 476-6873; www.riverside-inn.com. This full-service inn stands next to the Rogue River, where the Hellgate jet boats take off. It has an outdoor pool, a spa pool, and a restaurant. $$$$

Travelodge. 1950 NW Vine St.; (888) 515-6375 or (541) 479-6611; www.travelodge.com. A restaurant, continental breakfast, and laundry facilities make this a convenient place for families. $$$

IN JACKSONVILLE

Applegate River Lodge. 15100 Highway 238 north of Jacksonville; (541) 846-6690; www.applegateriverlodge.com. The best of B&B lodging—delicious hot breakfast and cozy rooms with down comforters—without the claustrophobia. This gorgeous spot on scenic Highway 238 overlooks the Applegate River and the historic Pioneer Bridge. Lots of

room for kids to walk or run on the grounds; each large room has a deck with a view and a soaking tub for Mom. $$$$

The Stage Lodge. 830 N. Fifth St.; (800) 253-8254 or (541) 899-3953; www.stagelodge.com. Resembling a 19th-century stage stop, this 2-story lodge has attractive decor that matches the rest of the town's ambience. They serve a continental breakfast, too. $$–$$$$

Wolf Creek Inn. 100 Front; (541) 866-2474; www.thewolfcreekinn.com. Eight rooms. One of the state's oldest hostelries, the inn originally opened for business in 1880 as a stop along the Oregon-to-California stagecoach line. The rooms have been restored to reflect the authentic pre-1900 style. Includes continental breakfast. $$

IN KLAMATH FALLS

Best Western Klamath Inn. 4061 S. Sixth St.; (877) 882-1200 or (541) 882-1200. Continental breakfast and indoor pool. $$–$$$

Best Western Olympic Inn. 2627 S. Sixth St.; (800) 600-9665; www.olympicinn.com. Kids will be fascinated by the hunting-lodge decor of the large lobby, and parents can feed hungry kids on free soup, salad, and sandwiches in the afternoon and warm chocolate-chip cookies in the evening. Large, clean rooms and a pool make this a favorite, even though it's a bit off the beaten path. $$$$

Cimarron Motor Inn. 3060 S. Sixth St.; (800) 749-2648; www.cimarroninnklamathfalls.com. Clean, modern rooms with microwaves and refrigerators, an outdoor heated pool, complimentary breakfast, and laundry facilities make this one of Klamath Falls' best values. Pet-friendly, too. $–$$

Maverick Motel. 1220 Main St.; (800) 404-6690 or (541) 882-6688. The rooms tend toward small, but you can stretch out in the summer at the outdoor pool. They serve a continental breakfast and welcome pets, too. $

Rocky Point Resort. 28121 Rocky Point Rd.; located on upper Klamath Lake off Highway 140 and FR 34, 25 miles from Klamath Falls; (541) 356-2287; www.rockypointoregon .com. Boat rentals, tent sites, and RV hook-ups as well as dining rooms, showers, and laundry facilities are offered. $ camping; $$$–$$$$ lodging.

IN LAKEVIEW

Aspen Ridge Resort. Located off FR 3790 about 16 miles south of Highway 140; (800) 393-3323 or (541) 884-8685; www.aspenrr .com; e-mail: aspenrr@gmail.com. Lodge rooms and self-catering cabins overlook a meadow where the ranch's cattle and buffalo roam. Horseback trips take you into the surrounding forest. In winter you can strap on cross-country skis or hop on a snowmobile. $$$–$$$$

Lakeview Lodge Motel. 301 N. G St.; (541) 947-2181. The motel has large, clean rooms, a spa pool, and an exercise room. Pets are welcome. $–$$$

IN MEDFORD

Best Western Pony Soldier Inn. 2340 Crater Lake Hwy.; (800) 634-7669 or (541) 779-2011; www.bestwestern.com. There's a restaurant on the complex, and continental breakfast is available. It also has an outdoor pool and a spa pool. $$–$$$

Cedar Lodge Motor Inn. 518 N. Riverside; (800) 282-3419 or (541) 773-7361. A restaurant and continental breakfast are conveniences available to inn guests. Pets are welcome. $–$$$

Hampton Inn. 1112 Morrow Rd.; (541) 779-0660; www.hamptoninn.hilton.com. Near Harry and David and the freeway, this clean hotel offers cribs and highchairs for kids, plus a pool to wash away road restlessness. $$$–$$$$

Windmill Inn of Medford. 1950 Biddle Rd.; (800) 547-4747 or (541) 779-0050. A playground nearby makes parents and kids happy. Laundry facilities and kitchenettes are available, too. $$–$$$

IN ROSEBURG

Big K Guest Ranch. 20029 Highway 138W near Elkton, about 40 miles northwest of Roseburg; (800) 390-2445 or (541) 584-2295; www.big-k.com. The Kesterson family welcomes guests in 20 modern, log-sided cabins and a log lodge on their ranch, which rests along 10 miles of the Umpqua River. They offer horseback riding, fishing, horseshoes, and lots of exploring possibilities. $$$–$$$$

Diamond Lake Campground. West off Highway 138 about 80 miles east of Roseburg on FR 4795; (877) 444-6777 or (541) 793-3310; www.reserveusa.com. Fireplaces, running water, flush toilets, and showers provide a little extra luxury to this camping experience. $

Diamond Lake Resort. 76 miles east of Roseburg along the N. Umpqua Highway; (800) 733-7593 or (541) 793-3333; www.diamond lake.net; e-mail: info@diamondlake.net. The resort offers the sparkling solitude of a Cascade mountain lake but with amenities to enhance your family's fun. Hiking, biking, and horseback riding are all available in the vicinity. Motel rooms $$–$$$; cabins $$$$.

East Lemolo Campground. North off Highway 138, located 75 miles east of Roseburg on FR 2610; (541) 498-2531; www.fs.fed.us /r6/umpqua. Fifteen pretty sites are located on Lemolo Lake. The campground has vault toilets, picnic tables, and fire rings, and the lake offers fishing and waterskiing opportunities. $

Howard Johnson Express Inn. 978 NE Stephens St.; (541) 673-5082 or (800) 446-4656. The full-service inn offers continental breakfasts, kitchenettes, an indoor swimming pool, and laundry facilities. $$–$$$

Rose City Motel. 1142 NE Stephens Rd.; (541) 673-8209; www.rosecitymotel.com. If you're a minimalist you may find the rooms a tad fussy, but the motel's cleanliness and hospitality, along with a lovely garden patio area, make this independent hotel a treasure and a great value. Rooms with kitchens and easy chairs are great for families. $–$$

Windmill Inn of Roseburg. 1450 NW Mulholland; (800) 547-4747; www.windmillinns .com. It has a swimming pool, whirlpool and sauna, guest bicycles, and a complimentary continental breakfast. Family packages available. $$

For More Information

Ashland Visitor Information Center. 110 E. Main St., Ashland, OR 97520; (541) 482-3486; www.ashlandchamber.com.

Discover Klamath. 205 Riverside Dr., Klamath Falls, OR 97601; (800) 445-6728 or (541) 882-1501; www.discoverklamath.com; e-mail: visit@discoverklamath.com.

Grants Pass–Josephine County Chamber of Commerce/Grants Pass Visitors and Convention Bureau. 1995 NW Vine St., Grants Pass, OR 97526; (800) 547- 5927 or (541) 476-7717; www.visitgrants pass.org or www.grantspasschamber.org; e-mail: vcb@ visitgrantspass.org.

Illinois Valley Chamber of Commerce. P.O. Box 312, 201 Caves Hwy., Cave Junction, OR 97526; (541) 592-3326; www.cavejunction oregon.com; e-mail: ivchamberofcommerce@ cavenet.com.

Jacksonville Chamber of Commerce. P.O. Box 33, 185 N. Oregon St., Jacksonville, OR 97530; (541) 899-8118; www.jackson villeoregon.org; e-mail: info@ jacksonville oregon.org.

Klamath County Chamber of Commerce. 205 Riverside Dr., Klamath Falls, OR 97601; (541) 884-5193; www.klamath.org /visitors; e-mail: inquiry@klamath.org.

Lake County Chamber of Commerce. 126 N. East St., Lakeview, OR 97630; (541) 947-6040; www.lakecountychamber.org.

Medford Visitors & Convention Bureau. 101 E. Eighth St., Medford, OR 97501; (800) 469-6307, or (541) 779-4847; www.visitmed ford.org.

Roseburg Visitors and Convention Bureau. 410 SE Spruce St., Roseburg, OR 97470; (800) 444-9584; www.visitroseburg .com.

Southern Oregon Visitors Association. www.southernoregon.org; e-mail: office@ sova.org.

Eastern Oregon

The rolling wheatlands of the Columbia River Valley give way to the high Blue Mountains and Wallowa Mountains before dropping sharply into Hells Canyon of the Snake River. Grande Ronde River's colorful carved canyons, the sage-scented high desert, and the painted hills around the John Day Fossil Beds testify to vast changes wrought over 50 million years of geological evolution. The landscape recalls the days of cowboys and bronco-busting, pioneers and wagon trains, sometimes so vividly that one feels transported back in time. One of the least-populated areas of the state, much of northeastern Oregon remains untouched, the terrain preserved as early pioneers would have encountered it. Walking in the actual path of the wagon trains and reading the words of the pioneer women and men who trod these paths impart a sense of the past your kids won't find in any history books.

Baker City

This Old West gold-mining town has recaptured its history by resurrecting its original name: Baker City. For years the name had been shortened to Baker, but with the approach of the Oregon Trail sesquicentennial celebrations, the town mined its roots for a wealth of historic interest. For a while in the 1960s, Baker was known as the site of "No Name City," the fictional location created for filming *Paint Your Wagon,* with Clint Eastwood and Lee Marvin. A complete frontier town was constructed for the filming, and a replica is displayed at the Baker Heritage Museum.

National Historic Oregon Trail Interpretive Center (all ages)
Located at Flagstaff Hill, about 5 miles from Baker City on Highway 86; (541) 523-1843; www.blm.gov/or/oregontrail; e-mail: Nhotic_Mail@or.blm.gov. Open daily Apr through Oct 9 a.m. to 6 p.m., Nov through Mar 9 a.m. to 4 p.m. $–$$ seasonally, children 15 and under free.

EASTERN OREGON

Pendleton

Wallowa

Enterprise

Joseph

Hells Canyon
National
Recreation
Area

La Grande

Baker City

Sumpter

John Day

Burns

Frenchglen

Plan to spend all day here. At the heart of the center are exhibits of life-size figures speaking out as if you're overhearing their conversations along the trail. The historical accuracy and details are absorbing for both parents and children. In three mini-theaters, well-made films integrated into a scenic backdrop provide insight into the experience of Oregon's early pioneers. Your kids can try to pack a miniature wagon with all the supplies needed to make the journey, having to make some tough choices about what to leave behind—a puzzle that can keep determined youngsters occupied for hours! Walking trails take you down the hill to several spots where wagon ruts are visible among the sagebrush. Some of the 4⅕ miles of trails are quite steep, so you'll want to be in good shape. Ticks, rattlesnakes, and scorpions are local pests to be aware of on your walk. Take water, too, especially if you're walking in the heat of the day. A pioneer encampment and an old mine site are additional attractions.

Baker Heritage Museum
and Adler House Museum (ages 4 and up)

(541) 523-9308; www.bakerheritagemuseum.com. $$ for both museums, $$$$ family, children under 16 free. The Heritage Museum is open daily 9 a.m. to 5 p.m. Mar through Oct and by appointment. Adler House is open Fri through Mon 10 a.m. to 2 p.m. May 15 through Sept 15.

The Baker Heritage Museum (2480 Grove St.) fills the 33,000 square-foot former natatorium (indoor swimming pool) with exhibits on the rich history and settlement of the region. Kids will love the rock and fossil collection (coveted by the Smithsonian Institution), the fire wagon, and old carriages. A schoolroom replica includes some old schoolbooks your children will enjoy looking through. Also visit the replica of the complete frontier town built for the filming of *Paint Your Wagon*. Take a guided tour of the Adler House Museum (2305 Main St.) and by appointment. $$ (includes Heritage Museum), $$$$ family, children under 16 free. The fully refurbished turn-of-the-20th-century Victorian home once belonged to Leo Adler, Baker City's greatest benefactor. Adler lived here from age 4 to his death at 98, and never replaced the original furnishings.

Fun Fact

In the 1860s gold was discovered just outside Baker City, spawning a gold rush that lasted more than 50 years. In the early 1900s Baker City was known as the "queen city" of the Pacific Northwest because it was the cultural center between Salt Lake City and Portland, with several exquisite hotels and restaurants, ballrooms for dancing, and an opera house.

Historic Baker City Walking Tour (all ages)

Maps at 2101 Main St.; (541) 523-5442; www.historicbakercity.com, **free.**

This self-guided walking tour takes you to many of the more than 100 buildings in the Historic District of downtown Baker City.

Leo Adler Memorial Parkway (all ages)

Contact Baker County Visitors Bureau, 490 Campbell St.; (888) 523-5855 or (541) 523-5855; www.visitbaker.com. Open daily, year-round. **Free.**

This trail along the Powder River was built in memory of Leo Adler, a bachelor who died in 1993 and left his $20 million estate to the community. Fishing, running, and bird watching are among the trail's attractions.

Elkhorn Drive National Forest Scenic Byway (all ages)

Travels in a 106-mile loop from Baker City through the Elkhorn Mountains to the not-so-ghostly ghost towns of Sumpter and Granite and the more ghostly Auburn; (800) 523-1235 or (541) 523-5855. An illustrated brochure is available from Wallowa Whitman National Forest; (541) 523-1932; www.fs.fed.us/r6/w-w/recreation/byway/byway-elkhorn.shtml. Always open. **Free.**

Once a wild frontier town where laws were posted on trees, Auburn grew to become the second-largest town in Oregon. Now it's marked only by the grave sites of those left behind. Be sure your gas tank is full. Gas is available only in Baker City, Haines, Sumpter, and Granite.

Sumpter

Sumpter, one of the most interesting of area "ghost towns," can be reached by Highway 7, south of Phillips Lake. You'll pass the **Sumpter Valley Dredge** (541-894-2486), a state park where a massive machine was used to dredge up the valley floor to be processed for gold. Point out to your children the long rows of rock piles left by the dredge all along the road. More than $10 million in gold came from dredging the Sumpter Valley alone.

Top Sumpter Events

Memorial Day, Fourth of July, Labor Day weekends

Sumpter Community Flea Market. This outdoor flea market spreads from the fairgrounds to the town area. The tiny town of Sumpter comes to life when literally thousands of visitors come through to look at the wares or enjoy an old-time fiddler's show. When the kids have had enough browsing, they can buy fresh American Indian fry bread or barbecued beef sandwiches at one of the food stands set up for the occasion. (541) 894-2314.

Sumpter Valley Railroad (all ages)

Leaves from the McEwen Station, 5½ miles down the valley toward Phillips Lake to the south end of Sumpter and back; (541) 894-2268 or (866) 894-2268; www.svry.com; e-mail: sumptervalleyinfo@yahoo.com. Operates the 5 miles between McEwen Station and Sumpter on weekends and holidays Memorial Day through Sept; call or check website for schedule and special events. $$, $$$$ family, children 5 and under free. Tickets can be purchased at either end.

No trip to Sumpter is complete without taking a train ride on the narrow-gauge steam locomotive as it whistles down 5 scenic miles of track. Vital to the settlement and development of eastern Oregon, the Sumpter Valley Railroad was one of the most colorful and longest-lived narrow-gauge railroads in the nation. Take a trip back in time to an era when steam locomotives were the main mode of transportation, and logging and mining were the mainstays of the local economy.

John Day

John Day Fossil Beds National Monument is one of the best reasons for traveling to this part of the state. Aside from their vivid beauty, the canyons of the John Day River provide a window on prehistory that will give your children a better understanding of the expanse of time captured in the region's geography. For more information, visit the website at www.nps.gov/joda.

Kam Wah Chung State Heritage Site (ages 5 and up)

Located adjacent to Gleason Park; (541) 575-0028 or (800) 551-6949; www.oregonstateparks .org/park_8.php. Open May through Oct daily 9 a.m. to 5 p.m. Free.

On personal tours the museum director explains the purpose of some of the more unusual items housed in the museum, which is maintained to preserve the legacy of the Chinese workforce in Oregon. Shrines in each room seek to appease various deities, such as the kitchen god. Do you have any aspiring doctors in the family? They'll be especially

Fun Facts

- The John Day River has more miles of wild and scenic designation than any other river in the United States. It's the second-longest undammed river in the country.

- After gold was discovered in 1862, $26 million of the shiny stuff was mined from the John Day–Canyon City region.

fascinated with the collection of more than 500 Chinese medicinal herbs that were once dispensed in the building.

Grant County Ranch and Rodeo Museum (ages 3 and up)

241 E. Main; (541) 575-5545. Open May through Sept Fri through Sun 10 a.m. to 4 p.m. or by appointment. $ donation requested for adults, but not required.

The Grant County Ranch and Rodeo Museum captures the legacy of local American cowboys and ranchers from pioneer days to modern times, with exhibits of ropes and saddles, bits and spurs, photos, tools, and literature. The museum is staffed by those who have lived the ranch and rodeo life and can tell a lively story to enchanted youngsters.

John Day Fossil Beds National Monument, Sheep Rock Unit (all ages)

Located 7 miles northwest of Dayville on Highway 19, just beyond the junction with US 26; (541) 987-2333; www.nps.gov/joda. Call for visitor center hours. Monument open daily dawn to dusk. Free.

An Adventure to Remember

The Kam Wah Chung & Co. building was constructed in the 1860s and served as a trading post on the main east–west highway during that period. The dim lighting that casts an eerie glow in the museum's rooms also beckons the curious to come explore its exotic ambience. You will see that Kam Wah Chung & Co. served as an efficient multipurpose pharmacy, doctor's office, general store, religious shrine, and opium den. The museum has been left in almost the same state that proprietor "Doc" Ing Hay left it when he locked the doors in 1948. Hay and fellow proprietor Lung On purchased the building in the 1880s, and the two men soon became important members of the local community. Lung On was a respected entrepreneur, and Hay was considered the most famous herbal medicine doctor between Seattle and San Francisco. You can spend well over an hour under this tiny roof as your imagination runs wild contemplating the clandestine opium exchanges and examining sundries that now lay dormant on dusty shelves. More than 500 Chinese medicinal herbs, along with gold-mining and logging tools, are wedged next to canned goods, tobaccos, and notions. Several Buddhist shrines still coated with incense are housed here, too, giving testimony to Hay's position as the region's chief priest for the Chinese. Don't miss this museum, the contents of which are said to provide the best historical account of the integration of Oriental and Occidental cultures in the United States, in addition to the prosperous gold-mining era in northeastern Oregon.

Top John Day **Events**

August
Grant County Fair and NPRA Rodeo. This county fair has all the fixings for a family weekend of fun, including flying dogs and performing pigs and kids' rodeo on Sunday. (541) 575-1900.

Grant County Kruzer Car Show. Classic cars are celebrated with activities at the fairgrounds and in the streets of Prairie City. (541) 575-2127; www.ortelco .net/~kruzers.

This historic visitor center and museum is a good place to begin accumulating information about the area. The museum has fossil displays of prehistoric creatures that once roamed this region—from saber-toothed cats to elephants and rhinos—between 6 and 50 million years ago. A 15-minute film presents a synopsis of the area's geological history in terms your children will understand. The grounds of the center make a perfect picnic spot. At a small laboratory in an old log shed, park rangers demonstrate some of the tools and techniques used to remove fossil specimens from the stone encasing them. Your children will be fascinated by the tiny jackhammers and will enjoy the idea of dental tools being used to scrape fossil teeth rather than their teeth. Park rangers guide walks on some of the trails throughout the summer. Pick up trail maps and program schedules at the center, then head up the road to explore. The monument covers 14,000 acres in three separate units, the largest of which is the **Sheep Rock Unit.** Trails in this section include two in the **Blue Basin,** with its stunning blue-green canyons, just 2½ miles north of the visitor center. About 3 miles farther north on Highway 19, you'll see the striations of **Cathedral Rock,** one of the hallmark images of this area.

Painted Hills (all ages)
Located northwest of Mitchell; (541) 987-2333; www.nps.gov/planyourvisit/painted_hills_ unit.htm. Open daily dawn to dusk. Free.

The monument's Painted Hills offer a close-up look at the eroded hills of multimillion-year-old colorful volcanic ash. The best views are at dawn and dusk after a rain, when the moisture brings out the spectacular hues in the mineral-rich clays. A ¾-mile hike leads to an outstanding rim view, and a short self-guided walk to **Painted Cove** offers a close view of the colorful clay stones.

Strawberry Mountain Wilderness (ages 8 and up)
Located 11 miles southeast of John Day; (541) 820-3311; www.fs.fed.us/r6/malheur/recreation. Closed due to snow during the winter and spring. Free.

Located in the **Malheur National Forest,** the Strawberry Mountain Wilderness has more than 100 miles of hiking trails as well as several campgrounds. **Strawberry Lake** is one of the more accessible lakes in the wilderness, although the trail climbs steadily for about

1³⁄₁₀ miles and can be tiring for little ones. From Prairie City head south on FR 60 to the **Strawberry Lake Campground,** about 12 miles south of US 26. You can set up camp here and take a day trip to the lake or backpack into one of several wilderness sites near the lake, where you must leave behind no trace of your visit.

Burns

When you get into the southeastern corner of Oregon, you're entering one of the least-populated areas of the country. Harney and Malheur Counties together account for 20,154 square miles of land—more than Massachusetts and New Jersey combined—and just a little more than 36,000 people, fewer than the student population of some universities. That's part of the reason you feel as if you've entered deep Australian outback when you're driving through this country of broad sagebrush deserts and lonely mountain crags. As the major population center in the southeast, Burns is a natural place from which to begin exploring the vast range of outdoor opportunities that awaits visitors. The city received its name because of the fondness early postmaster George McGowen, one of the town's founders, had for Scottish poet Robert Burns.

Rockhounding

An activity for all ages, rockhounding is one of the major tourist attractions in this area. Government-managed properties do not charge a fee for removing rocks, but call the Harney County Chamber of Commerce first (541-573- 2636) about the requirements for each area.

- **Burns.** Located off Highway 205. Agates are abundant at the quarry just south near the Narrows, the strip of land between Harney and Malheur Lakes.

- **Glass Butte.** Located 55 miles west of Burns on US 20. The butte is so named because it is composed almost entirely of volcanic glass, or obsidian. This area was used extensively by Native Americans for gathering obsidian used to make arrowheads. Collecting arrowheads is against federal law, so if you find any, leave them for the next person to appreciate. All kinds of obsidian can be found near here—lace, rainbow, mahogany, gold sheen, black, and banded.

- **Steens Mountain.** Located 60 miles south of Burns. Agate, jasper, obsidian, and thunder eggs can be dug near Buchanan Road at the base of the mountain.

Top Burns **Events**

April
John Scharff Migratory Bird Festival and Art Show. Watch thousands of birds as they rest and feed during their spring migration. You'll see every-thing—waterfowl, shorebirds, cranes, raptors, waders, songbirds. (541) 573-2636; http://migratorybirdfestival.com.

September
Harney County Fair, Rodeo & Race Meet. Rides, exhibits, food concessions, and broncos will fill your entire weekend. (541) 573-1616; www.co.harney.or.us/countyfair.html.

October
Burns Paiute Reservation Day Pow Wow. Held at the Burns Armory. Traditional dancing and drumming and dance contests will get your toes tapping and add another dimension to the culture and history of the area. (541) 573-2088.

Harney County Historical Museum (ages 5 and up)
18 W. D St.; (541) 573-5618; www.burnsmuseum.com. Open Tues through Sat 9 a.m. to 5 p.m. Apr through Sept. $, family of 4 $$, children under 6 free.

Look for the armored wagon at the edge of the parking lot. Once a brewery, it's now a hands-on museum where your kids can turn the apple peeler and lift the hand irons to get a feel for the work that had to be done to keep a family together a century ago. Northern Pauite artifacts tell another part of the story of western life, and kids will have lots of questions about the display of early medical and dental equipment.

Ochoco National Forest, Delintment Lake (all ages)
Located 42 miles northwest of Burns via FR 41; (541) 416-6500; www.fs.fed.us/r6/central oregon. Always open. Free forest access; Delintment Lake $ day-use fee, $ camping fee.

This lake was created by damming Delintment Creek. Campsites in the ponderosa pine forest are suitable for tents and RVs. A picnic area and boat ramp are also available.

Crystal Crane Hot Springs (ages 5 and up)
Located 25 miles southeast of Burns on Highway 78; (541) 493-2312; www.cranehotsprings.com. Open daily 9 a.m. to 9 p.m.; reservations recommended. $, private tubs $$, lodging $.

There's a naturally hot mineral-water swimming pool and bathhouse/spa for families and kids. Rustic cabins as well as tent and RV sites are available.

Sagehen Hill Nature Trail (ages 5 and up)

Located 16 miles west of Burns at the Sagehen Rest Area on US 20. Contact Bureau of Land Management, 12533 US 20W, Hines, OR 97738; (541) 573-4400. Always open. Free.

The ½-mile-long nature trail has 11 stations along the route that provide information on the trees, cultural history, plants, and, of course, sage hens, also called sage grouse. The trail goes through sagebrush, bitterbrush, and western juniper. Watch for sage grouse in May.

Frenchglen

Both the Steens Mountain Loop Road and the Malheur National Wildlife Refuge loop tours take you through this tiny town, perhaps best known for its century-old hotel.

Frenchglen Hotel State Heritage Site (all ages)

Highway 205, Frenchglen; (800) 551-6949 or (541) 493-2825; www.oregonstateparks.org. Operates Mar 15 through Nov 15. Call for rates.

Part of a State Historic Wayside Park, the 8-room hotel is an oasis for travelers to this region where many miles separate even the closest towns. The hotel provides lodging and meals for visitors coming to enjoy bird watching and wildlife. Whether or not you stay at the hotel, you can stop by for sodas or coffee, or just enjoy a picnic in the shaded yard. Breakfast, lunch, and dinner are served daily to residents and drop-in guests. Reservations are a must for dinner meals.

Fish Lake (all ages)

Located about 18 miles east of Frenchglen; (541) 573-4400; www.blm.gov/or/resources. Open dawn to dusk during season; closed Nov through mid-July. $ camping fee, free day use.

There's a boat ramp for nonmotorized boats, as well as more than 20 campsites in both shaded and open areas. A trail joins two sections of the campground on opposite sides of the lake. The wildflowers here—and all along the loop road—are stunning, especially in July. Page Springs, another campground, is just 3 miles east of Frenchglen. Open year-round, it has more than 30 campsites, toilets, water, fireplaces, and limited firewood. There's a $ camping fee when water is available. Watch for rattlesnakes, ticks, and stinging nettles in summer.

Peter French Round Barn (all ages)

Located southeast of Burns and Malheur Lake near New Princeton; road signs direct you to the site from Highway 205; (541) 573-2636; www.roundbarn.net. Hours change seasonally; call first. Free.

The barn is worth a stop for both historic and architectural reasons. Built before 1884 of native rock and juniper trees, the structure is fascinating. It's shaped like a Chinese umbrella, with timbered "spokes" leading to a central truss. Peter French used the barn as a winter livestock shelter and for breaking saddle horses.

Fun Fact

The town of Frenchglen was named for Peter French and Dr. Hugh Glenn, who established a 150,000-acre livestock ranch at the base of Steens Mountain in 1872. After French married Glenn's daughter, Glenn was killed by a man named Miller in 1883 on his Jacinto Ranch in California, where French once worked for him. French also met a violent end—he was shot and killed over a land dispute near his P Ranch. A large section of the ranch is now in the Malheur National Wildlife Refuge.

Diamond Craters (ages 8 and up)

Located 55 miles south of Burns on Highway 205; (541) 573-4400; www.or.blm.gov/burns. Always open. Free.

The craters were created in the last 25,000 years. They have been described as having the nation's most diverse basaltic volcanic features. There are craters, domes, lava floors and pits to explore.

Oard's Museum and Gallery (ages 3 and up)

Located 23 miles east of Burns off US 20; (541) 493-2535. Open Mon through Sat 8 a.m. to 6 p.m., Sun 9 a.m. to 5 p.m. Free.

This old-fashioned museum features authentic American Indian art and historic pioneer collectibles while the shop has contemporary arts and crafts. It's a fun break during a long day on the road.

Wild Horse Corrals (all ages)

Just west of Hines, on US 20 near milepost 122; (541) 573-4456 or (541) 573-4400; www.or .blm.gov/Burns. Open weekdays year-round 7:30 a.m. to 3:30 p.m. Free.

More than 2,600 wild horses are free-roaming, unbranded descendants of horses turned loose by, or escaped from, the US Cavalry, ranchers, prospectors, or Indian tribes from the late 1800s to the 1930s. At certain times of the year, you can see wild horses in the corrals operated by the Bureau of Land Management or at various viewpoints around the Steens Mountain area. The BLM operates an "adopt a wild horse program" to help control their population.

Malheur National Wildlife Refuge (all ages)

From Burns take Highway 78 south, turn right on Highway 205 for 28 miles, then left at refuge sign; (541) 493-2612; www.fws.gov/malheur. Visitor center open daily 8 a.m. to 4 p.m.; museum and refuge open daily dawn to dusk. Free.

Fun Fact

The greater sandhill cranes that return each year to nest at the Malheur National Wildlife Refuge belong to one of the oldest living bird species. Today's flocks descended from birds that lived more than 9 million years ago.

Located in the Blue Mountains south of Burns, Malheur is one of the best places to view birds and waterfowl in the state. Before leaving Burns, be sure to fill the gas tank; in summer, bring water and mosquito repellent too, and in fall and winter bring warm clothes for sudden winter storms. The refuge encompasses both Malheur and Harney Lakes, as well as a narrow stretch of land bordering Highway 205 south of Burns. Established by President Theodore Roosevelt in 1908, the refuge covers more than 187,000 acres and is home to more than 320 species of birds and 58 mammal species. Obtain a list of species at the headquarters, located on the south shore of Malheur Lake, 5 miles from Highway 205 along a paved road. The headquarters consists of both a visitor center and a museum, which contains nearly 200 mounted bird specimens. It's a great opportunity for your children to see up close the birds they might spot through binoculars on the refuge. The website has a "Bird Arrivals" page that lists approximate dates of arrival for migrating species. The big show of the year happens in Aug, when more than 200 pairs of greater sandhill cranes nest at the refuge.

Steens Mountain (ages 10 and up)

Located 60 miles south of Burns on Highway 205 toward Frenchglen; (541) 573-4400; www .blm.gov/or/districts/burns/recreation/steens-mtn.php. Road open July through Sept. Check road conditions before you visit. Free.

Steens Mountain Loop Road is the best way to explore the mountain; take a full day—or more—and drive the gravel-topped road, which is open only in summer. The road is rough in places, so you'll want to make sure your car is in good condition and has a full tank before you set out. One of the most dramatic geological features of the region, Steens Mountain is a 30-mile-long fault block that rises to an elevation of more than 9,700 feet. A breathtaking view from the rim looks down through the deep gorges of Kiger, Wildhorse, Big Indian, and Little Blitzen Canyons, carved by glaciers a million years ago, into the dry Alvord Desert more than a mile below. The highest road in the state, it stops just short of the mountain's 9,733-foot summit. A short climb on foot takes you to the top of the jagged peak. Be prepared for dramatic shifts in the weather, and keep a close eye on the children—the walls of the mountain are rocky and steep, and high winds can disrupt balance with surprising swiftness. Watch for raptors, such as falcons, hawks, and golden eagles, who use the updrafts from the Alvord to soar over the rugged countryside searching for food.

La Grande

One of the towns settled by pioneers traveling the Oregon Trail, La Grande takes its name from the lush Grande Ronde Valley and the river that flows through its center.

Meacham Divide (ages 6 and up)
Located 19 miles northwest of La Grande near Meacham; (541) 963-7122. Open late Apr through mid-Dec. Call for snow levels and opening status. Free.

Winter weather blankets the area with snow, making cross-country skiing a popular activity. You and your children can set out on more than 15 miles of groomed trails here, with diagonal and skate lanes. Hike or bike on trails in summer.

Anthony Lakes Mountain Resort (ages 5 and up)
Located 50 miles southwest of La Grande on I-84, 19 miles west of the North Powder exit; (541) 856-3277; www.anthonylakes.com. Call for hours and prices, including seasonal discounts.

The resort has rope tows or Pomalifts for beginners, chairlifts for experienced skiers, ski and snowboard rentals, and meals on-site. Anthony Lakes also offers more than 35

Top La Grande **Events**

June
Eastern Oregon Livestock Show and PRCA Rodeo. Take the opportunity to enjoy the oldest rodeo in the Northwest—since 1908! The event also includes horse racing, a carnival, and dancing. (800) 848-9969 or (541) 963-8588.

July
Elgin Stampede. Located in Elgin, 20 miles northeast of La Grande. Pro rodeo and a draft-horse pulling contest are featured, plus a carnival, dances, a parade, and races. (541) 437-4007.

August
Oregon Trail Days, Rendezvous, and Old-Time Fiddler's Contest. Besides good old-fashioned fiddlin', Trail Days features a pioneer encampment, a buffalo barbecue, and a Dutch-oven cookoff. (800) 848-9969.

kilometers of groomed Nordic trails looping the lake. Downhill, cat, and cross-country ski-ing are offered, and the lake is a popular fishing and canoeing spot in summer.

Eastern Oregon Fire Museum (ages 3 and up)

Located on the corner of Elm and Washington Streets; (541) 963-8588; call for hours and admission costs.

The museum is housed in La Grande's historic fire station, in uses from 1899 to 2002. Along with the usual displays, the museum offers chances to climb on vintage and historic fire trucks.

Lions' Birnie Park (all ages)

Located at the corner of Old Oregon Trail (B Avenue) and Gekeler Street; (800) 848-9969 or (541) 963-8588. Open dawn to dusk. Free.

Once a pioneer encampment, where wagon trains circled to rest and reenergize for the steep climb up the Blue Mountains to the west, the park now houses symbolic ceramic columns that mark the route taken by wagons as they climbed out of the valley and a life-size wrought-iron pioneer play wagon. Interpretive displays contain excerpts from pioneer diaries, extolling the beauty of the valley and describing the hardships of the journey.

Union County Museum (ages 5 and up)

333 S. Main St., Union, 15 miles southeast of La Grande; (541) 562-6003; www.unioncounty museum.org. Open Mon through Sat, Mother's Day through mid-Oct, 10 a.m. to 4 p.m., $, 6 and under free. Special tours by request.

Natural history and a Cowboys Then and Now exhibit will give you a glimpse into the region's early days and its cultural and geographic evolution.

Grande Ronde River (ages 8 and up)

Runs through La Grande parallel to Highway 244; (800) 848-9969; www.rivers.gov/wsr-grande-ronde.html. Always open. Free.

Summer temperatures in this high-country town call for cooling swims in one of several swimming holes along the banks of the river or in nearby lakes and reservoirs. The Grande Ronde River is a natural selection, especially at any of the parks or campgrounds along its shores. Mule deer, elk, black bears, cougars, and bighorn sheep inhabit the river corridor.

Fun Fact

The Grande Ronde River, at 180 miles long, is Oregon's second-longest free-flowing river and has been designated "Wild and Scenic."

Fun Fact

This area is known as Nicht-yow-way, homeland of the Cayuse, Umatilla, and Walla Walla—three distinct tribes now combined to form the Confederated Tribes of the Umatilla Indian Reservation. These tribes once numbered 8,000 people; now they have 2,719 enrolled tribal members.

Eagle Cap Excursion Train (all ages)

20 miles north of LaGrande in the town of Elgin; (800) 848-9969 (information) or (800) 323-7330 (reservations, which must be made by the Fri before the trip); www.eaglecaptrain .com. Board the train at 300 N. Eighth St. Trips Sat in summer and fall leaving Elgin at 10 a.m. $$$$, kids 3 and under **free.**

The Eagle Cap Excursion Train operates on a scenic 63-mile railroad, linking the communities of Elgin, Wallowa, Enterprise, and Joseph. The 3½-hour "Two Rivers" excursion passes through spectacular roadless areas as it follows the Grande Ronde River downstream to its confluence with the Wallowa River, then turns up the Wallowa for a few miles before reversing direction. Car hosts provide information about the history of the railroad and area, and help you look for wildlife. Lunch and a beverage are included and a gift shop and concession stand on the train provide additional diversion—but bring cash, as neither accepts debit cards.

Pendleton

History truly comes alive once a year in this cowboy town when the **Pendleton Round-Up** rears its raucous head. But if you're not in town for the rodeo or didn't plan well enough in advance to get tickets, your children can still get a taste of the Old West with a visit to the **Pendleton Round-Up Hall of Fame.**

Umatilla County Historical Society Museum (ages 5 and up)

108 SW Frazer; (541) 276-0012; www.heritagestationmuseum.org; e-mail: uchs@oregontrail .net. Open Tues through Sat 10 a.m. to 4 p.m. $, $$$ family.

Exhibits trace the region's history, beginning with the Native American tribes that settled along the Umatilla River and leading through the arrival of missionaries, sheepherders, ranchers, farmers, soldiers, and loggers. The museum, housed in the restored 1909 railway depot, contains a large collection of photographs and artifacts to accompany the tales from the Old West. Your children might enjoy what's next door most of all. Kids can compare contemporary classrooms with the restored one-room schoolhouse—an elementary, middle, and high school all in one.

Tamástslikt Cultural Institute (ages 3 and up)

72789 Highway 331 (take exit 216 off I-84 and follow signs to Wildhorse Resort); (541) 966-9748; www.tamastslikt.com. Open daily 9 a.m. to 5 p.m. Apr through Oct; closed Sun Nov to Mar. $$, $$$ families, children under 5 free.

The word *tamástslikt* means "interpret," and this center interprets the story of three distinct native peoples—the Cayuse, Umatilla, and Walla Walla tribes—whose histories came together over the past 150 years toward an alliance called the Confederated Tribes of the Umatilla Indian Reservation. The museum looks at the region from the perspective of these tribes—often a very different outlook than that traditionally taught in textbooks. Permanent and changing exhibits and regularly scheduled talks and demonstrations provide a rich experience in history. Permanent artifact collections and photography archives look to the past, while contemporary art exhibits display works by local and regional tribal artists.

Pendleton Underground Tours (ages 10 and up)

37 SW Emigrant; (800) 226-6398 or (541) 276-0730; www.pendletonundergroundtours.org. Open year-round, call for 90-minute tour dates and times, reservations recommended. $$ adults, kids 10 and up only.

Descend below street level and get a glimpse of remnants of a time when Pendleton was part of the rootin' tootin' Wild West, once boasting 32 saloons and 18 bordellos. The tours are tastefully presented, but parents of young children might not want to have to explain some of the references. Once a year the underground comes to life. Actors dressed as dance-hall girls, cowboys, Chinese laborers, and gamblers provide entertainment along the tour.

Bar M Dude Ranch (all ages)

58840 Bar M Lane, Adams; located 31 miles east of Pendleton in the Blue Mountains; (888) 824-3381 or (541) 566-3381; www.barmranch.com; e-mail: barmranch@eoni.com. Ranch open to guests mid-May through mid-Sept. Cost is $$$$ per week per person.

Home-style accommodations are offered on this working ranch. The main ranch house has 8 guest rooms. Other accommodations include three 2-room suites, 2 cabins, and 4 RV sites. Horseback riding, a recreation barn, natural hot springs, and meals to make any ranch hand's mouth water are all part of the experience.

Fun Fact

Pendleton's underground tunnels, dug by Chinese immigrants between 1870 and 1930, cover more than 70 miles underneath Pendleton's historic district.

Clockworks

If you walk to the corner of SE Fourth and Court, you can view the century-old clockworks through glass panels in the clock tower. The Seth Thomas clock is located in front of the Umatilla County Courthouse.

Blue Mountain Crossing Interpretive Site (ages 5 and up)
Located just south of Emigrant Springs; (541) 963-7186. Call for seasonal hours. $ trailhead fee (National Forest Day Pass).

During summer weekends you can meet some pioneers camped with their wagon at the 4,193-foot summit, awaiting the rest of their wagon train. Dressed as characters drawn from the past, the living-history pioneers tell tales sketched from diaries left by the emigrants. Three short trails take you past signs of their passage. Give your child the interpretive brochure to guide you to the numbered stops along the way.

Hat Rock State Park (all ages)
Located on the shore of a lake formed by McNary Dam, 29 miles northwest of Pendleton via Highway 37 and US 73; (800) 551-6949 for information; (800) 452-5687 for reservations; www.oregonstateparks.org. Closed in winter except for boat ramp. Free day use. Call for camping and picnic area reservations and fees.

This is the first Oregon landmark recorded by Lewis and Clark on their journey. The park has camping and picnicking facilities as well as boat access to the Columbia River. A private campground across from the park has a swimming pool. The large pond is a great place to picnic and spot the waterfowl—such as great blue herons, kingfishers, and friendly ducks and geese—that inhabit the area.

Top Pendleton **Event**

September
Pendleton Round-Up. One of the largest rodeos in the country, the Round-Up includes unusual events such as wild-cow milking and Indian and baton races. You'll want to don your 10-gallon hat and your cowboy boots (or your baseball cap and sneakers—there's no dress code) and join in the festivities. The nightly Happy Canyon Show, in which members of the local Umatilla, Cayuse, Walla Walla, and Nez Percé tribes present pageantry and tradition, is a spectacle to capture even the most jaded teenage interests. (800) 45-RODEO or (541) 276-2553; www.pendletonroundup.com or www.happycanyon.com.

Pendleton Round-Up Hall of Fame (ages 5 and up)

1114 SW Court St.; (800) 45-RODEO, (541) 276-2553; www.pendletonroundup.com or www.traveloregon.com. Open Mon through Sat 10 a.m. to 4 p.m. Free; donations appreciated. Tours available.

Displays of photographs of famous bronco riders and rodeo stars line the walls that commemorate the Wild West. There's even an old rodeo bucking horse, Warpaint, in full-body mount—a real kid-pleaser.

Pendleton Woolen Mills (ages 5 and up)

1307 SE Court Place; (541) 276-6911; www.pendleton-usa.com. Call for hours. Free 20-minute tours available.

When some people hear the word *Pendleton,* they have visions of soft woolen shirts and blankets instead of rodeos. Although your kids may not be thrilled to look inside a wool mill, they might at least appreciate the benefit of the warm winter clothing that can be purchased at the outlet here.

Hells Canyon National Recreation Area

What is the deepest river gorge in North America? Nope, not Arizona's Grand Canyon. It's right here in eastern Oregon: **Hells Canyon** on the Snake River. Forming the border between Oregon and Idaho, the Snake River carved a gorge more than a mile deep over the past 20 million years. The canyon's oldest rocks were formed as long as 280 million years ago at the bottom of a vast inland sea.

Designated in 1975 as a National Recreation Area within the Wallowa-Whitman National Forest, Hells Canyon offers many opportunities for family fun. The highest point on the Oregon rim of the canyon is **Hat Point,** rising 6,982 feet above sea level. A new road into the scenic overlook has made this vista available to motorists from mid-June through Oct. From Imnaha drive east on Hat Point Road. Gas up before leaving Enterprise or Joseph and carry drinking water; you'll drive 23 miles from Imnaha one-way to the Hat Point Overlook.

Hells Canyon National Recreation Area (ages 5 and up)

(541) 523-6391 (Bureau of Land Management) or (541) 426-5546; www.fs.fed.us/hellscanyon. Check first for road access during winter months. Free.

To explore the Hells Canyon National Recreation Area more deeply, look into guided trips by boat, on the back of a horse, or with a pack mule or llama. You can take your own float or powerboat trip along the "Wild and Scenic" Snake River if you are an experienced whitewater boater.

Hells Canyon Adventures (note age restrictions below)

Located 80 miles east of Baker City; P.O. Box 159, Oxbow, OR 97840; (541) 785-3352 or (800) 422-3568; www.hellscanyonadventures.com; e-mail: jetboat@hellscanyonadventures.com. Open Mar through Oct. Call for tour availability, schedules, and prices.

They are one of the few outfitters offering day trips rather than extended overnight floats. With one exception, the trips—either by raft or jet boat—navigate all of the major white-water on the river, including some Class IV rapids (not for the faint of heart). Children must be at least 12 to take a daylong raft trip. For those with hearts and stomachs made of weaker substances than steel, they offer "soft adventures"—2- and 3-hour jet boat trips that take you up to but not through the worst of the whitewater. Younger children are welcome on jet boat trips. All trips involve stops to explore an old homestead, ancient Indian pictographs, an abandoned Indian village, a deserted cave, or the Kirkwood Living Historical Ranch, a museum that was once the home of former Idaho governor and US senator Len Jordan.

Steen's Wilderness Adventures (ages 6 and up)

64591 Steen Rd., Joseph; (541) 432-6545; http://steenswildernessadventures.com; e-mail: steens@oregontrail.net. Trips run late May through early Sept. $$$$.

Take 3- to 7-day horse and mule pack trips into the canyon or into the Eagle Cap Wilderness, or a take a 3-hour horse trip to Minam River Lodge, where you can stay overnight in cabins ($$$$) or pitch a tent. Lodging includes family-style meals. With five generations of history in the region, Steen's Wilderness Adventures knows the canyon and its wilderness well.

Nee-Me-Poo National Recreation Trail (ages 8 and up)

Access to the trail by car (high-clearance vehicles strongly recommended) is from Imnaha, about 20 miles over rough, single-lane gravel-topped FR 4260; (541) 426-4978, ext. 5546; www.fs.fed/hellscanyon. Open year-round. Free.

The 5-mile (one-way) trail gives kids a strong sense of history as it leads into the Snake River Canyon, downriver from Hells Canyon. Nee-Me-Poo means "the real people." The evocative story of Chief Joseph and his flight from the Wallowa Valley seems to resonate through the valley as you walk in his footsteps. The trail ends at Dug Bar on the Snake, where an interpretive sign tells the story of the Nez Percé. When walking here, carry drinking water and be prepared for weather changes. This is a steep trail, with a 1,000-foot elevation change at each end of the hike. Be watchful for rattlesnakes and poison ivy.

Saddle Creek Viewpoint and Campground (ages 5 and up)

Located 18.8 miles out of Imnaha; (541) 426-5546 or (541) 426-4978. Open May through Oct, but always check first for snow levels. Free.

This area has both camping facilities and terrific viewing spots into Hells Canyon, where you also get a good view of the Seven Devils Mountains in Idaho. An interpretive sign helps you identify for your children the various geologic features they're seeing, and they'll enjoy scrambling over the rocky surfaces that surround the area. From here the road climbs in twists and turns another 4⁷⁄₁₀ miles to Hat Point. If you're not one for heights, you can enjoy the view from here while your kids climb the 92-foot lookout tower for an all-around view that spans northeastern Oregon and extends to northwestern Idaho. If you're camping, bring your own water, as there's no supply at the campground.

The Wallowas

The lush flatlands of the Wallowa Valley form a contrast to the abrupt rise of the mountains. The variety of choices for family adventure in this beautiful corner of the state is surprising for an area with such a sparse population. Magnificent natural beauty, much of it preserved in the **Wallowa-Whitman National Forest** and **Eagle Cap Wilderness,** captivates visitors and residents alike throughout the year. Winter snows cover the Wallowa Mountains—often called the Swiss Alps of Oregon—which offer downhill and Nordic skiing. Spring brings a time for alpine wildflower walks and fishing in the area's many lakes and streams. Summer invites hikers, mountain bikers, horseback riders, water-skiers, and swimmers. Autumn colors are spectacular, and so is the fishing during fall spawning.

Wallowa Lake, formed about a million years ago by glacial drift, is bounded on the east and west by lateral moraines (accumulations of earth and stones collected and deposited by a glacier) and at the north by a terminal moraine. The teardrop-shape lake is 283 feet deep and 6 miles long. Its name comes from the Nez Percé term for a tripod-mounted fish trap that was used in the lake. The south end of Wallowa Lake was first commercially developed in 1906. A dance pavilion and bowling lanes have given way to numerous resorts and lodges. Floating platforms dot the lake near the shore for swimmers and water-skiers to rest or picnic. Fishing is excellent both in the lake and in nearby streams for rainbow trout, kokanee (landlocked blueback salmon), Dolly Varden (char), sturgeon, and mackinaw (lake trout). Hiking trails take off into the Eagle Cap

Fun Facts

- When the Wallowa Lake Tramway was constructed, it boasted the steepest vertical lift for a 4-passenger gondola in all of North America.
- Eagle Cap Wilderness is Oregon's largest designated wilderness area.

Wilderness Area, or you can take horseback trips with a guide. Mule deer roam the area freely and are quite accustomed to people. Please don't feed the deer, as human food is bad for them. Also, these are wild animals, and their antlers and hooves are sharp and powerful.

Wallowa Lake State Park (all ages)

Off Highway 82, 6 miles south of Joseph; (800) 551-6949 or (541) 432-4185; www.oregon stateparks.org. Open year-round. Camping $.

Wallowa Lake's campground, with more than 85 tent sites plus yurts and RV sites, is ideally positioned as a base camp for nearby wilderness treks and water-sport fun in and around Wallowa Lake. From Memorial Day through Labor Day, this place is packed, so you'll definitely need to reserve your campsite. But if you're staying elsewhere, come out for the day to enjoy swimming, boating, fishing, or hiking the nature trails.

Wallowa Lake Marina and Store (ages 5 and up)

P.O. Box 47, Joseph, OR 97846; (541) 432-9115; www.wallowalakemarina.com. Open May through mid-Sept. Summer hours 8 a.m. to 8 p.m.; call for off-season hours and prices.

Reservations can be made for a 1½-hour lake tour aboard a pontoon boat, which is also available for rent. The marina rents canoes, rowboats, paddleboats, and motorboats by the day, half day, or hour. The kids will be delighted to find kiddie rides here. The store has basic provisions and snacks plus camping, fishing, and water-fun supplies.

Wallowa Lake Tramway (ages 5 and up)

59919 Wallowa Lake Hwy.; (541) 432-5331; www.wallowalaketramway.com. Open daily mid-May through Sept 10 a.m. to 4 p.m., to 5 p.m. July through Labor Day. $$$$ adults, $$$ kids, children 3 and under free.

Top Wallowa **Event**

July

Tamkaliks Celebration. Held annually, the Tamkaliks Celebration symbolizes the return of Wallowa Band Nez Percé descendants to their homeland. *Tamkaliks* means "from where you can see the mountains." Your children will be wowed by the traditional dancing in ceremonial dress, the rhythm of the drumming and singing, and the experience of a distinctive cultural tradition. The Nez Percé prepare venison, salmon, and traditional fry bread, and other area residents bring potluck dishes to share for the Friendship Feast on Sunday. Visitors are asked to contribute, too, either with a dish or a donation. Tepee, tent, and RV camping available. (541) 886-3101; www.wallowanez perce.com; e-mail: tamkaliks@gmail.com.

Family Favorites in Eastern Oregon

1. National Historic Oregon Trail Interpretive Center, near Baker City

2. Malheur National Wildlife Refuge, near Burns

3. Steens Mountain, near Burns

4. Nee-Me-Poo National Recreation Trail, Hells Canyon

5. Peter French Round Barn, near Burns

6. John Day Fossil Beds National Monument

7. Kam Wah Chung State Heritage Site, John Day

8. Pendleton Underground Tours

9. Umatilla County Historical Society Museum, Pendleton

10. Wallowa Lake Tramway

The tram takes you on an alpine ride on an amazingly steep incline. The elevation at the base is 4,450 feet, climbing to a breathtaking 8,200 feet at the crest of Mount Howard. Along the surprisingly brief (about 10-minute) ride, the gondola travels between 3 and 120 feet off the ground—be prepared for children's squeals of mixed delight and terror. From the top the spectacular vista encompasses **Wallowa Lake,** the **Eagle Cap Wilderness,** the **Seven Devils Mountains** in Idaho, the **Hells Canyon** area, and on really clear days the **Bitterroot Mountains** of Montana. Let kids work off pent-up energy walking the 2-mile trail that circles the summit, then stop for a bite to eat at the **Summit Grill and Alpine Patio.** June is the peak month for alpine wildflowers on the mountain.

Joe's Place Pizza & Bumper Boats (all ages)

72662 Marina Lane, Wallowa Lake; (541) 432-4940. Open daily Memorial Day through Labor Day. Call for prices and hours, which change seasonally.

The whole family can load into bumper boats or play mini-croquet or putt-putt golf at Joe's, and the kids will quickly gravitate to the arcade area. Order one of Joe's "gourmet pizzas" in between sessions or tuck into a great hand-dipped ice-cream cone.

Eagle Cap Wilderness Pack Station (ages 7 and up)

59761 Wallowa Lake Hwy.; (541) 432-4145; www.eaglecapwildernesspackstation.com. Call for hours and season plus pricing on various trips and activities.

This is the oldest horse-packing operation in northeastern Oregon. Your family can take a 1-hour, 2-hour, half-day, or all-day ride as well as a week-long excursion. All rides are accompanied by experienced guides. Deluxe summer pack trips come complete with camp setup, horses, guide, and wranglers (who take care of the horses and cooking).

Enterprise

This Old West town, named by a committee of early settlers who hoped the moniker would bring good fortune to the area, forms a gateway for vacationers heading into the Eagle Cap Wilderness.

Eagle Cap Wilderness (all ages)

Begins at the Hurricane Creek Campground, 6 miles south of Enterprise on FR 8205, a rough road suitable for slow travel with a passenger car but not recommended for RVs or trailers; (541) 426-4978, (541) 426-5546 for road conditions; www.fs.fed.us/r6/w-w/ecwild .htm. Call for hours, which vary seasonally (there's often snow in the area until July). $ vehicle fee (National Forest Day Pass).

Besides an easy hike, you'll have great views of Sacajawea Peak and the Matterhorn, Oregon's sixth- and seventh-tallest mountains, as you pass through meadows and forested areas along Hurricane Creek.

Stangel Buffalo Ranch (all ages)

Located about 1 mile north of Enterprise on Highway 3 at 65044 Alder Slope Rd.; (541) 426-4919. Always open. Free.

A wide spot on the road's shoulder invites you to stop and view the herd of 150 or more buffalo that are usually found grazing here. It's a far cry from the days of herds of thousands, but it's an opportunity for your kids to see creatures once native and wild in Oregon. Mules are another frequent sight around here.

Top Enterprise **Event**

September

Hells Canyon Mule Days. These long-eared animals are celebrated at this annual event. Mule owners from all over the state come together, and your family can join in a halter and trail class or just watch the parade down Main Street. Races, rodeo competitions, and mule rides are also part of the fun. (541) 426-3271 or (800) 585-4121; www.hellscanyonmuledays.com; e-mail: loziers@eoni.com.

Joseph

Named for the famous Nez Percé chief who led his people on a harrowing winter journey to avoid war, the town of Joseph remembers its history. Any resident could tell you the story of young Chief Joseph—the statesman and orator whose Nez Percé name was Hinmut-too-yah-lat-kekeht, which is said to mean "Thunder Rolling in the Mountains"—and his father, Old Joseph, who is buried at the north end of Wallowa Lake, where a roadside historical marker provides a brief history. Young Chief Joseph's peaceful band was ordered in 1877 to leave the Wallowa country, which had been granted to his people by treaty in 1855. After a few angry men seeking revenge for the deaths of two young braves killed some white settlers, Joseph led his people first to seek refuge with the Crow in Montana and then toward Canada and Chief Sitting Bull. They were pursued and captured after a 2-day battle within 50 miles of the Canadian border. In surrender, Chief Joseph spoke words that have rung through time: "Hear me, my chiefs! I am tired. My heart is sick and sad. From where the sun now stands, I will fight no more forever."

Ferguson Ridge Ski Area (ages 8 and up)
Located 8 miles southeast of Joseph; (541) 398-1167; www.skifergi.com. Open weekends and holidays only, 10 a.m. to 4 p.m. in winter. Call for times and prices.

Young downhill skiers can spend all day on the rope tow for a couple of dollars; adults ski from the T-bar for less than $20 a day. Equipment rentals and food are available at the

Top Joseph **Events**

Summer
Great Joseph Bank Robbery. At 1 p.m. nearly every Sat from Memorial Day through Labor Day, enthusiastic performers reenact the 1896 Robbery (always referred to in capital letters around here). Masked bandits gallop up to the bank, then come out a few minutes later with guns blazing (blanks, of course). (541) 432-1015.

July
Chief Joseph Days Rodeo and Encampment. During Chief Joseph Days the tiny hamlet of Joseph swells from its usual 1,000 residents to nearly 10 times that. The 5-day event packs a lot in, kicking off each year with a bucking horse stampede down Main Street. Other events include 4 days of rodeo (including one specifically for families), parades, a carnival, a Nez Percé encampment and friendship feast, an Indian dance contest, and a cowboy "breakfast" that starts at 11 p.m. and goes all night long. (541) 432-1015; www .chiefjosephdays.com.

lodge. The hill is owned by the Ferguson Ridge Ski Club and operated by members, so opening times are a bit sporadic.

Valley Bronze of Oregon (all ages)

307 W. Adler St. (foundry); (541) 432-7551; www.valleybronze.com; e-mail: info@valley bronze.com. Open daily Memorial Day through Sept for tours. Call or visit Joseph Gallery at 18 W. Main St. (541-432-7445) for tour reservations. $.

One of the more surprising elements of this small western town is its sizable arts community. While the idea of a trip through an art museum might not excite your children, they'll be enthralled by this bronze sculpture showroom that specializes in extremely detailed, realistic renderings of western themes, such as wolves, horses, mountain lions, eagles, cowboys, and Native Americans.

Wallowa County Museum (ages 4 and up)

110 S. Main St.; (541) 432-6095; www.co.wallowa.or.us. Open daily 10 a.m. to 5 p.m. Memorial Day weekend through the third weekend in Sept. $, children 12 and under free.

The Nez Percé history room contains a large tepee that your children will enjoy sitting in even if museums in general offer little appeal. Look for "buckskin bucks," money produced for trading locally during the Great Depression, when real money was scarce.

Where to Eat

IN BAKER CITY

Baker City Cafe. 1840 Main St.; (541) 523-6099. Signature menu items are "flaming pasta salads"—we won't spoil the surprise—as well as more traditional fare. $$–$$$

Inland Cafe. 2715 10th St.; (541) 523- 9041. Down-home cooking specialties are chicken-fried steak and pork chops. $–$$

Oregon Trail Restaurant. 221 Bridge St.; (541) 523-5844. Family dining with old-fashioned American fare. $$–$$$

Sumpter Junction. 2 Sunridge Lane; (541) 523-9437. A miniature replica of the Sumpter Valley Railroad runs on tiny tracks around the restaurant, alongside booths and over dining tables. Family dining with Mexican specialties. $–$$

IN ENTERPRISE

La Laguna Family Mexican Restaurant. 307 W. North St.; (541) 426-3500. Homemade Jalisco-style dishes plus chicken, steaks, and seafood. $-$$

Toma's. 309 S. River St.; (541) 426-4873. Family cooking. $–$$

IN JOHN DAY

Grubsteak Mining Company. 149 E. Main; (541) 575-1970. Pizza, steak, fish, and chicken specialties; open for lunch and dinner. $–$$

IN JOSEPH

Cheyenne Cafe. 209 N. Main; (541) 432-6300. Country cooking 7 days a week. $–$$

Old Town Cafe. 8 S. Main St.; (541) 432-9898. This tiny lunch and breakfast place offers hearty food at reasonable prices. It's the place to stop and fill up before heading out for a round of outdoor activities in northeastern Oregon. $

IN LA GRANDE

Boulder Creek Café at the Rock. 2301 Cove Ave.; (541) 975-2695. The cafe offers salads, sandwiches, and appetizers along with fish, steak, and seafood dinners.

Foley Station. 1011 Adams Ave.; (541) 963-7473; www.foleystation.com. Open for brunch, lunch, and dinner, this eatery offers gourmet dishes at reasonable prices. $–$$

Nells-n-Out Drive-Thru. 1704½ Adams Ave.; (541) 963-5733. This tiny gourmet burger stand has been running for more than 40 years and is still attracting locals from miles around. Best bets are curly fries, hand-made milk shakes, and a huge offering of Italian sodas and other specialty drinks. $–$$

Ten Depot Street. 10 Depot St.; (541) 963-8766. This casual restaurant is a good place to relax with a tasty meal and get a feeling for this friendly town. The owner also operates **Mamacita's** on the next block (110 Depot St.), which serves Mexican fare ($). $$

IN PENDLETON

The Great Pacific Wine and Coffee Company. 403 S. Main St.; (541) 276-1350. Get a good deal for your picnic lunch here and buy tasty sandwiches made on bagels or croissants. Then stuff your picnic basket with baked goodies. $

Main Street Diner. 349 Main St.; (541) 278-1952. You'd be hard pressed to tell you're not in a real '50s diner, except the menu goes beyond the standard burgers and fries. $–$$

Virgil's at Cimmiyotti's. 137 S. Main St.; (541) 276-7711. Cimmiyotti's was a steak-house institution in Pendleton; its replacement still has the old-school decor but updated (and some say improved) food. With a full bar inside and a honkey-tonk out back, this is probably best for families with older kids. $$$–$$$$

IN THE WALLOWAS

Russell's at the Lake. 59984 Wallowa Lake Hwy.; (541) 432-0591. Open May through Oct. Grab a hamburger and terrific fries (from potato to plate in 10 minutes) at this old-fashioned burger bar that has both outdoor and indoor seating. Russell's is popular for its almost-too-thick-for-a-straw milk shakes as well as its ranch-style breakfasts. $

Joe's Place. 72662 Marina Lane, Wallowa Lake; (541) 432-4940; www.wallowalakelodge.com. Enjoy Pizza and hand-dipped Umpqua ice cream while the kids play slot cars and putt-putt golf. $–$$

Where to Stay

IN BAKER CITY

Best Western Sunridge Inn. 1 Sunridge Lane; (800) 233-2368 or (541) 523-6444. An outdoor pool waits for you in the summer, and an indoor spa will warm your bones during the cold winter months. $$–$$$

Eldorado Inn. 695 Campbell St.; (800) 537-5756 or (541) 523-6494. A restaurant and indoor pool are among the amenities here. Pets are welcome. $$–$$$

Oregon Trail Motel. 211 Bridge St.; (541) 523-5844. Clean rooms (some with Memory Foam beds) and fridges in the rooms. Breakfast at the Oregon Trail Restaurant included. $$

Rodeway Inn. 810 Campbell St.; (800) 228-2000 or (541) 523-2242; www.qualityinn.com. The inn serves continental breakfast and welcomes pets. $$–$$$

Super 8. 250 Campbell St.; (541) 523- 8282. Laundry facilities, an indoor pool, and a spa pool help make family stays here more comfortable. $$–$$$

Union Creek Campground. Located on Highway 7 on the shores of Phillips Reservoir about 20 miles southwest of Baker City; (541)

523-4476. Fifty-eight campsites for tent and trailer camping. The swimming beach is a great place for your kids to enjoy a summer dip while Mom and Dad soak up some of this area's seemingly endless sunshine (in the summertime, that is). $

IN BURNS

Hotel Diamond. 10 Main St.; take Highway 205 south toward Frenchglen; (541) 493-1898. This century-old hotel has both charm and tradition. Adjacent to the Malheur Wildlife Refuge at the base of the Steens Mountains, it receives regular visits from deer and great horned owls. Breakfast is included, and the restaurant also serves lunch and dinner. $$–$$$

Silver Spur Motel. 789 N. Broadway; (800) 400-2077 or (541) 573-2077. Twenty-six units. Microwaves and refrigerators make this a convenient place for families to settle in for a day or more. Best of all, they offer a full breakfast buffet. $$

IN ENTERPRISE

Best Western Rama Inn & Suites. 1200 Highland Ave.; (800) RAMA-INN or (541) 426-2000. Continental breakfast is offered, plus an indoor pool, spa, and exercise room. Pets are welcome. $$–$$$$

Lick Creek Campground. 29 miles southeast of Enterprise on FR 39, Wallowa Mountain Loop Road; (541) 426-4978; www.fs.fed .us/r6/w-w. At the 5,400-foot elevation, nights are chilly, but the views from the ridge above the campgound are terrific. You can fish or hike from this campground, which also has trailer sites and drinking water. $

Wilderness Inn. 301 W. North St.; (541) 426-4535. This newly remodeled inn has private saunas, kitchenettes, and an adjoining restaurant. $$

IN FRENCHGLEN

Frenchglen Hotel. Located on Highway 205, 62 miles south of Burns; (541) 493-2825 or (800) 551-6949; www.oregonstateparks .org. Open mid-Mar through Oct. The hotel provides lodging and meals for visitors coming to Malheur to enjoy bird watching and wildlife. Breakfast, lunch, and dinner are served daily to residents and drop-in guests. Be sure to make reservations for dinner. $$

IN JOHN DAY

Budget 8 Motel. 711 W. Main St.; (541) 575-2155. Fourteen units. Your family will settle in nicely here, with a restaurant and laundry services plus an outdoor pool for those hot summer days. $$–$$$

Dreamer's Lodge. 11 N. Canyon Blvd.; (800) 654 2849 or (541) 575-0526; www .dreamerlodge.com. All rooms have refrigerators and microwaves, and family kitchen suites are available at this inexpensive independent motel. $–$$$

Riverside School House Bed and Breakfast. 28076 N. River Rd. (County Road 61); located 6 miles east of Prairie City, 19 miles east of John Day; (541) 820-4731; www.river sideschoolhouse.com. Here's a bed-and-breakfast that will give your children a new experience in going to school. Originally a 1-room schoolhouse, it is now part of a working cattle ranch. $$$$

IN JOSEPH

Flying Arrow Resort. 59782 Wallowa Lake Hwy.; (541) 432-2951; www.flyingarrow resort.com; e-mail: info@flyingarrowresort .com. Twenty units. This family-oriented resort with all the amenities—heated swimming pool, hot tub, sundecks, and barbecues—is open year-round. Cabins range from rustic to modern, with 1 to 4 bedrooms. Most are located on the Wallowa River, and all are fully equipped. $$$–$$$$

Indian Lodge Motel. 201 S. Main; (541) 432-2651; www.indianlodgemotel.com. Sixteen fresh and clean rooms with great views of the Wallowa Mountains. $$$–$$$$

IN LA GRANDE

Anthony Lakes Recreation Area. Baker Ranger District, on FR 73; (541) 523-4476. You can camp at Anthony, Mud, and Grande Ronde Lakes. Campgrounds are available for tents and trailers, and there are boat ramps for nonmotorized craft. $

Hilgard Junction State Park. Located on the Grande Ronde, at the edge of the Blue Mountains, take I-84 northwest about 9 miles to the Highway 244 turnoff and head west about ¼ mile; (800) 551-6949; www.oregon stateparks.org. Open mid-Apr to mid-Oct, weather permitting. The park lies along the path taken by pioneers on the Oregon Trail, and you can use the interpretive panels to share some of its history with your children. $

Historic Union Hotel. 14 miles southeast of LaGrand at 326 N. Main St., Union; (541) 562-6135; http://thehistoricunionhotel .com. Newly restored hotel with 16 theme rooms decorated around a historical character—your kids will have fun putting the clues together to learn more about each person. Great location near Union City Park and Catherine Creek. Eight full-hookup RV spaces available too ($). Lodging $$–$$$$

Stang Manor Inn. 1612 Walnut St.; (541) 963-2400; www.stangmanor.com. A stay at this small B&B will add to your list of memorable travel experiences. The stately Georgian manor was the home of a local lumber baron in the 1920s and is furnished with antiques. The spacious grounds are ideal for children to let off pent-up energy. $$–$$$$

Super 8. 2407 E. R Ave. at the I-84/Highway 82 interchange; (800) 800-8000 or (541) 963-8080. Sixty-four units. The simple rooms are comfortable, and the indoor pool and

spa pool offer a nice respite after a day of outdoor activities. $$–$$$

IN PENDLETON

Emigrant Springs State Heritage Area. Located near the summit of the Blue Mountains off I-84, 26 miles southeast of Pendleton; (541) 983-2227 or (800) 551-6949; (800) 452-5687 for reservations. Your family can stay in the Totem Bunkhouse, with 2 bunk beds (4 single beds) in each of 2 units. It's available year-round for winter cross-country ski holidays and summer camping. The campground offers a self-guided nature trail, a kitchen shelter in the day-use area, a horse camp with two corrals, and a horse trail that doubles as a cross-country ski trail in winter. $$

Holiday Inn Express. 600 SE Nye St.; (541) 966-6520 or (800) HOLIDAY; www.hiexpress .com. Indoor and outdoor spa and indoor swimming pool are offered. Continental breakfast is served. $$–$$$$

Rugged Country Lodge. 1807 SE Court Ave.; (877) 7-RUGGED or (541) 966-6800; www.ruggedcountrylodge.com. A sweet, clean, remodeled 1950s-era motel with continental breakfast; adjoining suites available. $$–$$$.

IN THE WALLOWAS

Eagle Cap Chalets and Park at the River RV Park. 59879 Wallowa Lake Hwy.; (541) 432-4704; www.eaglecapchalets.com. Twenty chalet rooms, 12 cabins, 5 condos, plus full RV hookups (no tent camping). All rooms and cabins have TV, coffeepot, microwave, and fridge. Indoor pool and spa at chalet. $ RV sites; lodging $$–$$$$

Wallowa Lake Lodge. 60060 Wallowa Lake Hwy.; (541) 432-9821; www.wallowalake.com; e-mail: info@wallowalake.com. Lodge rooms and rustic cabins are for rent at this historic resort. Cabins open year-round; lodge and restaurant available for conferences and

events from mid-Oct through Memorial Day .
$$–$$$$

For More Information

**Baker County Visitor & Convention
Bureau.** 490 Campbell St., Baker City, OR
97814; (888) 523-5855 or (541) 523-5855;
www.visitbaker.com.

**Eastern Oregon Visitors Association/
Oregon Trail Marketing Coalition.** P.O.
Box 1087, Baker City, OR 97814; (800) 332-
1843; www.eova.com.

Grant County Chamber of Commerce.
281 W. Main St., John Day, OR 97845; (800)
769-5664 or (541) 575-0547; www.gcoregon
live.com.

Harney County Chamber of Commerce.
484 N. Broadway, Burns, OR 97720; (541)
573-2636; www.harneycounty.com; e-mail:
info@harneycounty.com.

Joseph Chamber of Commerce. P.O. Box
13, Joseph, OR 77846; (541) 432-1015; www
.josephoregon.com; email: cjdays@eoni.com.

Union County Tourism. 102 Elm St., La
Grande, OR 97850; (800) 848-9969; www.visit
lagrande.com.

**Pendleton Chamber of Commerce/Visi-
tors & Information Center.** 501 S. Main
St., Pendleton, OR 97801; (800) 547-8911
or (541) 276-7411; www.pendletonchamber
.com; e-mail: info@pendleton-oregon.org.

**Wallowa County Chamber of Com-
merce.** P.O. Box 427, 115 Tejaka, Enterprise,
OR 97828; (800) 585-4121 or (541) 426-4622;
www.wallowacountychamber.org; e-mail:
info@wallowacountychamber.com.

Index